CHILDREN and FISH
DON'T TALK

Praise

for

CHILDREN and FISH DON'T TALK

"Leshek Zavistovski's searing memoir is not just the testament of a young man's survival in the soul-killing monochrome world of post-war Soviet-controlled Warsaw. It is the story of how Art and Love saved him from the overwhelming burden of his past and the shackles of his old-world Polish family. *Children and Fish Don't Talk* powerfully shows how Leshek transcended the extreme circumstances of his existence (and how many five-year-old children become the good luck charm to a Soviet Field General?) to carve out a life of beauty and meaning in a unique version of the Immigrant's Journey—with all its frustrations, humor and pathos—set in the world of classical music.

"At its root, Leshek's book represents a brilliantly crafted love story—to the human spirit (his!), to music, to his wife and children, and ultimately, to his adopted country."
—Bruce C. McKenna, writer, *Band of Brothers*; Emmy Award-winning creator, writer, executive producer, *The Pacific*

"*Children and Fish Don't Talk* is excellent and polished."
—Connie Martinson, writer, host of syndicated television show *Connie Martinson Talks Books*

"If it's true that we are the product of the challenges we face, then that must explain why Leshek is so extraordinary. His is a path of movie-worthy, epic struggle, great guardian-angel luck—interspersed with hilarious episodes throughout—and the mountainous obstacles he faced and overcame.

"I could never have dreamed that such a background was endured by the man with whom I've performed countless times at the Metropolitan Opera. I was agape from the beginning to the end of this book!"
—Susan Graham, internationally-renowned opera star

"Leshek Zavistovski has led a remarkable life and he writes about it vividly and passionately. His survival as a child, separated from his parents by war, and his subsequent career as a musician, should be the stuff of legends."
—Jerry Adler, senior editor, *Newsweek* (retired)

CHILDREN AND FISH
DON'T TALK

Adventures with Nazis, Communists, and the Metropolitan Opera

LESHEK ZAVISTOVSKI

in collaboration with

MONIQUE ZAVISTOVSKI AND TONI RAPPORT ZAVISTOVSKI

SUNSTONE PRESS

SANTA FE

Sunstone books may be purchased for educational, business, or sales promotional use.
For information please write: Special Markets Department, Sunstone Press,
P.O. Box 2321, Santa Fe, New Mexico 87504-2321.

Cover design › Monique Zavistovski
Book design › Vicki Ahl
Body typeface › Adobe Caslon Pro
Printed on acid-free paper
∞

Library of Congress Cataloging-in-Publication Data

Zavistovski, Leshek, 1938- author.
  Children and fish don't talk : adventures with Nazis, Communists, and the Metropolitan Opera /
by Leshek Zavistovski ; in collaboration with Monique Zavistovski and Toni Rapport Zavistovski.
    pages cm
Includes bibliographical references and index.
  ISBN 978-0-86534-957-5 (hardcover : alk. paper) -- ISBN 978-0-86534-958-2 (softcover :
alk. paper)
  1. Zavistovski, Leshek, 1938- 2. Cellists--Biography. 3. Polish Americans--Biography. 4. World
War, 1939-1945--Poland--Biography. I. Zavistovski, Monique. II. Zavistovski, Toni Rapport.
III. Title.
  ML418.Z39A3 2013
  787.4092--dc23
  [B]
                                    2013018752

WWW.SUNSTONEPRESS.COM
SUNSTONE PRESS / POST OFFICE BOX 2321 / SANTA FE, NM 87504-2321 /USA
(505) 988-4418 / ORDERS ONLY (800) 243-5644 / FAX (505) 988-1025

Dedication

To my beloved Toni (*Kotuś*) and Monique for their immeasurable inspiration and devotion, and to Tanya, Katia, Gregory, Adam and Chloe

Contents

1

A Century of Good Health

Brooklyn, New York, November 1964

Maria and Josef Mikrut finished Mass that Sunday morning feeling spiritually satiated. They wore the typical solemn expressions that were etched into the faces of all the Polish immigrants who filled the congregation, and their broad shoulders slumped under the weight of their piety. The flock was poor, elderly and pale—their skin looked like boiled chicken—while I was only twenty-six years old, far from devout or obedient, and achingly hungry for breakfast. But I deferred to the Mikruts and didn't hurry them along. Maria lowered her eyes in profound humility under her kerchief, hoping the priest would take notice, and as always, he did. Cupping her callused hands in his own, Reverend Jakubik offered his blessings while I stood aside, patiently. The Mikruts never ate before attending Mass; they made a point of fasting until receiving the Sacrament of Communion, and I felt obliged to honor them, my guardian angels. I was, after all, their resident fugitive. Carrying my cello in its second-hand case, I was happy to play Gounod's *Ave Maria* in their place of worship, on an empty stomach, in exchange for discretion and a roof over my head.

Maria took Josef's arm and I gripped my cello case as we finally headed home in the cold. I was starving for Maria's traditional Polish spread. Her tasty buttered *chleb*, accompanied by a dish of salt and an array of mouth-watering sausages—especially the finger-thin, semi-dry *kabanosy*, my favorite—was a savory reward after laboring over their faith. And, of course, the meal would always begin with a vodka toast to a century of good health, "*Sto lat!*"

We turned the corner onto Sixteenth Street and the first thing I saw was a long, black patent car parked in front of Josef's ailing Ford. The Mikruts noticed it too, I am sure, as each of us slowed our pace and held our tongues. Nobody in the neighborhood owned such a car. If I had been alone I would have thought twice about proceeding down the block. I may have stopped, coolly lit my pipe and changed directions, but I did not want to seem nervous around Maria, so I kept moving. Only a few feet from our brownstone, the car doors opened in unison and two men, with synchronized efficiency, stepped out onto the sidewalk in front of us.

They wore pressed, dark suits with starched shirts and striped ties. One of them took a brass badge from his pocket and identified himself as a U.S. Immigration officer. He asked if my name was Leszek Zawistowski.

"Yes," I responded, even though I hardly understood any English.

He continued, "Mr. Zawistowski, you are under arrest for remaining in the United States of America illegally."

The other man took my cello without a word, handed it to Josef who was in a state of shock, and snapped a pair of handcuffs on my wrists. I wanted to fall to my knees, but tears were pouring down Maria's face and if I crumbled she would have thrown herself on top of me and created a scene.

"*Nie płacz*, don't cry," I said. "I am going to be okay. Call Father d'Anjou and my lawyer, Lydia Savoyka, right away."

The dread that had been dominating my thoughts for years shot through me like rifle fire. The two officers were very orderly and polite—nothing like the KGB agents who beat the hell out of my father in the frost of 1945, leaving a trail of blood in the snow, or the Gestapo who seized my oldest brother Henryk with similar brutality—nonetheless, I was convulsing with fear. I tried to find reassurance in the words of my attorney, "*Bąć spokoiny*, be calm, I will protect you."

The officers on either side of me pulled me into the waiting car, and once more I pleaded with the Mikruts to call Savoyka. Maria acknowledged my request with a twitch and nod of her head between sobs. She cried for me as if she were watching her only son getting dragged away in shackles. My own mother would never have abandoned her fortitude in front of authority.

The car thundered toward Manhattan and with every bump in the road the handcuffs sliced into my skin. I told myself, *Arresting me is an absurd mistake. I am not a threat. I spent the night before entertaining New Yorkers at Radio City Music Hall, delighting them with holiday tunes in time to the Rockettes, whose perfume still lingers on my skin. This country is supposed to welcome me. That was Voice of America's promise. For god's sake, I am just a musician in search of freedom.*

When we arrived at an undisclosed location, my handcuffs were removed and I was put into a windowless holding cell. Alone, I closed my eyes and began to piece together my case. *How will I convince a judge that my only hope for a future is in his hands, and if he returns me to where I came from it will all be over? My argument will have to start with my earliest childhood, long before I defected, before I was a cellist, and even before I was abandoned as a four-year-old in the Polish countryside in war-torn Europe.*

❊

I was born in Warsaw, Poland, on Good Friday, April 15, 1938. The midwife warned my mother, "Your son will grow up to be a priest, or a thief."

I had two much older brothers, Zdzisław and Henryk. Zdzisław was the mean one. His face was long and narrow like a fox, and with his thin-lipped grin he would taunt me relentlessly, "You act like a scared sissy all the time." It was true that I was skinny (apart from my cherubic, full cheeks) and vulnerable as a little boy.

My early childhood overflowed with eerie stories about Slavic folk rituals and Polish pagan mythology. Across centuries, ancient tribes passed their beliefs from one generation to the next through spoken words that whispered between the branches and brambles of prehistoric forests and seeped into my bedroom at story time. Polish parents frightened their little ones into good behavior by warning of the *Boginki*, who steal babies from their cribs, leave changelings in their place, and sacrifice the newborns to river nymphs. Mother loved to tell me chilling tales about *Baba Yaga*, the witch who flies through the woods on her broomstick, snatching children and eating them alive. Such stories inflated my already brittle anxieties. But my mean brother was wrong about me; like my parents, I would learn how to conquer fear with sheer grit.

The first three years of my life were mementos in my mother's keeping. She always carried a pocket-sized photo of me on my first birthday. I am sitting atop a downy rug in a white eyelet dress that was customary for girls and boys, and look like a heavenly creature unspoiled by the tyranny of men. If not for this picture, and her tales, these early years would be lost to me.

Michalina Zawistowska, my mother, was born Michalina Rużik in 1910, the granddaughter of Jewish émigrés. The family moved from their native Czech Republic to Warsaw to provide their children with a better life and a superior education. Dating back to the thirteenth-century, Poland had been very tolerant of its Jewish community. At the time of my birth, the Jewish population of Poland was approximately three and a half million.

Michalina was pretty, but didn't boast of high cheekbones or blond hair, the trademarks of Slavic-Polish beauties. Her hair was curly and brown, her peach complexion slightly dark, and she had definite Semitic features. She was street smart, resourceful and fearless. If Michalina had a weakness it was that she was deeply superstitious.

Mother's father, Anton Rużik, was the manager of an upscale apartment building in the Jewish section of Warsaw. It was a very comfortable existence for him, his wife Ewa and the children until 1926 when Ewa developed cancer and died. This was a catastrophic loss for my then sixteen-year-old mother. Her devastation was compounded by the shocking discovery that after only a few months, Anton took a young, beautiful gypsy girl as his lover. In her grief Mother visited my grandmother's grave daily, begging her to help punish Anton from beyond. Poor Mother repeatedly cursed her father, whom she despised, and prayed that if vengeance could not be taken upon him, she herself wished to die.

The newly widowed Anton, on the other hand, felt flush with good fortune and went on to win an enormous sum of money in the lottery. Mother was not impressed and loathed him and his lover even more. Grandfather Anton decided to use his winnings to purchase a large estate in Lithuania, not far from Vilno, which in those days was considered Polish territory. He arranged for a coach and driver and, with his gypsy girl and a suitcase full of money, went to claim his manor.

Traveling from Warsaw to Vilno was an extremely risky adventure. In the eastern part of Poland were the most ancient European forests, which were said to harbor outlaws, primitive woodsmen and evil spirits. They were also the favored hunting grounds for Polish and foreign aristocracy, but neither would enter these lands unprotected.

With the confidence of a nobleman, Grandfather Anton ventured without guards through the Białowierza Forest. My mother never learned how far he got, but days later his mutilated body was discovered alongside the abandoned coach. There was no trace of the beautiful gypsy girl, or the money. Mother felt sure the mortal price he paid for his affair was her own wish fulfilled, and she suffered stinging feelings of guilt.

My father, Feliks Zawistowski, was not of Jewish descent. He was born in 1909 and came from the rural nobility, *Szlachta;* he was blond with sky blue eyes and carried himself with the dignity of his class. Like most Polish gentiles, his family was conservative Catholic. His parents, my Grandfather Constantine and Grandma Helena, owned large properties encompassing several villages in the very eastern part of Poland and had over one thousand peasant serfs cultivating their land. According to Polish custom at the time, property was inherited by the offspring who did not pursue a higher education. Because my father was sent to Warsaw to study at a prominent trade school, the equivalent of a university education in those days, he received an equal portion of the income from the harvest, but didn't own any of the land. Father eventually became an expert conservator and restorer of fine French antiques, especially of Louis XV- and XVI-style furniture.

In 1927 Feliks met seventeen-year-old Michalina, who was studying painting at the prestigious Academy of Fine Arts in Warsaw. Her eyes still bore the shadows of sorrow and guilt, as it had only been one year since she lost both her parents. Every bit the gentleman, Feliks kissed her on the hand and she fell in love. Of course, he greeted all the ladies with a kiss, which provoked Mother, and not even the couple's betrothal the following year would quiet her jealousy. Soon after the wedding they had their first baby, Henryk, and two years later Zdzisław was born. Father's aristocratic station afforded my mother a prominent place in society and their first few years together were happy ones.

My parents' house stood on Ulica Freta, the main street in the city's New Town. Freta was distinguished by a majestic, seventeenth-century Gothic church and the notable address, No. 15, where Maria Skłodowska-Curie was born across the street from our house. *It was a good place to begin my life.*

Our townhouse occupied four stories: my father's studio and workshop were on the ground level; a parlor, dining room and kitchen on the first floor; our bedrooms occupied the second; and on the third, in an extension of the attic, lived an old hunchback lady who rented the space. My mother believed hunchbacks brought good luck, so it gave her comfort to have the old lady living in our building. To my family's great embarrassment, every time Mother spotted someone in the street with that same pronounced slouch, their breathing labored under the steep curve of their back, she would discretely maneuver to touch them. Then she would smile and say to herself, *'Fortune is in my favor.'*

There is little I remember of my father's ancestral lands. I was told that my grandparents lived in a big, log manor house with a thatched roof, on the edge of a small lake. The property was south of the ancient forests where Grandfather Anton was murdered. To reach their land a traveler needed to embark from Warsaw by train. After crossing the River Bug and passing through Małkinia Górna (a large village that would serve as a railway junction to the infamous Holocaust city of death, Treblinka), the traveler would arrive in the dusty little station of Czyrzew. It was remote, desolate and primitive. To get to the estate from there, one had to continue east for many hours on bumpy dirt roads in a horse-driven wagon.

The inhabitants of this land lived no differently in the early twentieth-century than they would have one hundred years before, despite being a very short distance—approximately one hundred fifty miles—from the cultured and sophisticated city of Warsaw. They had no electricity, no running water, no proper schools. Almost everybody outside the *Szlachta* was illiterate. The only opportunity for some enlightenment was at the local Catholic Church. Once a week everyone gathered for Mass. On these mornings the villagers wore festive clothing, heard organ music, and listened to the priest's cautionary sermons about Satan and hell and a multitude of demons, who should be credited with building his church—the more wicked the story, the more full the coffers. The spirit of the flock was always heavy from sin when the sun went down, and almost everybody got drunk on homemade *bimber*, the predecessor to our famous Polish vodka.

The noble owners of these villages, like my grandfather, lived in splendid houses and had total control over their territory. Serfs were scarcely allowed the freedom to travel from one community to the next and needed approval from the landlord to marry. If permission was granted, the sanctity of the marriage was often interrupted on the wedding night in a tradition that appears in Mozart's famous opera, *Le Nozze di Figaro*. Known as "the right of the first night," or, "the lord's right," the medieval practice dictated that the nobleman could sleep with the bride before she consummated her union. I wondered if my grandfather ever took advantage of that barbaric custom.

As a child, my father frightened me with legends from the countryside and warned me never to enter the forests alone.

"The inhabitants of the woods are rough, suspicious, and ruled by mysticism," he said. "They wouldn't hesitate to plunge a knife through your little heart."

He learned his lesson as a student in 1924 when he and two friends took a bicycle trip to his parents' rural estate. As soon as they crossed the River Bug, they biked into more and more isolated territory, pedaling through increasingly dense brush. Reaching a clearing deep in the forest, Father and his friends came upon a group of locals who responded in horror at the sight of them. The woodsmen gave chase with pitchforks and sickles, throwing stones at their backs and driving them out of the village quickly. In the age of automobiles and the first airplanes in the sky, it had not occurred to my father that there could still be people who never saw a bicycle. In the minds of these backwoods denizens, the young men riding through the forest were devils in their midst.

The history books describe how vulnerable Poles are as a people, as a nation. They also chronicle our resilience. Though I have always been wary of what lay in Poland's borderlands outside the city, I do share an important trait with my countrymen from the woods. It is not in their nature to back down from a fight, nor is it in mine.

2

Run

Poland's borders had been redrawn time and time again in its history. My country had been overrun by the Swedish, bitten in the ass by the Ottomans, squeezed by Prussia and then Russia, carved in half, seized, annexed, occupied, swallowed up, spit out, eviscerated, and in 1939 it was about to happen all over again. Mother loved to reminisce with deep bitterness that the five months after her pocket photo of me as a baby was taken marked Poland's last as a free nation.

That summer when I was only one year old, Nazi propaganda trumpeted relentlessly that Poland was a military threat to the Third Reich. Dark clouds had been gathering for a long time, portending the storm coming from the West. War was inevitable. Considering such uncertain conditions, Mother collected eleven-year-old Henryk, nine-year-old Zdzisław and me, and we escaped Warsaw's anxious atmosphere by taking cover in Father's parents' estate in the eastern part of Poland.

A nobleman, my father was automatically drafted into the Polish Army as a lieutenant. In the coming months we lost all contact with him. Then, on September 1, the Wehrmacht Army crossed into Polish territory, and so began that horrible chapter in history. On September 17, Stalin's Red Army stunned Poland by attacking from its eastern borders and, although our leaders never surrendered, Warsaw and the rest of the country buckled in defeat in a matter of weeks. The majority of the Polish Army fled to the East, only to be ensnared by the Russians. Soviet occupation of the region beyond the River Bug was total and included my grandparents' estate. Mother and her three sons were wedged between two armies in a fiefdom where the rules were swiftly changing. The Soviets promised to free the serfs from the despotism of the aristocracy, as they had a few decades before. Landowners, like my grandparents, suddenly felt hunted.

The early winter had already turned the ground cold, but Father, with a small group of partisans at his service, made a brave and desperate attempt to rescue us. He crossed German and Russian lines and appeared like a ghost one evening at my grandparents' house. With no time for packing, he led us on a wildly dangerous journey back to Warsaw.

We traveled at night, disguised as peasants. During the day we sought refuge in barns under stacks of hay, only to emerge after sundown and proceed quietly by moonlight. One of Father's men always walked ahead of us to warn of possible danger. It was my presence that was probably the biggest hazard to our safety. I was only one and a half years old, with the loud cry and restless spirit of most toddlers, which threatened to give our position away. In order to keep her little one quiet, Mother fed me milk heavily spiked with vodka. I passed the journey mostly asleep in a drunken stupor.

Trudging forward just east of the River Bug, we were able to conceal ourselves behind the thick tree limbs of the forest. We moved like nocturnal creatures, trekking through hostile woods and muddy swamps, slowly, but poised for action. Coming upon a clearing at the river crossing, we were spotted by a Russian Army patrol and they started to shoot. Our partisan escorts returned fire, and we slipped back into the cover of night. Father kept us on the edge of the forest like a pack of starving animals for a day, maybe more, until we were able to move ahead undetected toward Warsaw.

When we finally reached the city, Mother was on the verge of collapse from physical and mental exhaustion after carrying me on her chest for over one hundred miles. Looking like city beggars, dirty and in rags, my parents crossed the bridge toward Ulica Freta and saw their home lying in ruins. Our beautiful townhouse was a victim of one of the Nazi's first air attacks. A bomb had pierced directly through the roof of the building, causing its total destruction. Father's meticulous restorations, Zdzisław's toys, Henryk's books, our cozy beds, were all gone. But, the old hunchback lady, who was in her attic apartment at the time, miraculously survived. The city rescue team found her sitting, only slightly injured, on top of the rubble. Mother was not at all surprised.

My father found a dinky, two-room apartment for us on the other side of the Vistula River from the Old Town, in a dreary, working class neighborhood called Praga. We lived across the street from the train depot, and day and night we felt under siege by the constant screeching of locomotive wheels.

Had we not escaped my grandparents' estate, our fates would have been far worse. Within days of our departure the Russian police descended on the village, lined up the residents and asked not for identification papers, but rather for a show of everyone's hands. Men and women, children and adults alike, stood with their palms facing the heavens, waiting for judgment. People like my grandparents, the local priest, teacher and dressmaker, who did not work the land, whose hands were soft, clean and un-callused, were taken away. I would never see my grandparents again. They disappeared without a trace.

Having settled us into our dismal living quarters, Father left once more to rejoin the resistance movement. The opposition activities began immediately after the invasion of Poland, and the underground army quickly grew into the largest resistance force in the whole of Europe. Four hundred thousand men fought under the name of the Home Army. Called *Armia Krajowa* or *AK*, it evolved into a semi-secret state with a very organized chain of command.

The Nazis began to Germanize Poland with mass arrests and executions of its scientists, professors, doctors, lawyers, writers and artists, in an effort to turn my country into an intellectual wasteland. The victims were sent directly to labor camps and were the first to be killed. Father was trapped behind the fast-advancing German Army and went into hiding. He evaded capture with the Underground and was able to receive news of the terror in the East. Under Stalin's orders, the Soviet Secret Police, or *NKVD*, was also organizing mass deportations of all Polish intelligentsia, sending them to the remote gulags of Siberia. A million and a half of these deportees ultimately perished. The most haunting Soviet purge was the Katyn massacre, in which over twenty thousand retreating Polish officers were executed under the dark canopy of Russia's Katyn Forest. The majority of the dead were men like my father, upper class reservists and the scholarly elite of Poland.

Life in Warsaw was extremely hazardous. Schools were shut down, social and cultural activities prohibited. Anyone daring to listen to the music of Fryderyk Chopin could be shot. Jews were systematically corralled and arrested. Mother, with her Jewish family background, was always on high alert. Father demanded she wear a chain with a cross and a pendant engraved with the image of the Virgin Mary prominently displayed on the outside of her blouse at all times. For her it was a superstitious measure; she liked to believe such a talisman would protect her from the Nazis.

To keep us safe, on most days Mother sent my older brothers to the local Catholic Church for some clandestine school instruction and kept me indoors with her. Whenever possible, she loved to escape from our tedious life and visit the rubble of our townhouse. In August of 1940, when I was almost two and a half years old, Mother took me for a walk in the section of the Old Town where I was born. Feeling bold, she ventured into a royal park built by King August the Saxon, the beautiful Saski Gardens. We passed a German soldiers' patrol. They surrounded us and Mother snatched me up in her arms. I was frightened and began to cry hysterically.

One of the soldiers pressed his gun against my forehead and asked, in his broken Polish, "What's the matter, boy? Don't you like us, you little Polish pig? Are you afraid of Germans?"

My terrified mother and I both wet our pants. The soldiers laughed and called us dirty Polacks, but allowed Mother to run from them without further harm. After this incident she spent almost an entire year shuttered with me inside our apartment. She would only risk an outing when it was absolutely necessary.

For every act of sabotage or murder of a German soldier in Warsaw, the Gestapo conducted a collective punishment. They would close both ends of a city block, and whoever was trapped on the street would be lined up against a wall and executed. The numbers of innocent victims could be ten, or could be a hundred.

In the spring of 1941 Mother was caught in such an unfathomable situation. Dozens of men, women and children were herded at gunpoint onto a sidewalk, some mere steps from their homes or shops. With arms raised above their heads, everybody faced the wall as they waited to inhale their last breaths. An execution squad arrived alongside a truck equipped with large speakers blasting the Fuhrer's favorite music, a Wagnerian death knell. Mother was standing in the middle of the group of detainees, next to a young woman who was sobbing uncontrollably.

"I don't want to die; I have a newborn baby at home," she wailed over and over.

Mother barked at her, "Shut up and listen to me. We might have a chance to survive."

The Nazis conducted all of their activities very efficiently, but in the din of the music and the shouting of orders, Mother whispered to the young woman, "I will count to three."

Then she said she would scream as loudly as she could, and run.

"I will run left, but you run to the right for your life!"

Mother needed to act quickly. She surveyed her surroundings once more and prepared her frozen muscles to flee. Briefly, she considered her leather shoes. Mother never wore shoes without heels, and never rubber because she couldn't stand the smell. It would be hard to run in these shoes.

"One, two, three," she said in a forceful whisper, and then she yelled, "Run, run, RUN!"

The young woman sprinted in the opposite direction and the rest of the captives followed suit. Mother created total chaos. Of course, the Gestapo started shooting furiously at anything that moved. Splattered blood and bodies covered the street. Mother bolted like a maniac into one of the building's courtyards. Since many of the city's older structures did not have plumbing, outhouses were stationed throughout. She tossed herself into one of them and dropped down its shithole, into that disgusting, stinking human waste. Shaking and vomiting, there she remained late into the night when she could no longer hear a sound. Her courage had betrayed her own terror; she had truly expected to get a bullet in the back. Mother never learned if her young accomplice lived to see her baby again, an unanswered question that tormented her for years.

In June, Hitler's army broke its non-aggression pact with Stalin, and with all their military might quickly took Eastern Poland from the Russians. For my father it was a welcome change, as he and his resistance fighters now only had to deal with one enemy—the Nazis. He would also have easier access to his ancestral lands. His cousins and a handful of faithful peasants occasionally smuggled onions and potatoes to us. This was our basic means for survival.

Even though her husband was absent and war was raging outside her window, Mother took impeccable care of the household and herself. She was meticulously clean and had a vain obsession with her skin. Every night she went to bed with goose fat or, in lean times like these, some sort of cheap cream smeared all over her face. In the mornings I would peek up into her cracked mirror and watch while she applied lipstick before doing anything else. She did this religiously, despite the fact that she stayed mostly at home.

While my father served his country, Mother became very friendly with his younger brother Kostek, who lived just outside Warsaw. I was almost four years old when Mother and I cautiously started to visit him in the afternoons. He would pat me on the head and give me some snack or other, which was a rare treat.

"Go outside and amuse yourself!" he would say.

On one such afternoon I became bored with my solitary play and ventured inside. There were strange noises coming from Kostek's bedroom, and when I opened the door I saw my uncle on top of Mother. She was only partially dressed and I thought he was hurting her. I let out a shriek. Uncle abruptly slammed the door and a few minutes later Mother grabbed my arm and dragged me from the house.

On the way home I got a severe spanking.

"Don't you dare tell anybody what you saw," she warned.

I didn't breathe a word to my brothers. We never visited Uncle Kostek again and he never came to our door. Nobody in the family even mentioned his name. He simply disappeared. Later in life I wondered if my father and his devoted band of partisans had anything to do with Kostek's disappearance, or if he was just another victim of the Reich.

❈

At four years old, I was living in that bleak apartment with my mother and two older brothers who wanted nothing to do with me. My only toy was a rusty, little metal airplane. The plane and I were inseparable. Father was gone and I no longer visited my nice uncle. The summer of 1942 was hot, tense, and full of danger everywhere. *This* I remember.

On a sunny September day Mother was in the city with Zdzisław and me in tow. Henryk, fourteen years old at the time, remained alone at home.

Our pockets were heavy with smuggled food rations. We were turning the corner of our city block when the neighborhood watch group stopped Mother.

"Michalina, turn around! Don't go back to your apartment. The Gestapo is waiting for you. They took your son away."

I remember Mother's rosy complexion turning ashen in an instant. She didn't audibly cry out, but tears were streaming down her face, and when she grasped our hands I could feel her whole body shaking. We turned and headed in the opposite direction. I also began crying quietly. I just wanted to go home and play with my toy plane.

Henryk was arrested as a Jew. The Nazis had finally come after us.

Through a secret line of communication Mother got in touch with Father, whom we hadn't seen in months. He led us to temporary safe quarters, and a few days later arranged for Zdzisław and me to be separated from our mother and sent to a distant town as parentless victims of the war. We were torn from each other. I watched my mother drowning in her tears and kept my eyes on her in desperation until they shut the doors, and she was gone from my sight.

Father then sent Mother to the south of Poland. He thought she would be safe in the city of Częstochowa, hiding in the famous Catholic monastery, Jasna Góra, with its miraculous black Madonna. With my father's aristocratic background, the monks took Mother under their protection. She brought no belongings with her—except for the small photo of me in my white dress—and lived under their roof as a servant woman with no access to information about her children or her husband.

I didn't know what organization took responsibility for Zdzisław and me in the absence of our mother. I assume Father's Home Army, with the help of the Red Cross, arranged for our safety. My brother and I, with dozens of other orphaned children, were taken to Warsaw's train depot and we boarded a coach heading east. I was the youngest in the group—only four and a half—and was so scared being separated from Mother.

Arriving at the Nurzec River stop, we were hoisted onto a horse-drawn wagon and continued on our journey. We passed by village after village with thatched roof houses nestled in the raw landscape. The locals were very friendly and gave us fruit, bread and delicious fresh milk to drink. The aroma from the haystacks, freshly harvested wheat and cornfields, and the pollen from the abundant wildflowers, permeated the air. We didn't ask questions, but I had so many, *'Where are we going; what is going to happen to us?'* We sang songs and tried to enjoy ourselves, while misshapen willow trees leaned across the roads from both sides and hovered over our wagon. The deeper we passed into their clutches, the more grotesque and animate the trees seemed. My brother's presence gave me the only shred of security that remained during these hours of transit.

By sundown we arrived in front of a white wooden church in the center of a very small village. It was a primitive hamlet. A dirt road divided each house from its barn and stable. All the homes were made of sturdy logs, had straw roofs and were colorfully painted. The setting was as magical as the fairy tales Mother used to read to me, while I was safely tucked in the bed that no longer existed.

I was very tired and particularly upset and teary because Zdzisław stopped paying attention to me. He became friendly with the other twelve-year-old boys during the trip and was increasingly annoyed by his little brother. We climbed off the wagon and were greeted by an overweight priest who lined us up in front of a group of waiting villagers.

The priest showed off each boy, pointing out the broad shoulders of some and the strong arms of others. The villagers were only interested in the older boys, including Zdzisław, and took them to work on their farms. Zdzisław jumped onto a stranger's wagon and, without even saying goodbye, he left me. I was sure I would be abandoned and yearned for my mother.

I was the only child remaining in the dusty square, alone with the priest. He begged several of the lingering villagers to take me, but nobody wanted the burden of a four-year-old city boy dressed in a silly blue sailor suit. I tried not to cry. The local tailor finally approached the priest. He had recently lost his wife and was raising a daughter my age. As a gesture of mercy, he took me as a companion for his little girl. The priest complimented him and showed great relief at not having to take care of me himself. I clearly remember the tailor's bony hand clasping my own as he dragged me down the road toward his house. I felt helpless.

As we crossed the village, the locals peered at me curiously. Through doorways and fences I saw strange people gawking at my clever starched collar and the soft curls framing my face. Polish storybooks warned of the *Polewiki*, spirits who appeared at sunset waiting to murder those who wandered astray, and the one-eyed *Licho*, the skinny old woman dressed in black who personified evil. I was suddenly terrified that the demons in my imagination were real. The strong grip on my hand was pulling me against my will. The villagers on the side of the road seemed like witches eager to scratch me with their long, monstrous nails. The horses looked like dragons with taut, angry muscles and mouths full of powerful, razor sharp teeth, and the birds in the air were like vampire bats thirsty for my blood. The sun was already very low on the horizon. I wanted to close my eyes, but was too afraid. I just stared ahead into the blinding light, and with my eyes on fire I spotted the very last building along the main dirt road. It was the tailor's house, and it would be my new home.

3

Losha

What a relief to be inside. The place was warm, and skipping toward me across the dirt floor was a ragged, barefoot child with a broad smile who was exactly my size. She seemed overjoyed at the sight of me. Maybe she expected an older boy, a muscled ruffian who would boss her around and smash her toys.

She came close to me, her nose practically touching mine, and said, "My name is Marysia, what's yours?"

The tailor, who had barely said a word, introduced me and told the two of us to sit and eat as he served cold, sour, homemade yogurt with hard, undercooked potatoes. I hated the taste of it. Every spoonful was a struggle to swallow. Marysia kept her eyes and grin fixed on me while she spooned the yogurt into her mouth. I was on the verge of throwing up, but terrified of what would happen to me if I did. So I ate.

It was before dawn the next morning when the tailor woke up in the dark to warm our breakfast. The strident sounds outside the front door from hundreds of birds greeting the new day were completely different from the city sounds I was accustomed to hearing. Marysia and the tailor took me outdoors to show off their horse, cow, chickens and geese (who arched their necks more like snakes than fowl as they hissed and snapped at me), their barn, modest vegetable garden, and the little courtyard with its stone water well that plunged into creepy darkness. Even though they were very nice to me, I was still afraid— only a week earlier I spent every hour of the day protected by my mother. But, after a day of playing with a cheerful and mischievous companion my age and surrounding myself with animals and nature, I began to feel somewhat safer in this stranger's house in the woods.

Every dwelling in the village looked alike, except for the tailor's house, which to my small eyes was the largest. It was shaded by dense willow and birch trees and was the only building with a brick exterior and a crude, wooden spinning wheel that was taller than I. In the corner of the dirt-floored main room, which also functioned as a kitchen, stood a roofed fireplace used for cooking. On top of the fireplace was a narrow sleeping area with a straw-filled mattress. This became my bed. I loved its height and its warmth; it was my nest.

The tailor was slight of build, with a mousey gray beard. He was a sad man who kept to himself, but looked at me with kindness in his eyes. I never learned his name and always addressed him as *pan,* mister. As winter loomed he made a fire in the big cast iron wood-burning stove every morning. Then he would take a seat at his spinning wheel and disappear under hunched shoulders for hours. The foods that made up our meals—flour, potatoes, carrots, onions, apples, preserves, honey—were given to the tailor as payment for his work. The villagers didn't trade in money; everything was bartered. My duties included feeding the oven with wood while the tailor labored over his sewing, and chasing the geese into the barn before nightfall. I had to carry a long stick to defend myself against these vicious birds.

All the villagers rose with the first rays of the sun and went to bed at dusk. Candles were costly and lit only for emergencies. Electricity and running water did not exist, so everyone used outhouses. Folk medicine was the only kind available—vodka was the remedy for scrapes and cuts, leeches were applied for purging (every household had a bottle of these bloodsuckers), and a plate of moist bread covered with greenish mold could always be found in dark storage spaces. Without penicillin, the peasants relied on the same homegrown fungus they had used for centuries to treat infections.

Winter came and with it an abundance of snow which kept us inside, mainly in the kitchen with its large shepherd fireplace. My fifth birthday was fast approaching—without my knowledge—and life with my new family was uneventful. Marysia and I had a daily routine and many domestic responsibilities, and while she never tired of it, for me the magic of her forest hamlet vanished early on. The three of us ate the same meal of chilled yogurt and potatoes very often and over time I got used to it. The wicked trees that once loomed like talons ready to pierce my eyes, soon looked like harmless, brittle sticks. The geese never warmed up to me and neither did the neighbors. My only excitement came from going to church on Sunday mornings.

When I entered the immense and gleaming white building for the first time—which I can only assume in retrospect was actually a worn and parochial church with a crackly, eggshell coat of paint—I was overcome by its majesty. A sea of worshipers was lifting its voice in song, led by the powerful music from the church organ. The vibrations resonated through my entire body, and I tried hard to learn the hymns so I could sing in a bold, proud voice along with everyone else. On a few occasions I saw my brother in the church. He was usually sitting with his older friends and made no attempt to communicate with me. Sometimes he waved, but nothing more. *I hate him. What have I done wrong?*

I didn't consider myself Jewish and neither did any of the villagers. My skin is fair, my hair blond, my eyes blue, and my identification papers claimed I was a baptized Christian. So when we saw German soldiers, which was rare, they had no interest in me. Their only concern was arresting Jews, or partisans. The partisans they hunted would often sneak into the village at night. They came for supplies, to get drunk on *bimber* and, I later learned, to satisfy their sexual urges with the young women. In return they fed us information about what was happening in the war. In the spring of 1943 the village was abuzz with talk about the advancing Soviet army. German columns were retreating westward from their failed Russian campaign with badly frostbitten, hungry soldiers who rampaged our village for any provisions they could find. Watching these men, mad with desperation, tearing into the tailor's cupboards and stealing our last stores of food, was terrifying.

My father's Home Army, in the meantime, was extremely organized and active, sabotaging Nazi supply lines, blowing up railroad tracks, moving east and inflicting many German casualties. The Nazis started to lose battles on both their eastern and western fronts, and in response, they stepped up their mass exterminations of Jews.

By April 19, 1943, when only seventy thousand of the original four hundred forty thousand inhabitants of the Warsaw Ghetto were still alive, a couple of hundred young Jewish fighters took up arms against the Nazis. Many of them were only children—boys and girls armed with pistols and Molotov cocktails. They were reinforced by a small group from the Home Army who supplied some weaponry and a few fighters. Father was one of them.

At the end of the first day, the Germans waited until sundown and then stormed the ghetto. They were quickly repelled with heavy casualties, including the loss of a tank. The following day the Jewish fighters raised two flags atop one of the tallest ghetto buildings—the red and white flag of Poland and a blue and white flag which would become the symbol of Israel. It was a message to the entire population of Warsaw that their fight was not over. This act of rebellion caught the Nazis by total surprise. For the "master race" it was a crushing, humiliating blow.

The Warsaw Ghetto Uprising lasted for three horrific weeks until May 9 and resulted in the deaths of over thirteen thousand inhabitants. Many of the fighters, on the verge of capture, chose death by suicide as a more honorable end than what faced them in the concentration camps. Roughly one hundred fighters from my father's Home Army were killed, but Father made it out alive.

Hundreds of miles away, in the safety of our village, Marysia and I reveled in the spring weather. We played outdoors for hours, while the tailor worked. Along with the heat and humidity came an infestation of pesky flies, mosquitoes and spiders. The villagers made use of the abundant *fly amanita* mushrooms, with their poisonous red and white-spotted caps, as an effective repellent. They soaked them in saucers filled with milk, placed them on windowsills and tables, and watched as the scarlet seductress attracted its prey. Dozens of pests lay dead on the same table where we ate our meals. This repulsive sight was even more of a reason to stay outside.

The next-door neighbor had a beautiful cherry tree growing just off the tailor's property. It was full of ripe, deep red cherries ready to harvest, and Marysia and I wanted so badly to taste the fragrant fruit. One day, while lazily bothering some spiders that nested in the firewood, we watched as the neighbor rode away on his horse. The moment he was out of sight we dashed over to his yard. I managed to climb the tree, stuffed a few cherries in my mouth, and threw a handful down to Marysia. In the midst of our indulgence I heard a distant pounding of hooves from the neighbor's horse. He was galloping up the main road and saw us on his property.

With cherry juice dripping down my chin, I yelled down to Marysia, "*Uważaj*, watch out! He's coming back!" and she sprinted for home.

For me it was too late. Awkwardly, I tried to jump out of the tree, but in the process broke one of its branches and tumbled to the ground. As quickly as I could, I fled for safety into the tailor's barn and climbed on top of one of the hay bales.

The enraged neighbor ran after me, grabbing a sickle along the way. He stood outside the barn cursing and screaming threats. The tailor appeared and tried in vain to calm him, but the neighbor was unappeased. He stormed into the barn and wildly thrashed at the straw with his razor-sharp sickle. In sheer terror I burrowed myself as deeply as possible under the straw. The mad man was on top of me, ready to kill me. His cherries meant much more to him than my life, I was sure of it. The tailor ran home frantically and fetched a bottle of vodka, which he used to pacify the neighbor. It was a more than generous exchange for the few cherries I stole. So, begrudgingly the neighbor accepted the bottle and headed for home. I stayed in hiding for a long time, shivering, my senses on high alert. It felt like an eternity of silence passed before the tailor and Marysia came to tell me it was safe to come out.

This was the only time the tailor hit me. The lashings themselves were not nearly as painful as the humiliation and alienation I felt afterward. Only then did it strike me, *I really am an orphan. Nobody loves me.* I never again wandered into the neighbor's yard.

❀

On a cold March evening in 1944, my second winter in the village, I stepped out of the house and into the shadowy night to collect firewood from the barn. The snow was deep and I wasn't wearing any shoes. With every breath I could have fogged up the moon, but there was no moon to be found in the darkness of the woods. I was struggling with a bundle of logs when two large beasts suddenly appeared from behind me. They were sinister figures on horseback, and before I could run, one of them grabbed a hold of my shirt and lifted me, tummy down, onto the horse. With lightening speed we galloped away from the village and rode deep into the forest.

I thought I had been snatched by devils. The local priest delivered count-less sermons from the depths of his stern, swollen belly on the treachery of our souls and the demonic punishments that awaited us. I never felt personally subject to his warnings. If anything, I liked to think he was preaching to the neighbor who couldn't control his temper, to the witchy women who showed no affection for a skinny city boy, and to my brother who treated me like a pest. On this night, however, bruised and strapped to the back of a fierce animal with an even fiercer rider, I was so afraid.

There were dozens of these strangers in the forest, and they looked very different from the men of the village. Their hair was long, they displayed thick beards and mustaches, and they were foul-smelling, even to a dirty little boy. They were Cossacks, partisans like my father, scouts for the advancing Russian army. The Cossacks came from the territory of the Ukraine and the very eastern parts of Poland, and were descendants of nomadic, Mongol tribes dating back to Genghis Khan. Riding miniature Steppe horses, they were a free brotherhood of warriors. When they came upon me—a small, shivering urchin, barefoot and dressed in rags—maybe they thought I could provide some valuable information.

A few of the men surrounded me. They gave me woolen socks, wrapped my ice cold feet with leather straps, and put a thick sheepskin fur on my back. One of them asked me questions in poor Polish.

"I don't have parents," I said. "This village isn't where I was born, but I live with the tailor and his daughter Marysia."

I answered all his questions while the men fed me unfamiliar food and gave me a warm drink, probably horse milk. Very soon, overwhelmed and tired, I fell asleep.

When I woke the next morning, they doted on me like Marysia had when I first arrived. So, I roughhoused with them and watched as they galloped at full speed, sometimes not even on the horses' backs, but hanging onto their sides or dangling under their stout stomachs. We idled away the time for a few days until a fully equipped Russian armed force joined us, and together we marched into the village with tanks, trucks and hundreds of men. The commanding general took over the tailor's brick house as headquarters. Poor Marysia and the tailor were thrown out. After spending a year and a half of my life with them, they were suddenly gone.

The soldiers questioned the locals about me, and the villagers confirmed I was indeed an orphan. Since I didn't belong to anybody, they decided to claim me as their own and took me to an officer. A very tall and handsome man, he stood like a giant, dressed in a pristine uniform, wearing high, shiny black boots. I was extremely intimidated. I could see my reflection in his boots, and I was shaking like a little squirrel.

"We found this orphan boy alone in the woods. He was almost frozen to death."

The officer, with his penetrating blue eyes that locked on my own, asked me in Polish, "What is your name?"

"Leszek," I answered, meekly.

He grinned at me, shook my small hand and said, "Little Losha, don't be afraid. I will tell you a secret. I am an orphan too, so we will take care of each other."

I smiled at him, and he ordered one of his men to arrange for a Russian army uniform in my size.

And then he said, "Come, you will stay with me."

Back in the tailor's house, now the officers' quarters, I reclaimed my warm bed on top of the fireplace. All the soldiers called this man "General," so I did, too. And for him I was "Losha."

I wondered what happened to my friendly playmate Marysia and the tailor, who rescued me when I was standing by myself in that dirt square. I didn't have the courage to ask.

4

Lost

My life changed dramatically with the Russians. All of a sudden, my friends were the invading force and their general became my foster father. For the first time since the start of the war, I didn't have to fear for my safety. The scared little rabbit became a fox.

I didn't think of the Cossacks and the Russian soldiers—whose families were hundreds of miles away—as my new "family." They were more like a rowdy pack of wolves looking for someone to toy with and lift their spirits. At night they gathered around a fire to play their *balalaikas* and *domras* while one guy accompanied them on his rhapsodic accordion. Bottles of vodka were passed from man to man, as they sang patriotic folk songs and impressed each other with wild Cossack dances.

They included me in their revelry, boasting, "You will bring us luck on the front lines!"

I tried to learn their Russian lyrics, mimic their *Kazatsky*, knee-bending dance moves, and make them smile as often as I could. We became close, even though the ties that bound us were circumstantial and fragile.

I loved my new freedom. The soldiers carried me around the village on their shoulders while the locals watched with disdain. I had no responsibilities, except for enjoying myself. Occasionally, I was taken on patrols close to German lines. The piercing sounds of gunfire and exploding bombs were frightening at first, but soon became another thrill on my growing list of pleasures. I was well-fed like never before and ate all my meals with the general. Above all, I didn't have to go to bed at sundown. I felt more grown-up and would tell myself, *I don't miss my mother any more. I don't even feel like an orphan.*

The troops positioned a large machine gun in the courtyard of the tailor's house, precariously aimed at the nasty next-door neighbor's barn. For me it was the sleekest, most sophisticated toy imaginable. I was envious of the soldier standing in front of its trigger, and I pleaded with him to let me take his place.

"I have nothing else to do, I can stand guard for you!" I implored.

He laughed at me, "You are too short and your skinny fingers are too small. You can never make it fire!"

Without any combat missions that day, the soldier grew bored. As the afternoon wore on, his resolve to keep me from the gun wore off. He positioned me behind the mount, angled the weapon skyward, and wrapped my fingers around its trigger. It must have been an arresting picture—a pink-cheeked child at the command of a firearm whose barrel was twice as long as he was and whose steel was unyielding. The man shook his head and watched me struggle. I pulled as hard as I could on the resistant trigger, but nothing happened. I was embarrassed and willed my fingers to squeeze harder. With all my determination I pulled hard enough to bring the barrel down to eye level, parallel with the ground, and it went off. To everyone's shock, especially my own, a stream of burning bullets exploded toward the neighbor's barn.

The battalion went berserk, screaming orders, diving under trucks and into houses, cocking their weapons, and then freezing to look and listen in the direction of the barn. We all saw smoke puffing out of the loft, followed a moment later by wild flames raging from every crack in the building. As soon as the rest of the battalion figured out that I had fired the gun, they stood and glared at me. The general was infuriated and shouted for his men to put out the neighbor's fire, but I had to bite my cheek to avoid laughing. I felt proud, rather than guilty. *Let it burn. This is my revenge.*

❧

It was April and I had just turned six years old. The Red Army used the village as an outpost for a month before they received orders to push west. Their departure was as swift and unruly as their arrival, and I felt so relieved when the general took me along, even though I didn't have a chance to say goodbye to Zdzisław. If I had been left with the villagers—who were glad to see me go—they probably would have murdered me. I had a greater chance of survival marching onto the battlefield in the largest theater of war in human history.

This was the first time ever that I would ride in a car. The general seated me next to him in our car that was flanked by armored vehicles thundering down the main road. We advanced toward Warsaw for three perilous months and came across countless dead and wounded Russian soldiers. A few had familiar faces. The ones who were still alive terrified me with their wild eyes and pained expressions. The dead ones sometimes looked like they were taking a nap. I often recognized them as playmates from the forest and tried to wake them up.

"Hey, hey . . ." I whispered, hoping they would open their eyes and say, "Hello, Losha! Do you want to go look for mushrooms, or hunt for deer?"

But they remained still. I was very confused, and it took a while for me to connect their torn flesh and bloody uniforms with their silence. We passed through many burning villages strewn with dead bodies. The deeper we traveled into the destruction, the more upset I became. *I don't want to die.* I stayed very close to the general and didn't wander astray with the soldiers.

Though they treated *me* well, the Cossacks were not nice people. They were heartless and cruel; their victims—German soldiers, civilians and, I later learned, members of my father's Home Army—faced a hideous death. During one of our offensives, the Cossacks captured an SS officer and delivered him to the general's headquarters for interrogation. Even though I was evicted from the room, I crouched under the window to eavesdrop. I heard a few muffled hits and grunts, but the Nazi didn't utter a word. Soon after I went to bed, the man began to scream in excruciating pain. His howling lasted throughout the night. I was told the next day that his interrogators introduced him to a big, hungry rat in a cage. When it became clear he had no intention of talking, the Russians strapped a metal pot onto his naked abdomen with the rat inside. The creature ate its way through the flesh and guts of the captive. I had nightmares for months afterward and would wake shaking, looking for rats under my covers.

Our battalion made rapid progress west across Poland and soon came upon what turned out to be my grandparents' properties. According to accounts from surviving residents, the general's first orders were to burn the local church and then to set Grandfather's manor house on fire. I was incredibly fortunate that none of the locals could identify me, and that I had no recollection of the place. If the general discovered I was of noble descent, my family enemies of the Bolsheviks, and my father a beneficiary of those lands and an officer in the Home Army, he would probably have thrown me into that burning building.

By July we approached Warsaw. The Germans desperately tried to stop the Soviet advance on the eastern side of the Vistula. With the Soviets on Warsaw's doorstep, the Polish government, exiled in London, issued an order to the Home Army to liberate the Polish capital ahead of the advancing Russians. The idea was to drive the Germans out of the capital city and establish legitimate Polish authority, preventing the Soviets from taking control. It was a daring nationalistic act of resistance.

Operation Storm started on August 1, 1944. With citizen soldiers, including women, teenagers, the last surviving Jewish people, forty thousand poorly equipped underground reservists and my father, the Home Army reclaimed a major part of Poland's capital city within days. Hitler was outraged. The city had been his first capital conquest of the war, and now it was trying to defeat and humiliate him. He ordered it destroyed. Heinrich Himmler proclaimed,

> *Warsaw will be liquidated; and this city . . . that has blocked our path to the east for seven hundred years . . . will have ceased to exist!*

Hitler emptied his German prisons to form monstrous military units made up of convicted murderers, rapists, crooks and ex-Soviet traitors, and he unleashed them onto the streets of Warsaw. Their role was to decimate the civilian population and slaughter without mercy, while the sophisticated SS command targeted the Polish resistance movement. German tanks rolled in full force, and there was heavy bombardment from the air.

The brave Polish soldiers fought house-to-house, door-to-door. Children threw gasoline bottles at tanks, women built street barricades, and no bullet was spared in the effort. The only way to move around the city was through its sewers, and in the dark, putrid maze of underground tunnels, many people drowned. The SS used flamethrowers to flush fighters out of buildings, and the whole of Warsaw was enveloped in thick clouds of ash that draped the battleground, like a shroud.

While Warsaw became a raging inferno, the Russians sat and waited on the other side of the Vistula River, making no effort to assist the Poles. The orders from Stalin (who called the Uprising a "criminal adventure" led by a bunch of "Fascists and reactionaries") were to delay the advance of the Red Army. Stalin joined with Hitler in the hopes of eliminating all non-Communist elements of the Polish resistance. For over two months, day and night, Father heroically fought for a free Poland, unaware that his son was on the other side of the river living with his adversaries. And at the same time, of course, I had forgotten my real father even existed.

After sixty-three days the Uprising was brutally crushed. Only a few hundred freedom fighters survived, having escaped through exit points in the sewers. Under international supervision from the Red Cross, the Germans honored the Geneva Convention and treated some of the survivors as POWs. Father was among them. He was dragged out of a sewer hole, arrested, and shipped in a cattle car to the Ohrdruf labor camp near Buchenwald, not far from Weimar, the Germans' cultural shrine. For him, more than five years of hiding and fighting the Nazis had come to a devastating end.

When the Soviet forces finally liberated Warsaw in January of 1945, they found eighty-five percent of the city totally destroyed. By the end of the month, the fast approaching Red Army freed Krakow in the South, along with its neighbors, Auschwitz and Częstochowa, the place of Mother's hiding. She had reference letters and a little money from the church, and left the monastery as quickly as possible heading northeast. Every town she passed was in ruin, and the people were in various stages of recovery. Many were vigorously rebuilding their homes, shops and churches, while others teetered like zombies in a fog, detached from the chaos around them. Mother, like thousands of courageous Polish mothers, was focused on a desperate search for her missing children. Hitchhiking almost the entire way, she arrived in Warsaw within a short time.

The city's eastern section, Praga, was largely intact, making it prime real estate for refugees and returning residents. Our miserable two-room apartment had been taken over by a different family. Mother applied to reclaim our old place, and after a contentious, humiliating fight with newly-appointed, disorderly bureaucrats who were running the city, she managed to obtain an order for permission to split the apartment in half. She and her youngest brother, my sweet uncle, Stasio, moved into that one room.

Having secured a roof over her head, she set out in search of Zdzisław and me, knowing the name of the village where we had been sent for adoption. After a couple of weeks of arduous travel, Mother arrived at the wooden church in the forest. She found Zdzisław without any problem. But I was missing, gone.

The villagers told her I left months ago with the Russian Army advancing west. They said I was under the protection of one of Stalin's most formidable generals, a man who was, remarkably, of Polish descent. His name was Konstantin Rokossovsky. *'Good riddance to the both of them!'* was the locals' sentiment. Mother returned to the city with Zdzisław and devised a plan to track me down. Unfortunately for her, I was hundreds of miles away, riding in a Jeep alongside my beloved general on our way to Berlin.

❊

Meanwhile, at an historic meeting between Winston Churchill, Franklin Delano Roosevelt and Joseph Stalin in the resort town of Yalta on the Black Sea, Poland's future was sealed for the next half century. Stalin convinced the ailing American president that his chief aim was to protect Poland,

To create a mighty, free and independent Poland.

And furthermore,

Because the Russians have greatly sinned against Poland . . . the Soviet government is trying to atone for those sins.

Roosevelt was idolized as a great leader in the eyes of the American public, but Poles had quite a different view. We saw him through the lens of war, as an old man who made a reckless deal with our deceitful enemy. Roosevelt handed over the Polish nation, disregarding our suffering and the incalculable sacrifices we made in combat on two fronts. Poland once again lost its sovereignty, and with it, our dream of a democracy vaporized.

By April all of the western territories were liberated up to the Oder River. Before the war that region had been considered Germany's Eastern Prussia. A few men in the Red Army treated the German civilians with good will, while others demonstrated a bloodthirsty brutality that could only be rationalized as revenge for Stalingrad. There were reports that General Rokossovsky tried to hold his men to standards of good conduct, but at this late stage in the war, many soldiers had long since abandoned their decency. I was old enough to recognize that human rights of some sort were being violated when I witnessed the treatment of women. With most of the German male population enlisted in the armed forces, groups of defenseless women—old ladies and very young girls among them—were rounded up and abused. Their arms were strapped to fences and poles that were low to the ground. In this way they could be raped from behind at any time of day or night. I could see there was no hope for them and, in fact, history recounts that many of these victims ultimately took their own lives. I stored their suffering somewhere far away from consciousness, along with my growing collection of unbearable childhood memories.

While Berlin was under siege and Hitler was contemplating suicide, Russian, American and British troops were liberating concentration camps all over Europe, one after the other. Millions perished, but thousands of prisoners were still clinging to life. The first camp to be liberated by the Americans was Ohrdruf where Father remained a prisoner throughout the winter of 1945. When the U.S. Army's Fourth Armored Division and Eighty-ninth Infantry Division entered the camp, Father was found locked in a torture chamber, one of the few prisoners who had not been evacuated on a death march toward Buchenwald. Perhaps it was his good fortune that shortly before the death march, a Nazi guard caught him stealing a single potato. He was confined to a very narrow compartment and forced to stand naked in a foot of water with a thin stream dripping incessantly on top of his head. After three days and nights under such excruciating conditions, the doors to the chamber were opened and, semiconscious, my father collapsed at the feet of his liberators.

Although photo and film documentation of Nazi atrocities had existed for almost a year, since the liberation of the Majdanek Camp in Southeastern Poland, the larger world was not yet ready to believe that the Nazis operated death camps. Rumors of gas chambers and mass exterminations were too nauseating for any civilized public to stomach. So, on April 12, U.S. Army General Dwight D. Eisenhower, the Supreme Commander of the Allied Forces, along with Generals Bradley and Patton, visited Ohrdruf to see the evidence for themselves. In a cable to the head of the Joint Chiefs of Staff, Eisenhower wrote,

> *The visual and the verbal testimony of starvation, cruelty and bestiality were so overpowering as to leave me a bit sick ... I made the visit deliberately, in order to be in a position to give first-hand evidence of these things if ever, in the future, there develops a tendency to charge these allegations merely to 'propaganda.'*

Patton himself was physically unable to tour certain sections of the camp for fear he would vomit. The Nazis' torture chambers, the piles of hundreds of badly mutilated and half-burned corpses, and the appalling condition of the surviving prisoners were more than even the most hardened warriors could bear.

Eisenhower ordered photographic documentation; he sent his army units to tour the camp to show his soldiers the depraved nature of their enemy, and he forced the local German population to visit the site and come to grips with their countrymen's heinous crimes against humanity.

After many days spent receiving medical treatment, Father was incorporated into the United States Army as a POW officer. Dressed in a U.S. Army uniform with the insignia of Poland on his breast and arm, he was assigned to the army's supply company in Germany.

On May 9, Germany's surrender was total. The wild celebrations throughout the world are legendary. But for me, the end of the war was not automatically a good thing. I had been born just before the war began, and my first seven years were spent amidst its fury. War was all I knew. The thought of peace was abstract and it made me feel anxious and uncertain. My soldier friends were overjoyed because they were going home, back to their mothers, wives and children. *What will happen to me? I don't have parents or a place to call home.* After the general told me he had a wife and a daughter waiting for him somewhere in Russia, I was terrified he would send me back to the village alone.

Mother had to rely on Soviet officials for help tracing the general's route across Poland and into Germany. She was moving west alongside thousands of feeble and sick refugees in rags, often holding each other for support. By the beginning of June, my brave and determined mother finally appeared at Rokossovsky's headquarters in the city of Statin. At the first sight of me she burst into tears. I was almost unrecognizable. I stood in front of her dressed like a little Russian soldier and didn't fly into her arms as she had expected. She was shocked. I pretended I didn't know who she was and wanted nothing to do with her.

I told the general in Russian, "She is not my mother. Get rid of her."

He was very amused by my behavior and said to her, "He doesn't know you. He doesn't even look like you. You cannot expect me to let him go with a stranger. The boy is more my son than yours!"

Mother presented him with a handful of documents—my birth certificate, an official letter from someone in command in Warsaw, the paperwork for my transport to the village—but the general was unmoved.

Through his dazzling smile he said, "Your husband is probably dead. Why don't you marry me?!" he mocked.

Of course, he failed to mention he already had a wife.

The general pointed to a room full of looted furs, clothing, china, piles of valuables, and declared, "They can all be yours. If you go back to Warsaw, you will have nothing but a miserable life."

Mother was silently outraged. She hated Russians and only wanted her youngest son back, but she was afraid to offend the very powerful Marshal of the Soviet Union, their highest-ranking officer.

She graciously declined his offer and asked, "How would it look if you were to marry the widow of a Polish aristocrat?"

It was an impossible proposition. The general had to let me go.

When my mother and I boarded a Russian military transport train heading east, I was still very angry at her. After all, she abandoned me when I was so small. The general had been good to me and kept me safe. I couldn't imagine that I would never see him again. To Mother's amazement, I was treated like an army dignitary as we rode toward Warsaw. The Polish passengers rode on top of mounds of coal in the rear of the locomotive, while Mother and I were comfortably seated inside warm, cozy cars. The soldiers who rode alongside us sang songs with me and enjoyed my company. I didn't pay attention to Mother and refused to speak to her in Polish. By that time I identified myself as Russian.

My wartime adventures ended abruptly back inside our cramped Praga apartment with a brother I barely liked. Zdzisław was not pleased to see me either. Mother burned my uniform and dressed me in worn, ugly rags, the only ones she could find. She was overly protective and severely restricted my freedom. Uncle Stasio was my only comfort, with his caring manner and reassuring male presence. I missed the general and the friendly soldiers. I missed my uniform. I missed the soulful sounds of Russian folk songs and the exuberant Cossack dances. I missed the excitement of the war. I missed the general's good food. Every day Mother made some kind of thin soup we had to be grateful for. We were lucky to have a piece of bread. Most days I felt hungry and lonely, locked up in our dreary apartment. We had no choice but to embark on an impoverished life in the newly created Republic of Poland.

And then one day Mother announced to me, "You will go to school after the summer."

I could finally get out of that hole Mother called home. I longed for some fresh air and playtime with other children, whose voices I heard through our fractured brick walls.

I imagined that my life would change and I would be free again, just like I was with the general.

5

A Typical Boy

After Germany's surrender, Father stayed with the Americans for six months, clearing remnants of the Nazi resistance. For his contribution the American authorities granted him, and his entire family, immigration papers to the United States. Many of Father's compatriots, having heard discouraging reports from the homeland about Soviet oppression and arrests, took advantage and emigrated to the U.S. Not my father. He was proud of his wartime achievements and noble heritage, and believed his place was in a free Poland with our family. In robust health and dressed in his American serviceman's uniform, Father began planning his trip back to his wife and sons and the home he hadn't seen for years.

Warsaw in 1945 was a very dangerous city. The population was beyond impoverished and lacked many basic needs. There was an abundance of guns and ammunition in the streets, and we very often heard about or witnessed terrible accidents. Adults and children alike were routinely mutilated by unexploded shells. It was only by sheer luck that we were not counted among the victims.

With our apartment came a small storage space in the basement. One morning Mother discovered several weapons, including grenades, hidden under a sack of potatoes and coal bricks, which Zdzisław found and was storing with a teenager's fascination. A single spark near his stockpile could have blown up the entire building. Zdzisław was furious when Mother disposed of his dreadful collection. He was an angry adolescent and hated me more than ever, as if it were my fault.

Since our one room had two windows, it was very bright. Three beds lined the walls—Mother's on one side of the room, opposite mine and Zdzisław's (we slept together), and in between us, under the windows, was Uncle Stasio's bed with its threadbare mattress. Everybody in the building had a terrible infestation of bed bugs, and on many nights I was bitten to the blood all over my body. How I hated those parasites. I was grateful when Mother got a hold of several cans of DDT. We sprayed the toxic white powder indiscriminately, under the beds, onto the mattresses, into the cracks in the walls. After inhaling so much of it, I am sure the poison is still swimming through my veins.

We had a large armoire to store our clothes, a table with four chairs, and no other furniture. The lone ornamentation in our drab room was a kitschy tapestry depicting a deer by a brook in the mountains that Mother found lying in the street while scavenging through rubble. I remember how proud she was to hang it on the wall, as if it elevated our nonexistent social status.

We cooked on a small coal-burning stove, and running water for the apartment was only available in a communal sink in the hall. Everybody used a dark, fetid outhouse in the courtyard. I was petrified every time I had to go there; closing myself inside felt like being locked in a crypt and surrounded by spooks.

I had no toys. The first thing I did when we came back to Warsaw was to search for my rusty little plane, but it was nowhere to be found. So I made my own playthings. I would find empty spools of thread, pieces of wood and cardboard, and make wagons, toy soldiers and horses. Mother would occasionally find crayons or pencils and bring them home, encouraging me to draw. Every stubby crayon would occupy me for hours, breaking the monotony of my days. There was hardly anything I enjoyed more.

Despite shortages of everything, Mother was as committed to her appearance as ever. She never went without stockings, which were a prized luxury, and she spent every evening after dinner mending them at the table. Mother was also extremely tidy and demanded the same from her children.

The atmosphere at home was not a loving one; she was always edgy and bossy, often reminding us, "You are lucky to have me and four solid walls. Shut your mouths and stop complaining."

That autumn I was enrolled in an elementary school just two blocks from our building, and every morning I walked with my brother for formal study.

Mother and Uncle Stasio worked from morning until sometimes very late at night. Just across the street from the school was a Silesian Church, the Basilica of Holy Jesus Heart—the biggest church in Warsaw—that miraculously survived the war intact. Its mission was to provide care and comfort for the youth of the city. The priests kept us off the unsafe streets, which gave Mother much-needed peace of mind. Zdzisław and I did our homework, played games and ate simple suppers. I played soccer and sang in the choir, which I loved, even though performing in such a huge space in front of a large crowd made me so nervous I peed in my pants during Mass one Sunday.

Compared to the first seven years of my life, I began to lead a normal existence as a typical boy.

❁

On an early evening in November there was an unexpected knock at our door. To the astonishment of Mother, Zdzisław and Uncle Stasio, Feliks Zawistowski stood in the hallway, a tall apparition delivered to us from a darker time and place. As soon as they realized he was no ghost, there was an outpouring of joy.

Mother cried, running to embrace him.

I, meanwhile, had no idea who Feliks was. I was seven and a half and hadn't lived with my father since I was a baby. *Is this proud man with his gentleman's mustache really my father?* The stranger looked so dashing in his impressive United States Army uniform, much better than my Russian general (although there was an eerie resemblance between the two men). I wished I could wear my old uniform and appear as dignified to Father as he did to me. All of us wept and laughed jubilantly, miraculously reunited, but for the terrible absence of my oldest brother Henryk.

We cobbled together a welcome home party in our one little room. Father unfastened the sack of packages he carried on his back and emptied it onto our small table. It was stuffed with SPAM, sardines, dried fruitcakes, chocolates and candies—all American goodies with exotic English labels beyond my imagination. I had never seen so many delicious treats. I swallowed my fill and ran around the table, high on sugar, and played with my father the same way I used to fool around with the general.

By nightfall, Father, Stasio and a neighbor were very drunk.

"Bring us more vodka," they demanded.

I was in such a playful mood, instead of obeying, I pleaded with my father, "Chase me, chase me!"

Father sat in front of me with his head buried in his hands over an empty glass of liquor. Again he ordered me to fetch more vodka, and again I defied him. He grabbed hold of me, raised me high in the air, turned me upside down and, with Mother screaming next to us, threw me head first onto the floor. I landed awkwardly on my neck and shoulders, but with my skull intact. I was in pain, scared and stunned, but did not dare cry. The general would never have done that to me. My father took a dreadful form in that instant. The gallant soldier became a monster.

In the eyes of the neighborhood, Father returned a war hero. Word of his survival spread quickly and gave everyone a bit of optimism, which was in scarce supply. But, late into the third night after Father came home, there was heavy banging on our door and then the shattering sound of a forced entry. It was dark, but I could vaguely see a band of armed men who stormed into our apartment. Some of them wore Russian Army uniforms. Father was dragged out of bed in his underwear and taken away.

When the sun rose the next morning and illuminated the events of the night before, we saw that the hallway outside our apartment was stained with blood. Mother made an official inquiry about Father's whereabouts and was told that he had been taken by the KGB. They accused him of being a Western reactionary spy. The Home Army officially disbanded in 1945, but the Communist Party authorities hunted every former member with a vengeance, imprisoning, or simply eliminating, as many as they could. After his brutal arrest, Father was sent to one of the Soviet gulags. Mother was convinced Rokossovsky was behind it.

"Your general took my husband away!" she shouted at me.

I didn't try to defend the general or myself, knowing it was best to remain silent. For the first time since the war began, Mother believed she would become a widow. I, on the other hand, was silently relieved that the man who hurt me so badly was gone.

❊

My music teacher at the basilica was an energetic, young priest named

Jacek Kochanski, who was the church conductor and also played the organ and violin. Father Kochanski was outgoing, always walked at a very rapid pace, adored music and was deeply committed to instilling his passion for music in all his young charges.

He said to me, "You have a good voice and excellent pitch, so I am giving you solo soprano parts to sing."

The next thing I knew, the priest handed me a cello and told me he would teach me how to play. The instrument was taller than I was, stately and shrewd, yet it showed signs of wear. Blunt wounds interrupted the smooth surface of its otherwise golden wooden skin, in the same way a returning soldier bears the marks of war. The notion that I would learn how to master this towering instrument was as exhilarating as firing that machine gun into the wicked neighbor's barn.

I had only begun my studies when the elder cellist in the church Baroque ensemble passed away, and Kochanski needed someone to play in the upcoming Christmas celebrations. I took cello lessons every day, and after about four months of intensive coaching, I managed to get through the holiday performances. In the spring of 1948, around my tenth birthday, Father Jacek had a serious talk with Mother about my musical training.

"Leszek is a very talented boy and I am not really a qualified teacher. It is time to find a professional cellist to give him proper lessons. I will look for someone good, and if it's too expensive the church will help."

He found a highly regarded cellist, the principal of the Warsaw Philharmonic, Tadeusz Kowalski, a true gentleman of European style who had lived in Paris for many years. In post-war Poland his appearance was quite remarkable; vanity was displayed proudly on his sleeve. He always wore gray cotton gloves, his hair was slicked back, and he had a valet walk behind him carrying his shiny cello in its wooden case. I was very intimidated by his formal and haughty manner and understood the seriousness of our arrangement. Twice a week Mother would take me to Kowalski's apartment for lessons, which usually lasted two hours. Every day after school I completed my homework and stayed indoors to practice the cello. ·

My new teacher was a tyrant who never hesitated to yell and even throw things at me. During the war years, I developed strong survival skills, but in Kowalski's presence I cowered and couldn't defend myself. I cried my way through many lessons. At ten years old, under Mother's, the priest's and Kowalski's constant supervision, I was forced to abandon everything for music. No more coloring or playing soccer with my friends. When I was alone with my cello, tuning it or holding it at arms length to study its features, I tried to blame it for my troubles. But I couldn't. The truth was, the cello took on a very special meaning in my life. Not only did I take great pleasure in the beauty of its sound, the cello was something I could call my own. In school the kids would make a mental tally of what each had lost during the war. This boy has a toy plane, that one does not; one has new shoes, another does not; some have family, many do not. Forget my absent friends, the cello took the place of everything I had lost.

By then Father had been gone for nearly three years, and Henryk's whereabouts remained an unsolved mystery, despite Mother's relentless searching. With their shadows gnawing at her ceaselessly, my mother struggled with her day-to-day routine. The practical hardships she had to overcome did little to distract her from the emotional void that was created by the absence of her husband and son. She wore a tired and vacant look on her face almost all the time and only made modest attempts to be an attentive mother to Zdzisław and me for a few brief moments before bedtime. In her scavenging she had found a gorgeous collection of hardcover Polish poetry—eleven of the twelve books intact—and she read them to us occasionally. But that was all she could muster.

I barely had any recollection of Henryk and never really gave him a thought. After all, I was only four years old when he was taken away. For Mother, however, our family was incomplete, and I didn't blame her for the cloud of despondency that hovered over our household.

Years earlier, while riding out the war in the secluded Częstochowa Monastery, Mother had a dream. She described to us how she saw Henryk, as tangible in her vision as if he were sitting beside her on the bed, the warmth of his breath and his smell as familiar as her own. Henryk leaned over, embraced Mother and gave her a kiss on the cheek. In the dream, her spartan cell suddenly took on an extraordinary glow and appeared as big and bright as the afternoon sun.

Mother asked Henryk, "How are you? I was looking all over for you, but you found me first."

He answered cheerfully, "I am fine. I just want to say goodbye before my long trip."

"What trip?" Mother asked. "Aren't you going to stay with me?"

"Oh, I am on my way to a beautiful place. Some day we will be there together."

At that moment, Mother awoke in great distress. In her cold room she found herself drenched in sweat, trying desperately to control her trembling body. She knew something terrible must have happened to her firstborn son. By the summer of 1948 she had recounted this dream to Zdzisław and me many, many times, as if retelling it would give her some comfort.

It was on a typical Sunday afternoon that we had a surprise visit from an unfamiliar young woman.

She introduced herself as Helga and said, "A few years ago, I knew a boy named Henryk."

The woman, in her early twenties, looked German, tall with straight blond hair and blue eyes. She had an air of calm and seemed trustworthy. Helga took Mother's quivering hands in her own and they sat down as dusk settled outside the apartment.

She came from Silesia, a territory in Southern Poland that through history had switched hands from the Austrians to the Germans and back to the Poles. Her family's situation was very common. Before the war they were Polish. During the Nazi occupation they became German. It all depended on the direction of the political winds. They owned a large farm just outside of Auschwitz, which, by 1942, had became a full-scale death camp. In 1943, at the age of seventeen, Helga's daily duties included assisting her father in supervising the property. Because of her unique proximity to the camp, the Polish Underground recruited her to work as an informer. She told us she hated the Nazis enough to take that risk.

All the production from her family farm, whose workforce consisted of prisoners assigned to slave labor, was destined to supply SS personnel in the Auschwitz and Birkenau camps. Walking through the muddy fields one day, Helga came upon a young, good-looking boy dressed in the familiar Auschwitz garb—tattered pajamas with blue and white stripes. He was disheveled and very emaciated. It seemed obvious to Helga that he was from the city because he looked uncomfortable with farm work. Without the SS guards taking notice, she carefully reached into her pocket and slipped a small piece of bread into the boy's palm. Then, as discretely as she could, she asked him a few questions.

"What is your name?"

"Henryk."

"How old are you?"

"Fifteen."

They were practically the same age.

"Henryk was frightened and spoke in whispers," Helga told us. "But he seemed eager to speak to someone from the outside."

"I am here as a Jewish prisoner, but I do not understand why. My father is Catholic. I have always believed my family is Catholic. I did nothing wrong. I am innocent."

Though their first encounter was brief, Henryk's soft, sweet manner made an indelible impression on Helga. She looked for him almost every day, surreptitiously bringing him a morsel to eat whenever possible. In that harrowing environment the two of them tried to share a smile. No matter her strong connection to him, she was helpless to change his circumstances. After months of almost daily meetings, suddenly Henryk failed to show up on the farm. Helga missed the boy and could not stop thinking about him. Almost two years passed before Auschwitz was liberated, and by that time, of course, Helga feared the worst.

She told us, "The Russian army rounded up all Nazi collaborators. My parents were taken away from our farm, but I was granted protection. The Russians were aware I had been watching the camp, and they assigned me to an official post. You see, the SS thought they had destroyed all evidence of their murders, their tortures, but the Russians knew thousands of documents and personal items survived, and they needed someone to sort through and catalogue all of it. This is my job." I noticed that her voice was shaking as she continued, "The first thing I did was to search for what happened to Henryk. I found a piece of paper, a camp record. It stated his name, his age (fifteen) and the cause of death. Heart failure."

Thousands of Jewish children were classified as having died from coronary diseases. No mention of starvation, beatings, gassings. Helga was unable to establish the actual cause of Henryk's death and could only relay to us the perverse lies of the Reich.

It had been six years since Henryk was taken from our apartment. Obviously, Helga's story was absolutely devastating, for Mother in particular. I was more affected by the dreadful narrative than by the absence of my brother. This terrible finality provided no solace, but Mother was profoundly grateful for Helga's kindness toward Henryk. We continued to see her from time to time, and Mother treated her like a daughter. But, the severe hardships of life in Poland were difficult to endure, so Helga eventually managed to escape to Western Germany where she moved in with surviving relatives. We lost contact with her and she faded out of our lives as seamlessly as she had appeared.

Mother and Zdzisław mourned Henryk's loss for a long time. I felt guilty for not feeling the same pain, but I couldn't relate to their suffering. When I was with the Russian troops during the war, I saw so many dead children. I tried very hard to imagine one of them as my brother, but it wasn't until many years later, as an adult, that I could begin to conceive of the weight of Henryk's death.

6

A Total Stranger

The population of Warsaw more than doubled in the three years following the end of the war. Displaced Poles flooded into the city, fiercely determined to rebuild their capital as the cultural center of Poland. When Mother and I first returned in 1945, everything around us was dirty, covered in dust and ash, fragile and infinitely spooky. We all lived in abject poverty, with strict food rations and minimum comforts. However, by 1948 signs of infrastructure began to emerge as rubble was cleared from the sidewalks and roads. Streetcars were rebuilt one at a time, using parts from demolished vehicles. Daily newspapers were printed and circulated; Chopin was played in sitting rooms once again. A virtual wasteland was quickly transforming into a livable society. The authorities ordered every resident of Warsaw to perform mandatory public service. One day each week, all men and women worked together to clear the rubble, build new structures and reconstruct old buildings. Consequently, Warsaw came back to life at a remarkable pace.

In the summer, for the first time in years, I started to sleep alone. Dear Uncle Stasio, who worked tirelessly to support his sister and us, was assigned the night shift at a local factory, leaving the mattress under the window vacant for me. My brother couldn't kick and punch me in bed any longer.

Uncle Stasio was four years younger than Mother and the most Semitic-looking of the Rużik family, with dark hair and a large nose. He stood barely five feet in height, was warm and gentle, and wore a sweet smile on his face. Even though he worked like a dog, my uncle always made time to play with me. Born a twin, Stasio was goodness personified, but his brother was an alcoholic and very nasty. One evening before the war began the bad twin had an accident. He staggered drunk through the streets of Warsaw, was hit by a train and died.

Stasio was the only member of the family who was not educated, but he was industrious, intensely loyal and loved his sister; she, in return, exploited her kid brother. Mother adored him, but expected Stasio to provide for all of us in my father's absence. Her domination over him was total and he submitted to her every request.

Meanwhile, I was losing patience with my mother's control over my life long before I would ever let her know it. Outwardly I was a well-behaved, dutiful ten-year-old son. She didn't have to make much of an effort to bend me to her will. Unlike Zdzisław, I always waited to indulge in my mischief unnoticed, leaving my reputation intact.

Mother had a government-issued day job, and Stasio, whom she trusted implicitly, was always home to supervise my schoolwork and cello practice, and to make sure I did not succumb to childish impulses. What Mother didn't realize was, her exhausted brother often slept late into the day. I could barely stand to read my books with him snoring like a dying cow across the room.

One fall afternoon, with Stasio passed out cold, I invited my friend Jerzyk over to play. He lived in the building and knew my mother quite well.

"What if your mother finds out?" Jerzyk sounded worried.

"I do what I want!" I assured him.

With no toys to amuse us, our eyes fixed on a big burlap sack of flour staring at us from the corner of the room. Once a month, Stasio would heave a ten-kilo bag of flour rations up the stairs and into our kitchen.

"A cake," I announced. "Wouldn't it be fun to make an enormous cake from all that flour, bigger than any in the whole wide world?"

We practically broke our backs lifting the sack onto the table in the center of the room. After emptying its contents, we poured a large bucket of water—which was most likely our washing water for the evening—over the huge mound of powder and began to knead. In no time we were covered up to our elbows in goopy dough.

This was no cake. It was an enormous, sticky, dripping, gooey mess. Mother would be home soon and we had to get rid of our unruly creation quickly. The window! We decided to throw the mixture out onto the street and Mother wouldn't be the wiser. Of course, my uncle was an obstacle sleeping under the window, but somehow it had to be done. Very carefully we stepped onto his mattress and each launched a handful out of the apartment.

Over and over, we scooped and tossed and set the dough free into the open air. There was yelling and swearing from the pedestrians on the sidewalk below who were accidentally pelted. This only encouraged us. Our mission was firm.

Curse me all you want, you bastards. I imagined myself a sniper in a turret.

We had almost cleared the table and unloaded the last remnants from our hands. Breathless and hysterical, suddenly we heard a howl from the street. Jerzyk and I poked our heads outside one more time and, to our horror, we caught sight of an outraged Army officer covered with dough from his head down to his polished boots. Cursing and waving a pistol in his hand, he spotted us. We dove under Uncle's bed. Within minutes there was a ferocious banging at our door.

Stasio woke up with a start. Disoriented and seeing the unbelievable mess all over the room, he yelled for me. Jerzyk and I lay still, frozen with fear. The officer was screaming and kicking from the hallway. My uncle struggled to his feet, pulled his suspenders over his belly and opened the door. He was met with disbelieving looks from the officer and the curious neighbors. There they stood—the officer with a dough-splattered uniform and a gun in his hand, and Stasio, plastered with goo from head to toe like a mad man, with a confused, wide-eyed expression on his face. They both looked like sorry visitors to a pigeon coop. By this time Jerzyk and I had emerged from under the bed.

"*Wariaci! Wariaci!!!*" the officer shouted, calling us crazy ones.

He glared at Stasio. "Are you insane? Have you no control over your children?"

After a barrage of verbal insults for half a minute, the officer abruptly turned around and left in a huff. We were lucky that he was Polish, not Russian, and that he didn't haul us away in handcuffs.

For the next week I suffered the consequences of my disobedience. I was spanked, had my ears pulled, couldn't leave the apartment, did extra chores, and was forbidden from playing with other boys in the building. Zdzisław was delighted, of course, and tried to add to my misery by accusing me of more misdeeds, all fabricated.

"Leszek told me he hates you. He was poking holes in your stockings, but I stopped him." Zdzisław said to Mother.

I paid dearly for my devilishness, but bore the punishment stoically and without remorse. It was a risk I knew I would be willing to take again. I refused to accept the notion that anyone, including my mother, could force me to surrender my free will.

❦

For my family, the war finally ended in November of 1948. Father, for the second time, came home unexpectedly. After years of being interned by the KGB in one of their gulags, he appeared in our doorway looking gaunt and wearing oversized, shabby clothes that hung over his skeletal body. He was obviously malnourished and his U.S. Army uniform was gone.

Mother was overcome with joyful disbelief. She wept in his arms while Father stood unresponsive. He was a changed man, no longer a tall, proud, noble Polish officer. The years of living in sub-human conditions—enduring torture in a German concentration camp and a Soviet prison—altered him. My father hardly spoke and looked at us with a haunted, lifeless gaze. He seemed off balance most of the time, afraid of his own shadow.

I was filled with terrible conflict. I wanted desperately to have and to love a father. But this man whom I was going to live with, wake up with and end every day with, who was he really? A total stranger. Even Mother and Zdzisław stepped cautiously in his presence at first. I was grateful Mother wouldn't allow him to take a drink, knowing he probably would have gotten out of hand. He brought the unbearable wounds of war into our household and we all felt their weight.

Father was never given the reason for his release. Mother often praised God for His salvation; nobody was ever expected to come out alive from a Soviet gulag. I thought General Rokossovsky's position of power was a more logical explanation for my father's miraculous survival and decided that my general had given the order as a final gift to me. Of course, I never shared my opinion with anyone.

Sadly, with Father's homecoming my treasured Uncle Stasio had to move out. There were too many bodies crowded into our one room. Eventually, he met and married a younger woman who was very amiable and twice his size. When they stood with their arms around each other, Stasio only came up to her armpit. We were all happy he found love.

Under Communist rule, every resident was required to register with the authorities and work at some job or other, not of their own choosing. Private enterprise did not exist; everything was nationalized and run by the government bureaucracy. Father was employed in a factory as a manual laborer. His expertise in the conservation and restoration of fine antiques became obsolete after the war because there were no French antiques in Warsaw anymore.

When Father saw the cello I was playing, he was struck by its terrible condition—badly scratched and full of open cracks. He vowed to repair it in a gesture that went a long way toward establishing a relationship with me. He undertook the task with an enthusiasm I hadn't seen in my father. For Mother it was a small reminder of the man she married. As a restorer of fine antiques, the repair of string instruments was a new, but not very difficult challenge. In a few short weeks he restored my cello to perfection and transformed it into a thing of beauty. Father Jacek and my cello teacher Kowalski were amazed. The priest asked my father to go to the church after work and look at the other instruments that needed repair—a few violins, cellos and a couple of basses in equally poor shape. Father accepted the project readily. The church provided him with a worktable and all the materials he needed. After some months these instruments, too, were restored by his gentle, able hands and became among the best in the whole city.

Word spread quickly. In those days Warsaw had only one professional luthier, an old man from Czechoslovakia. Kowalski brought my cello to the Philharmonic to show Father's work to the other musicians, and his reputation was sealed. By the next spring the authorities ordered Father to take a position as a luthier in the city's only music school, which was within walking distance from our apartment. He was given his own studio and could quit struggling in the factory. My father worked on the delicate instruments quietly and shut himself off from the outside world. I remember visiting him and watching with fascination, and admiration, as he concentrated on his beautiful restorations.

Healing those wooden, stringed bodies was Father's best therapy and gradually his sense of dignity returned. He began to dress each morning in a freshly ironed white shirt with a tie, pressed trousers and brightly polished shoes. Much to our amusement, he also grew a debonair mustache.

Besides my father's government salary, he took on private clients who understood his professionalism and paid him well. Our household income rose substantially and Mother did not have to work on the outside any more. She spent her days at home cooking, cleaning, washing and ironing, and she particularly loved to embroider. With great pride she designed beautiful linen tablecloths and napkins in the traditional Polish spider web embroidery style.

Corruption was a way of life in Poland. Everybody had greasy hands. With Father's new connections to bureaucrats from the Ministry of Culture, and surely some heavy bribes, in the summer of 1949 we moved to more comfortable living quarters. Our new apartment was not far away from the old, on the same street. It was a third-story corner walk-up in the back of the building, facing a courtyard with tall trees. The kitchen was large enough for a proper dining table and had a functioning sink and stove. There was one bedroom for all four of us and a guest parlor for entertaining, like in the old days. In postwar Warsaw, this was true luxury. For the first time in my life, we had a real bathroom with a large tub and a toilet. No more going to the creepy, disgusting outhouse. I loved to sit on the toilet seat in the quiet of this space and read books. At first, Mother was puzzled by my lengthy disappearances until she discovered I was reading happily in the sanctity of the bathroom.

"You are *meshuggah!*" she would say.

With renewed energy and her resourcefulness, Mother went in search of furnishings and even found a rug. Of course, once again the tapestry with the deer by the brook was prominently displayed.

One afternoon, shortly after settling in, we were surprised by the arrival of a moving company that brought us a stunning upright piano made by the famous French piano company, Pleyel. Father Jacek purchased it in gratitude for my father's restoration of the church instruments. That evening Jacek came for dinner and used the occasion to have a serious talk with Mother and Father about my musical future. I listened to him insist that taking cello lessons for two years was not enough.

"Leszek should start music school. Without harmony, solfeggio and music theory classes, not to mention chamber music coaching, his development will be incomplete."

He was adamant. My parents were very excited to hear that their son's musical gift was worthy of such serious study. I didn't share their enthusiasm. My life was sure to become more restricted, but I had no say in the matter. Within the next two weeks, I was enrolled in the music school where Father had his luthier shop. Mornings were swallowed up by regular public school, and in the afternoons I attended music classes, had private cello lessons with the strict Professor Kowalski (who still liked to slap me with his gray-gloved hands), and had to complete homework assignments, all under Mother's rigorous supervision. She demanded that I excel as a student *and* a cellist.

The piano became our family's most prized possession. Owning such an instrument was an impressive symbol of status in Poland and a nostalgic link to our bourgeois past. My mother loved to show off her son's talent. As often as possible she invited Father Jacek, or another pianist, to come over and play duets with me for the enjoyment of family and friends. Of course, she took all the credit for my accomplishments as if they were her own and spent many social evenings bragging. Unfortunately, the little recitals didn't last after we received a letter from the Ministry of Education.

The piano that resides in your apartment is needed at the music school. Since there is no person in your household who plays professionally, it is your civic duty to provide this instrument for use by the school's piano students. The Ministry assures you that the piano continues to be owned by you, but must be relocated from your premises to the school.

My parents were enraged. It was said at the time, "Communism means equality for all." In other words,

What's yours is mine . . . but don't dare touch mine!

Under Stalin's tyrannical rule, fear and suspicion reigned as his pervasive spy network infiltrated the populace. The first question asked in meetings about official dictates was, "Is anybody against it?" No one dared to step out of line and contradict the state. Dissenters were never put on trial. They simply vanished.

At school I was subjected to relentless indoctrination into the glories of the system and its ideals, but at home I listened to my parents rant against the regime.

Mother complained bitterly, "They call us, 'the Polish People's Republic.' But we, the people, have no voice."

At the age of eleven, I understood what it meant to be hungry for freedom, for the autonomy to act independently, to be left alone and to reject brainwashing from either side. My mind was awakening from a childish slumber.

7

Gefilte Fish

Our family entered the realm of the middle class (if there was such a thing) and began to eat sufficiently—by post-war Polish standards—almost every day. The Socialist pay structure was bizarre; laborers were rewarded above specialists, hospital nurses were paid more than doctors and, in the case of my father, his craft as a woodworker at the music school earned him far more money than the teachers. With the extra income from his private clientele, we could even afford tickets to concerts and the National Opera, and to entertain guests for dinner from time to time.

Mother prepared many of our meals in accordance with Jewish customs passed down from her dearly departed mother Ewa, which meant never buying dead fish or poultry. Mother brought the live fish home several days in advance of the winter holidays because they were in scarce supply and stores ran out quickly. She kept them swimming in our bathtub, like pets before slaughter, and until Christmas day, none of us could bathe. We probably smelled like peasants on a Polish train. Before cooking, in their last seconds of life, Mother whacked the unsuspecting creatures on the head, sliced them into steaks and tossed them into a skillet sizzling with butter. Zdzisław and I watched in horror as our dinner twitched in the scalding grease, protesting the betrayal that sent them so suddenly to their deaths.

Chicken or goose dinners were far worse. Father would take the bird outside, chop its gullet with an axe, and hold it upside down until it was drained of blood. On a couple of occasions he lost his grip on the poor, headless bird and it ran frantically around the courtyard like a ball of feathers plugged into a live electric socket and let loose. Father gave chase in a grotesque comedy routine that ended when he breathlessly handed the beast to me or to my brother.

"Pull out the feathers!" he would demand. It was a hateful task.

Mother was envious of our friends who left for Israel. It was not the idea of world travel or building a new communitarian society in a foreign land that appealed to her (she was fiercely patriotic and openly xenophobic), but rather she lamented not having an escape from the tyranny of Communism. If not for *Radio Free Europe* and *Voice of America*, which my parents listened to at night and in secret, my mother would have had no outlet for her profound anti-Soviet sentiments. I did not pay much attention to my parents' politics, but instinctively understood I couldn't breathe a word about what they heard across the airwaves. Anyone caught listening to foreign broadcasts of Western propaganda faced arrest.

The only Polish institution that escaped dominance was the Catholic Church. It was an independent body within the government, under the umbrella of the Polish nation, and was the only significant source of resistance against Stalin's puppet regime. Cardinal Stefan Wyszynski and the Archbishop of Krakow, Karol Wojtyła—who was ordained Poland's revered Pope John Paul II many years later—fought for the return of the exiled government in London. The two clergymen were the most outspoken supporters of anti-Communist groups and they were endorsed by almost the entire civilian population.

By the end of the war, only a small number of Jewish families survived in Poland. They dreamed of a utopian society, not so different from Lenin's ideals. Many escaped the Nazi death camps by fleeing to Russia, and when the war was over they came back to Poland with the Red Army. While some of the returning Jews were true believers in Socialism, most shared the Zionist vision of a Jewish national state. A few were rewarded for their defense of the Soviet regime with comfortable managerial jobs, which fanned the flames of resentment against the Jewish community, ceaselessly accused of being Communist sympathizers. It seemed as if everything that went wrong in Poland—the world's most Catholic country—was blamed on the Jews. Suffering extreme poverty and daily harassment, by 1947 most of their remaining population left. They emigrated to Israel, Western Europe or the United States, in search of the freedom they would never find in Poland.

Several of my parents' friends were Jewish and often came to visit. One of Father's clients, a double bass player named Sam, was a tall, overweight fellow who had a belly the size of his bass. I was especially fond of him because he sang Russian songs with me, and also because he had two very pretty daughters my age. Girls started to capture my attention; I would catch myself staring at them, mesmerized by the way they moved, the softness of their hair, the allure of their smiles. At the same time that I began to recognize the symptoms of desire in myself, I sensed my mother had a growing fondness for Sam.

I was happy when she asked me to deliver a platter of food to Sam's apartment one spring afternoon. I knocked on his front door holding a lovely array of gefilte fish, symbolic of good fortune and fertility, sweetened with sugar and garnished with horseradish. I heard Sam and his daughters laughing from inside. After a minute, heavy footsteps approached the door and it swung open. Sam was grinning down at me with his daughters smiling at either side. He was stark naked. Bushy black hair covered his body and, although I tried not to look, he had a penis as big as the pike Mother used to stuff the gefilte. It was a miracle I didn't drop the dish. All of my carefully laid plans to flirt with Sam's daughters were obliterated.

"Why don't you stay for a while?" the girls asked.

I responded by handing them the plate, turning on my heels and running home.

"Did he like the fish?" Mother asked.

I told my parents what happened, about their naked friend confronting me with his penis hanging almost down to his knees. Mother smacked me hard across the face.

"Shut your filthy mouth!" she snapped.

We stopped socializing with Sam's family until they invited us to a farewell dinner many months later on the eve of their emigration to Israel. My mother was very happy to see her old friends, but for me it was an extremely awkward affair. Every time I looked at Sam I imagined his huge cock. Father drank more vodka that night than I had seen him consume since his return from the front in 1945, and just as before, all reason left him. In what was perhaps their last chance to express tender feelings, Sam affectionately kissed Mother goodbye. Father lashed out in a jealous rage. He cursed wildly at the man, called him a dirty Jewish pig and, to our great horror, spit on him. I was so ashamed. Mother stopped speaking to her husband.

After a week of silence, she shouted at him, "What a fool you were, returning to Poland after the war instead of taking us to America when you had the chance!"

Father's work kept him out of the house six days a week and he cherished the solitude. During our occasional social gatherings at home, he always sat quietly while Mother held court commanding everyone's attention. Father preferred it that way. He found a delicate equilibrium where he could exist comfortably in his own world while keeping the demons that haunted him tightly sealed away. It was a critical balance he made sure his sons did not disturb. My brother and I were never allowed to speak without permission at the dinner table. If either one of us dared utter a word, Father wagged a threatening finger and glared from under his furrowed brow, *"Dzieci i ryby nie mówią*—children and fish don't talk!"

❧

Zdzisław would finally graduate from high school in June of 1950 and be out of the house. Since he was a poor student, not a single university accepted him. All young men in his situation were automatically drafted into military service, so my brother left to begin basic training. His absence brought with it an ocean of relief for me. I no longer had to endure his bullying and didn't miss him at all. My school days, on the other hand, continued to be challenging. I was an oddball who played the cello and had no time to participate in sports.

That spring I outgrew my shoes and needed new ones badly. When Mother and I got to the store, there was only one pair in my size, but the soles were not attached. The salesperson grumbled that the factory didn't have any glue.

"If you want the shoes, fix them yourself!" he snarled.

Mother took some glue from Father's workshop and connected the soles with careful attention, as if they were the seams of a cello. They would be my shoes for the next year, and they were really ugly. I was embarrassed to walk around in them.

Whenever the school gathered for a commemoration of any kind—Stalin's birthday, Lenin's birthday, Pushkin's birthday, the anniversary of the October Revolution, the anniversary marking victory over Germany—I was asked to play on stage in front of a full assembly. The boys would make menacing faces at me and whisper insults in my direction. Mother was always present in the audience on these occasions, easily spotted by her lipstick. She prided herself on having total control over my musical development and, although Professor Kowalski forbade her from sitting in the studio during my cello lessons, she would position herself just outside the door so she could hear every note. I felt like a caged animal, but knew I had to be obedient or suffer the consequences.

By the time I turned thirteen, I wanted nothing to do with my mother. Sometimes I would invite a girl over to our apartment to study, which annoyed her beyond reason. She was barely hospitable to my female guests, calling them *shiksa* under her breath, but loud enough for me to hear. For a long time I thought the word referred to a girl with a low reputation and was amused when I found out that in Yiddish it simply means 'not Jewish.' Mother used a lot of Yiddish words at home—never in public—most of them complaints or insults. One of her favorites was calling me a *chozzer*, a pig who eats a lot, despite that I was lean and never put on any pounds no matter how much of Mother's beloved carp I consumed.

My parents and I rarely attended Mass, but in 1952 Father Jacek asked me to learn Gounod's *Ave Maria* to play for his congregation of thousands. It was an unexpected, but thrilling request. At our first rehearsal I was startled by the huge cello sound vibrating off the granite columns in the basilica, and when the organist played at full volume I thought the reverberations would knock me to the floor. My proud parents went from one end of Warsaw to the other boasting to their friends and neighbors about the upcoming event. On that appointed Sunday I played during Mass while the faithful received their Sacraments of Communion.

My life took on a new glow. The church performances became a weekly routine, and girls started to pay attention to me. Playing music made me feel singular among my peers in a society where no one was supposed to stand out. I learned Bach's *Air*, Massenet's *Meditation* from his opera *Thaïs*, and my favorite, Schubert's *Ave Maria*, all appropriate for various church occasions. I also played for weddings and funerals and was well paid. To my parents' surprise, I sometimes brought home the same amount of money Father earned from his job at the school. Of course, I had to give every penny to Mother.

At the end of the school year, I was sent to summer camp in the mountains of Zakopane for a month of music and fun. What a relief it was to be away from home and out of Mother's reach. I played in the orchestra, swam, went on nature hikes and flirted with the girls. It was the perfect environment for playing practical jokes. I hid frogs and garden snakes under my tent mates' blankets and was especially proud of the time I cut a hole in my counselor's straw mattress, put a bucket full of water in its place, and covered it with his bed sheet. The counselor, after climbing into bed and sinking into the bucket, with his ass soaking wet and freezing, cursed all of us at the top of his lungs. I was never caught.

When camp was over I spent a few days at home before an unwelcome trek to the village of our ancestors. Father's youngest brother Antoś, and his wife Janina, survived the war and still owned a parcel of land from the scorched estate of my grandparents. The authorities distributed farm territory equally and everybody got approximately twenty acres. As sons of the former estate owner, Antoś and my father were each given twenty acres as well. Since Father had no interest in the farm, Antoś took charge of the entire forty-acre property. Substantial bribes were paid to the local Communist Party supervisor for Antoś' excessive share. While I was packing for the trip, I thought about the prospect of spending two weeks without my cello and felt very glum. Making matters worse, with Father at work and Zdzisław in the army, Mother and I were to travel alone.

My uncle built a rustic cottage of modest size on the property without electricity or running water so, once again, we all used an outhouse. For a city kid like me, it was miserable and a bitter reminder of my past. I watched my uncle take care of the horses, milk the cows, and collect wild mushrooms to pass the time. He taught me how to tell the difference between toxic and non-toxic fungi by their color, texture, shape and smell; how to distinguish the elegant, abundant chanterelles by their apricot (rather than peach) color, and false gills from true gills that separate easily from the cap; where to search for the prized porcini that weighed a half kilo; and to avoid the "magic" mushrooms with their bell caps that stood a head above the rest and were said to turn a person into a viper.

The highlight of my stay in the village was a daily visit to the black-smith. I spent many hours watching in amazement as he worked with burning iron, shaping the unyielding material into any form he chose. The blacksmith was responsible for shoeing the village horses, repairing the farm equipment, making tools and household objects. No rural community can exist without its blacksmith, the most indispensable person in the village. The joke goes,

If the blacksmith commits a crime, the authorities hang the tailor.

Standing in front of Uncle Antoś' cottage was an antiquated water well. To one side grew two large weeping willows, and in between was a pond with ducks and geese swimming contentedly in the summer heat. I couldn't resist stepping into the water one sweltering afternoon. The cool sensation on my perspired body was as erotic a feeling as I had yet known. I spent a long time listening to the sounds of the warm wind in the tall grasses, the dragonflies zipping across the water, and meditating on the designs my movements formed as I waded across the pond. When I emerged and climbed onto the bank, I was spotted like a leopard. I tried to wipe away the slippery black spots, but couldn't. As soon as I realized my legs, belly and backside were covered with pulsating leeches, I ran screaming for help to Aunt Janina, who was amused and not at all surprised.

"Oh good," she said, grabbing an empty glass jar. Slowly, one by one, in a most disgusting and painful process, she yanked the awful creatures off my body and stored them, delighted to have a fresh supply. Medicinal care was substandard, necessary drugs were lacking, and everyone, including my family, relied on old-fashioned remedies. If I had a cold or the flu, Mother rubbed alcohol on the inside rims of small glass cups, lit a match to set them on fire, and immediately suctioned them to my back or chest. It was medieval torture. For days and days afterward I looked like a branded pig—a *chozzer* indeed. But, even worse was getting rid of intestinal worms, which were very common because of poor sanitation. The cure for these nasty parasites was kerosene. Mother would force me to drink a couple of tablespoons of that rocket fuel and I thought I was going to die. Almost instantly I would become violently ill.

"You could have killed me," I would say to her when I recovered.

"On the contrary. The worms are dead and you are alive!" was her answer.

One of Father's cousins from the village was getting married at the end of the summer and, of course, our family was invited to the wedding. In fact, since everyone knew everyone else the entire village participated, and each household brought food and wedding presents of down feather pillows, quilts, chickens, noisy geese, *bimber* and more. Mother brought one of her embroidered tablecloths. The villagers were dressed in beaded, vibrantly colored clothing. Men wore festive jackets and women braided ribbons into their hair. Horses and wagons were also decorated with flowers and folk art, and the setting exploded with color. The ceremony was very sober, but the celebrations that lasted for two days and nights afterward were wild, with dancing, singing and drinking late into both nights.

When the sun set on the first evening, some of the local men—friends of the groom—noticed a former boyfriend of the bride from a neighboring village who hadn't been invited. The men were strong and drunk and surrounded the intruder. They pummeled him, stripped him of his clothes, held him down, and proceeded to smother him with black tar and feathers. To everybody's delight, they chased the poor fellow out of the village with horsewhips. I was terrified by their barbarity and looked for an escape. Without announcing my departure, I crept away to Uncle Antoś' house and in a corner of the dark room, curled myself into a ball on top of a mound of pillows and closed my eyes.

Some time later I was startled awake when the newly married couple careened into the room. They were falling over each other, thoroughly intoxicated, and collapsed onto the bed. After a few minutes of awkward fumbling, they fell into a deep sleep, snoring loudly. Watching from my safe corner on the opposite side of the room, I thought they looked pitiful. I wanted to tiptoe out, but suddenly the door flung open and a villager entered. He was burly and disheveled and grumbled to the newlyweds, trying to provoke some response. They were silent. He rolled the woman off her husband and made another unsuccessful attempt to wake them. Then the man pulled down his trousers and proceeded to have sex with the sleeping bride. I covered myself with the pillows, hardly breathing, panic-stricken at the thought that I might be discovered. As soon as the villager satisfied himself he departed, leaving the bride, still lying motionless next to her husband, with her wedding dress pulled up revealing her open, naked legs. When the first man left, another followed, and another. After what seemed an eternity, the raucous sounds of celebration began to die down outside the cottage, and the orgy of raping ended as well. I crawled from my hiding place, snuck out of the room in a daze, and ran for safety to the barn.

I did not dare tell anyone what happened. If word got out I would be afraid for the bride's life, as well as my own. Had the groom discovered what happened on his wedding night, retaliation against the bride for his shame would be swift and beyond barbaric. I was told that some women who were caught committing adultery were tied to a pole and set six feet above the ground. The offended husband would put a long, narrow, sharpened wooden stick into the woman's vagina. Loosening the ropes on the pole, the woman's body would slowly sink and she would be penetrated in unimaginable torture. After perpetrating such hideous acts, these people, who were also fanatically pious and deeply concerned with their salvation, would exonerate themselves in confession. The priest would forgive them their sins.

I begged Mother not to take me to the countryside again. I wrestled with horrible nightmares and conjured up every possible excuse to convince my mother that we should stay in Warsaw the following year.

"The peasant girls try to seduce me. They don't wear underwear and show me their bare bottoms."

This was my strongest argument and it worked. Mother called those young women *shiksa kurva*, gentile whores, and we never went back to the village.

8

The Communists

The Polish People's Republic was under the total domination of the central committee of the Communist Party. Opposition parties didn't exist and corruption was rampant. We waited for hours in long lines outside government-run stores, only to come away with a fatty scrap of pork, a few carrots and a potato or two. With severe shortages of everything, the black market flourished. Books sold illegally made their way into our household via underground trading. Every night when the lights in our apartment were turned off and my parents went to sleep, I would disappear under my covers with a flashlight and escape into the pages of Alexander Dumas' *The Three Musketeers*, James Fenimore Cooper's *The Last of the Mohicans*, Hemingway's novels, or the mysterious and sexy stories of Alberto Moravia. A number of foreign writers were translated into Polish and printed mostly by the clandestine press. In the upper echelon of Polish society, there was a great attraction for anything coming from Europe or the United States. A lucky buyer would read a book and sell it back on the black market, hopefully for a profit. This practice was patently against the law, but the hunger for Western literature was greater than the risk.

I was fourteen years old when Stalin ordered another round of sweeping investigations of the Polish intelligentsia and the few surviving remnants of the Home Army. The KGB showed up on our doorstep and extensively interrogated my father. We were petrified. Arrest would have meant never seeing each other again. Father answered their questions with the humility and skill of a man who knew his enemy almost better than they knew themselves, and he managed to avoid being taken away.

Massive persecutions continued throughout '52 and into '53. Any Jews who remained in Poland were targeted as Zionist spies for Israel and the West. Scores of priests were also arrested, including a leader among them, Cardinal Stefan Wyszynski. The authorities tried to starve and ultimately dissolve the influence of the Catholic Church on the populace. Everyone trembled in fear, and there was no relief in sight.

Then, on March 5, 1953, Joseph Stalin died. He wielded a bloody, thirty-year reign of terror that resulted in the murders of tens of millions of Russian citizens and Europeans of other nationalities who perished in his Siberian gulags. Yet, he was discovered in his bedroom like a helpless infant in urine-soaked pajamas.

The day after his death my entire school assembled in the auditorium. On that morning, red kerchiefs were distributed for us to wear around our necks—morbid reminders of Stalin's chokehold. Standing shoulder-to-shoulder, we were forced to listen to an amplified broadcast of his state funeral. Stalin was given a twenty-one-gun salute followed by dreary music and insipid propaganda speeches about the glorious life of our leader. As the hours passed my classmates and I grew restless. We fidgeted and became giddy, pinching and tickling each other while trying desperately to maintain a solemn outward appearance. At one point in the midst of this drawn out, dismal affair, one of the boys could no longer control himself and impulsively burst into loud laughter. School security grabbed hold of him immediately and took him away. He was barely fifteen years old and was never seen or heard from again. *It could have been me.*

My high school—built before World War II of beige limestone with wide hallways and tall windows in a style that portended the Soviet occupation—was an enormous structure that took the space of a city block. An equally huge basilica stood diagonally across the street and they faced each other like two kings on a chessboard. They were the most imposing architectural landmarks in our poor neighborhood, standing proud and obstinate, having survived multiple air raids. The student body was subjected to rigorous discipline and had to wear uniform scarves and hats identifying our school.

Russian lessons were mandatory for one hour every day. My classmates were very resentful, but I actually enjoyed using the language I spoke during my years with the Red Army.

Mother forbade me from participating in any popular activities with my peers and, to make matters worse, I was the only student in the whole school who walked through the corridors carrying a cello. The jocks called me the class *dziwak*, weirdo. The friends I did have liked me because of my mischievousness, not my musical talent or academic diligence. When a frog leaped out of the teacher's desk drawer and onto her shrieking breast, they knew who was responsible. Their respect for me was cemented on the day of an important test. I brought a bottle of cheap wine to school and lured a group of students into the locker room before the exam. Each of them took a big swig, not knowing I had spiked it with a heavy dose of laxatives. The exam began and one by one my classmates, red in the face, asked to be excused. They ran to the bathroom clutching their rear ends. The teachers concluded the class was suffering from food poisoning and cancelled the test. I was a hero that day.

Besides studying Russian, once a week we were forced to read *Das Kapital* and *The Communist Manifesto* as our indoctrination into nineteenth-century Communist philosophies. The teacher who introduced us to Friedrich Engels and Karl Marx was a short, stocky, older man who had a very poor grasp of Polish vocabulary. He was Russian and reviled by students and teachers alike. Every time he told us to turn a page in the book, he stumbled over the pronunciation of the word "page." In Polish, "page" is phonetically pronounced *strona*, but the similar-sounding word, *struna*, means a string on the violin or cello. The next time the teacher labored over the same request, I piped up and said, "It's *struna*." He thanked me profusely and for the rest of the semester told us to, "Please turn to the next string."

Since I was advancing musically very quickly, in 1955 Mother enrolled me in Warsaw's top music school. On most afternoons I trekked a long distance to the school, taking a streetcar first and then walking up and down a mile of hilly city blocks. My cello case tugged so heavily at each arm, I had to switch it from time to time to give my aching muscles some relief. It was a workout as good as any the jocks were getting.

The school faculty included several of the most important names on Warsaw's music scene. Professor Kowalski, the principal cellist of the National

Philharmonic, was among them. His vanity compelled him to prepare me for a Communist Party propaganda show called *The World Festival of Youth* in Warsaw. Much to his delight, the government chose me as one of the young musicians representing Poland. I was seventeen years old and no longer a child; my soft features had given way to an angular jaw and dignified brow, becoming for a performer. I was to appear as a soloist with full orchestra playing a concerto by the female Polish contemporary composer, Grażyna Bacewicz. It was a daunting prospect—something I had never done before. On the night of the concert I strode weak-kneed onto the stage to face the audience. My heart was pounding so fast, I was afraid I wouldn't make it to my chair on the raised platform in front of the orchestra without passing out. The opening phrase needed to be played boldly, so I had to commit to the music from the start. The moment I drew my bow across the string, Bacewicz's composition took over and I charged through the performance despite my nerves. It must have gone well because Mother and Kowalski were very complimentary.

My friends greeted me like a star when I went back to school, which led me to think seriously about my future after leaving those limestone hallways. It was exciting to consider music as a profession, and I made a firm decision, announcing to my parents, "I will attend the Music Academy of Warsaw University after graduation."

My public recitals continued and I toured with Father Jacek for two weeks during the summer. We performed in seminaries around the country for young men who were studying for the priesthood. They usually came from the poorest and lowest class of Polish peasantry and were inspired by our flashy programs. Jacek and I stayed in towering, ancient monasteries and dined on delicious food with the presiding clerics after every concert. Most Poles were destitute and knelt before their priests seeking comfort from sermons touting the virtues of poverty. They donated their meager *zloty* to the church coffers as faithful servants, while the clergy filled their bellies like kings behind closed doors. Every man of the cloth I met had a domestic staff and took pleasure in creature comforts unheard of in Poland. I watched my close mentor, Father Jacek, enjoy the spoils of his privileged station in society. He relished having a personal secretary who was a young, attractive woman. At first I felt flush with the indulgences and didn't think about the hypocrisy. Eventually, the excesses made me squirm.

It never occurred to me that Jacek could be sexually active until we took a train to a resort on the Baltic Sea one day. Jacek walked out of his room dressed in civilian clothes and declared, "Let's go to the beach!"

I loved everything about the seaside, especially the pretty girls frolicking in the warm sand wearing their skimpy bathing suits. It puzzled me why Jacek was lying on his stomach, looking from one side of the shore to the other, but not getting up. After a couple of hours I insisted he join me for a swim and, to my astonishment, when he stood I could see he had been hiding an erection. He obviously had problems with his vow of celibacy.

After a particular Friday evening performance in a very old monastery, and dinner with wine, I was ushered to my sleeping quarters by the host priest. The small cell, with its medieval brick walls, floors and ceiling, was like a dungeon, dark and smelly, but I was very tired and fell asleep as soon as I hit the bed. In the middle of the night I woke up with a start. My body felt as if it were on fire. I turned on the lamp and was horrified that I was covered from my hair to my toes with hundreds of jumping, biting fleas. The bed sheets were black with them. I ran out the door, screaming for help at the top of my lungs. Father Jacek appeared in the hall with a few sleepy priests, who all thought I was having a bad dream. They took one look at me and knew it was no dream. I tore off my pajamas, they poured pure alcohol over me, and I nearly fainted from the sting. Then they immersed my burning body in cold, soapy water. Wearing a fresh set of pajamas, one of the priests escorted me to a new room. Of course, I couldn't sleep for the rest of the night and constantly checked my mattress for those tiny, somersaulting fleas. When I saw myself in the mirror the next day, I looked like I had smallpox.

On our way home Father Jacek, in a very apologetic tone, said, "Your room had been occupied by a very sick, old priest who was found dead shortly before we arrived. He'd died in his sleep and his body wasn't discovered until after the fleas moved in. Unfortunately, no one cleaned or disinfected the bed after his corpse was removed. The man in charge of arranging the guest rooms took you to the dead man's bed by mistake. Maybe he had too much wine," he said with a weak chuckle, but I was not amused. Again he apologized, "I am so sorry."

This trip marked the end of my recitals with Father Jacek. I couldn't fathom traveling with him again and he understood.

In 1956 Nikita Khrushchev came to power in Russia. Under his more liberal leadership, the church unofficially agreed to stay out of politics and the government consented not to interfere in religious life. In October the Communist Party authorities finally released Cardinal Wyszynski from internment where he had been held for four years. All of Poland celebrated the Cardinal's freedom as if it were a national holiday. Thousands gathered in front of his residence holding candles and strewing flowers. After a celebratory mass in Warsaw's main cathedral with bishops from Poland and abroad in attendance—including Archbishop Wojtyła and a cardinal from the Vatican who was an emissary for the Pope—there was a welcome banquet followed by a concert. I was among the performers at the event, accompanied by Father Jacek.

When we entered the room the Cardinal, dressed in his bright red cassock, was sitting on his throne encircled by the hierarchy of the Polish Catholic Church. About twenty feet from the holy collective a chair was set for me. Wearing a long, white, altar boy shirt, I approached the clergy, knelt down and bowed low, as low as I could without landing face down on the floor. I tried hard to avoid His Eminence's gaze and felt insignificant and intimidated as I sat with closed eyes and started to play my old favorite, Schubert's *Ave Maria*. It was as if I were performing before a god. When the final notes rang out through the hall, I kept my eyes tightly shut and rested my fingers on the cello in silence. Father Jacek escorted me to Wyszynksi's throne, and once again I knelt in front of the Cardinal and kissed the ring on his finger. He blessed us and we walked out of the room. My parents, especially Father, beamed with pride.

The school bully, on the other hand, who was twice my size, viewed my public appearance with derision. It was our final year in high school, and while it could have been argued that his future was doomed to mediocrity, mine was looking up.

One morning before class he shoved me against the wall of the locker room and shouted, "You are nothing but a mother fucking *dziwak*."

I pushed him back, but the first bell rang and the altercation ceased abruptly. We went our separate ways to class.

After school the lout was waiting in a courtyard behind the building. His gang of thugs surrounded me while my friends waited off to the side. I did not want to fight, afraid of injuring my hands, but had no choice. He turned toward me, his athletic arms poised to punch me in the face. Before he could hurl the first blow, with all my strength I kicked him in the shin. He grimaced in pain, doubled over to grab his leg and I kneed him smack in the face. His nose gushed with blood, and he rolled around on the ground crying out in agony. His cowardly friends ran away, but mine stood by me, gloating in admiration. As I turned to leave I gave the bully a good kick in the balls. *A small gift to seal the deal.* For the next few weeks, until graduation, nobody bothered me again. And I was no longer called *dziwak*.

During my last semester of high school I became infatuated with a smart, beautiful girl named Basia. Of course, Mother never allowed me to invite her to our apartment.

Basia was an excellent student, and since Mother desperately wanted me to be at the top of my class, I told her, "If Basia comes over to study with me, I will do better on my exams."

Mother begrudgingly allowed a visit. When Basia and I were working alone in the parlor, I could not resist planting a passionate kiss on her eager lips. The door to the parlor flung open and Mother, who had been peeking at us through the keyhole, stormed into the room with a broom in her hand.

Waving it at Basia, she shrieked, "Get your filthy hands off him," and she chased Basia out of the apartment.

Shortly before graduation exercises I learned that Basia was very ill with an advanced case of tuberculosis. There was no treatment for it, and she died within weeks. I was devastated. Even my mother expressed genuine sorrow.

TB was widespread in post-war Poland and took several classmates and neighbors as its victims.

"As soon as you walk out our front door," Mother warned us, "you will be exposed to that deadly bacteria. Drink your cod liver oil."

We swallowed the horrid-tasting stuff every morning and, sure enough, none of the Zawistowskis contracted the ghastly disease. Naturally, Mother took credit for saving our lives.

In June I graduated. During the commencement ceremony the principal announced, "Leszek Zawistowski will receive top honors as the highest-ranking student in the class of 1956."

I was ushered onto the stage along with the second- and third-ranked students. The principal gave a long, boring address about our obligations as citizens of the Polish People's Republic and then called us up, one by one, to receive an award. The fellow in third place got a bouquet of flowers. Number two, much to his surprise, was given a beautiful red bicycle. I was bursting with excitement in anticipation of receiving my prize. *If number two got a bicycle, I will get nothing short of a motorcycle!* With a proud smile plastered on his bureaucratic face, the principal handed me a heavy book.

"I give you this book in recognition of your academic achievement," he proclaimed. "It is signed by the Minister of Education and is about the celebrated life of Joseph Stalin."

A little involuntary laughter came from my friends in the auditorium who wondered if it could be a joke—payback for my pranks. The principal shot a stern look over the assembly. Clearly it was no joke. I was flabbergasted. My pent-up hatred for Stalin and all the damned Communists overwhelmed me and I couldn't control my emotions. When I played a short piece at the end of the graduation ceremony, tears of disappointment and anger ran down the fingerboard of my cello. The bureaucrats in attendance who were smiling up at me probably misinterpreted my tears as gratitude for their gift. My father was outraged and understood how humiliated I felt. A week later my parents presented me with a gorgeous racing bicycle.

Graduating at the top of my class granted me automatic entry into any academic curriculum at any university in Poland, but I wasn't interested in academics. I was really looking forward to my studies at the Music Academy. Music had saved me, and I was determined to spend my life returning the favor. My parents understood that music education was of value; it taught me great discipline and also gave them personal pleasure. But Mother had a different plan for me. She decided it was time for her son to pursue a more prestigious and practical profession.

"You are going to be a doctor," she said, her mouth pinched into an expression of resolve.

The education system allowed students to go directly from high school into a pre-med program, so Mother applied to medical schools behind my back. Only then did I realize why I was forced to take extra courses in Latin, biology and chemistry. Obviously, she had been plotting this move for a long time. I protested vehemently, but without success. Mother's decision was irreversible and made me regret the hard work and good grades.

I had to escape the toxic atmosphere at home and decided to go on a bicycle trip to the countryside with some close friends. Mother tried every weapon in her arsenal to stop me from going and finally resorted to guilt.

"How could you abandon your cello and not play for a month?" she challenged.

My answer was, "Mother, if you want me to be a doctor, fuck the cello! Just leave me alone."

In the autumn of 1956, with a heavy heart, I entered the pre-med program at Warsaw University's School of Medicine.

9

Revolt

Mother was victorious. Her son would be a doctor and not, as she liked to tell me with keen derision, "a cheap klezmer musician humiliating yourself in *Plac Zwycięstwa* (the sardonically named "Victory Square").

My pre-med classes were set to begin in September. While I remained bitter about my forced enrollment, the school was not a terrible place to be. It was founded in 1816 and, although a young institution in comparison to Jagiellonian University in Krakow, it was the largest and most prestigious in the nation. The main campus was located on the city's most beautiful boulevard encompassing the Royal Castle, the Presidential Palace and the Academy of Sciences. Several of the school's buildings were converted eighteenth- and nineteenth-century palaces. Mother, in her youth, studied painting at the Academy of Fine Arts across the street, in what was perhaps the most magnificent structure of all. Passing the Fine Arts building from time to time, I imagined my mother as a beautiful and vibrant young woman, indulging in her creative talents. How could she deny me the same right?

There were roughly four thousand students enrolled at Warsaw University in my first year, and its grandeur inspired exuberant idealism. The campus grounds teemed with young people who felt empowered to dream of a better world within those valiant walls. In a softening of Stalin's dreadful domestic policies, Khrushchev kicked off the era of de-Stalinization, causing anti-Soviet sentiment to proliferate across Poland. Long-repressed dialogue was whispered in every dormitory and department of the school. It was a liberal atmosphere, closer to free expression than anything I had known since I was a small boy in the company of the Russian troops.

I was at the university for only one month when, on October 4, the student body staged a large protest. Our request was simple: All uniformed city police be ousted from school grounds. Many of the students around me were beaten in the campus square and arrested, but negotiations were taking place and our demands were eventually met. In our naïve hour of triumph, it did not occur to us that the removal of uniformed officers would in effect double the number of undercover security forces in our midst, and that such a pyrrhic victory would set the stage for a return to iron-clad control over all of us.

There had been a string of uprisings since June, as thousands of factory workers in the city of Poznań organized massive demonstrations for better working and living conditions. Food prices had risen too high for their meager wages and their banners read simply, *"Żądamy chleba!* We demand bread!" The demonstrations were met with a violent act of military repression ordered by, of all people, General Rokossovsky, now Poland's reviled Minister of Defense. He sent thousands of troops and hundreds of tanks into the city, and there were tragic reports that over fifty workers had been killed with larger numbers wounded and arrested.

Rokossovsky's message to the populace was, "Mess with the state and we will squash you."

As a child I trusted and loved the general more than my own father. All these years later, Rokossovsky's terrible acts of brutality against my fellow citizens tore me apart, and there was no one to help me sort out the conflicting emotions. My parents wouldn't have listened, and I certainly couldn't divulge my connection to the general to any of the student demonstrators on Warsaw University's campus. I marched with them, chanted their slogans and struggled to separate my childhood memories from my humanistic beliefs.

By the end of October we were absorbed by the news coming from Budapest. Tens of thousands of Hungary's citizens erupted into spontaneous revolt. Flooding the streets and demanding an end to Russian control, they called for the Premier, Imre Nagy, to form a new democratic government. With the majority of the Hungarian Army personnel joining the demonstrators, the revolt evolved into a national insurrection against Soviet rule. Poland was proud of its courageous neighbors to the south with whom we'd always had friendly relations. Soviet troops and tanks attacked Budapest and other Hungarian cities. We read in the newspapers, and heard on the airwaves, heroic stories of Hungarian resistance.

With escalating hostility toward the Russians, we could think of nothing but the taste of freedom. Staged demonstrations took place in solidarity with our Hungarian brothers and sisters. Nobody attended classes. Posters and banners calling for the Russians to "Go home!" were displayed all over the school. The fever of rebellion was contagious. The tug-of-war between our fears and our desire for a Polish democracy reached its peak. Then, on November 7, the Hungarian Uprising was successfully crushed by Soviet troops and all our hopes were dashed. Completely demoralized, the public went back to its dreary daily routine. Khrushchev began a process of dismantling the Soviet gulags and General Rokossovsky left Poland.

We were as far from achieving our democratic aspirations as we had been when the bloody revolts began. A popular bit of black humor at the time was:

The difference between Western democracy and our "people's democracy" is the difference between a chair and the electric chair.

❊

I was still living with my parents, but spent most of my days immersed in academic life and away from Mother's meddling. The progressive environment on campus held my interest, but I loathed medical study and the intense workload that came with it—mind-numbing courses in chemistry, biology and anatomy. I attended boring lectures, wrote tedious papers about subjects totally alien to my sensibilities, and made the rounds at city hospitals—with my annoyingly diligent classmates—to observe doctors and nurses at work.

As first years we were assigned the most filthy, unpleasant chores, cleaning the vomit and fecal messes of the sickest patients, tasks that left me constantly nauseated. Worst of all was the sight of blood, which made me ill. My heart ached remembering the countless blood-soaked soldiers and civilians from the war. *How can I be a doctor?* My only relief came during the rare moments when I returned to my cello. But I could not truly relax and enjoy playing under the weight of my course load. Only a few months into my studies, I came to the conclusion there was no pursuit more detestable than medicine.

Philosophy was the only class that inspired me, the only outlet to openly argue and tap into great creative minds. Debate made me feel drunk with excitement. Late into my second semester I submitted a paper to the professor and waited outside his office while he looked it over. He was an elderly and stately, if not madcap, sort of scholar whom I respected as a pillar of academia. He barely gave my work a glance. After a few minutes he called me into the room, scrawled something across the first page, and threw the paper out of the open window.

"Now get out!" he shouted.

I ran down several flights of steps as fast as I could to collect my paper, anxious to see his remarks. When I retrieved it I was a bit startled, but also very amused, to see he had written in capital letters the word, "*IDIOT.*" I was not the least bit concerned about my standing at the university, so I returned to his office and knocked loudly on his door.

"Come in!" he barked.

"Excuse me, Mr. Professor," I said with feigned deference as I pushed my paper toward him across his desk, "I see you've clearly signed your name . . . but you haven't given me a grade."

The old man stared at me in astonishment for some time, and then burst into hysterical laughter.

He stood up, looked at me with a straight face and said, "Mr. Zawistowski, I think you have the potential to become a very good philosopher."

He scribbled something above "*IDIOT,*" shook my hand, and gave me my paper marked with a "*Five,*" for *excellent.*

This was probably my crowning achievement at the university. I was miserable otherwise, and felt imprisoned. Taking classes I so disliked, having no time for a social life, and more importantly, for playing the cello, living in a society without hope for a better future, and having to return home to my parents every night, I felt more and more mutinous. My ability to hide my festering discontent was putrefying at a faster rate than the cadavers in anatomy. I waited anxiously for the summer months when I would be reunited with my cello.

As soon as the school year ended, I gathered enough confidence to announce to my parents my intention to quit medical school and apply to the Music Academy at Warsaw University.

"It is obvious that I hate medicine and would be a terrible doctor. I want to be a cellist. You must respect my right to decide for myself!"

They were shocked. Father became characteristically quiet while Mother worked herself into a frenzy. Her face turned beet red, she refused to listen to me, made threats, yelled and cried like an unruly child until she was thoroughly exhausted. And when she realized her emotional outburst had no effect, she came very close to my face, looked me hard in the eyes and said something I will never forget.

"If you want to be a thief swindling the public with your cheap music, and not a doctor, I don't want to know you." She continued, "I am sorry I gave birth to you. From now on you are not my son. You are not a member of this family. Take your things and get out of my sight!"

Father's face was pale and still. He sat in silence with his eyes closed.

I packed a little suitcase with a couple of shirts and pants, underwear, a toothbrush and hardly much else. I took my cello and some music and left the apartment feeling scared. My heart was broken, but I knew I could not reverse course just to please my mother. It was my life and I would now have control over it. I was nineteen, and on my own.

My relationship with Zdzisław remained nonexistent. He made no effort to contact me after I was thrown out of the house, or during my first difficult months of transition to an independent life. I saw him one afternoon when I was walking with my cello case through Victory Square. He flew past me riding my precious bicycle, which he had taken for himself. If I had seen Mother, I would have told her that she does indeed have a thief for a son, but it isn't me.

For the first week I hung out in dormitories with various friends and colleagues, sleeping in a different room almost every night. I contacted the church organist I used to play with for weddings and funerals and accumulated enough paying engagements to support a meager existence. Professor Kowalski and my fellow musicians were thrilled that I decided to apply to the Music Academy. With support from the faculty, I was awarded one of ten spots for cello students. But, enrollment added immense pressure to my mounting financial strain, and I knew weddings and funerals would keep me afloat for only so long.

A block away from the university were the city's two grandest hotels—Hotel Europejski and, overlooking the courtyard of the Presidential Palace, the elegant Hotel Bristol. The Bristol, which was once owned by the famous Polish pianist and former Prime Minister, Ignacy Paderewski, boasted an old world, elegant café where a piano trio entertained customers every night with Viennese-type arrangements of popular operettas and other schmaltzy music. When I heard that the cellist for the trio passed away and the remaining players were looking for a replacement, my cello and I appeared at the café within an hour, inquiring about the job.

The pianist and violinist were old-fashioned European gentlemen, about the same age as my father. They looked at me with skepticism, but invited me to play. They were skilled café players and I was very nervous having to sight-read unfamiliar music. Since I was classically trained, my style was very different from theirs. Of course, I needed work desperately and, if there were any hope of being hired, I knew I better start imitating them fast.

At the end of a half hour of play, the two old fellows gave me the job. The basic pay was very good and the extra tip money we made was a welcome bonus. From seven to eleven in the evening, six times a week, I played café music. During the day I aimed for the lofty heights of Bach, Beethoven, Haydn, Dvořák; at night I was a gypsy cellist. Mother would call me a klezmer, but I didn't care. I was earning an honest living.

In 1958 one of the most famous Polish pianists, Arthur Rubinstein, the world's foremost interpreter of Chopin, came back to Poland after a twenty-year absence. He had escaped the Holocaust by emigrating to the United States, but almost one hundred members of his family perished in the Nazi death camps. His return to Warsaw was a highly celebrated event and very emotional for everybody who loved music. He and his wife Nela were distinguished guests at the Hotel Bristol, and after a triumphant concert at Philharmonic Hall, Rubinstein, with his entourage including the Dean of Music from the University, showed up at the café.

I had been working happily with the trio for months and was very comfortable with the repertoire.

As soon as Rubinstein took his seat, the violinist leaned over and said, "Leszek, let's play the arrangement of the Chopin *Nocturne* in honor of our eminent guest!"

Rubinstein listened respectfully, but when we put down our bows he approached us.

"Gentlemen, you play very well, but it is late and you must be tired. Please take a break."

It seemed he didn't want to hear café musicians butchering his beloved music.

The following day I was called to the dean's office. He was outraged.

"You have brought shame to the Music Academy by playing such low-brow music. Quit your café job immediately, or face expulsion!"

I resigned from the trio at once.

That same year I entered a national cello competition for young musicians under the age of twenty-one. I played concertos by Haydn, Lalo and Saint-Saëns, and practiced six to eight hours every day. My hard work paid off and I won first prize. It was a fantastic break and validated my decision to quit medical school. This was proof that I was right and Mother was wrong. After this bit of success, I was engaged for solo and chamber music concerts, respectable in the eyes of the dean.

One summer afternoon I played a solo performance at the Saski Gardens, precisely the place where, in 1940 as a two-year-old in the arms of my mother, a German soldier put a gun to my head. There were roughly a hundred people sitting in the park lounging on benches, with dozens more strolling past. When I finished playing and stood to acknowledge the flattering applause from the audience, I spotted Father and Mother walking toward me. I had not seen them, or any other family members for that matter, in over a year. Mother had rendered me an outcast. Despite this, she approached me smiling, as if nothing happened between us, and complimented me on my playing. Although Father was mute as usual, I sensed he was pleased to see me. Perhaps because of the softness in his eyes, alongside the wickedness of Mother's idle chatter, I was torn between joy and anger. By then I had my own place and was proud to be a musician able to support myself. I was no longer a child and didn't care what my mother thought. Gradually, I accepted their gesture of peace and we regained some semblance of family life, seeing each other occasionally.

Later in the summer I was hired to play another park concert outside the city. It was unbearably hot and humid that evening, and when I took my seat on the open-air stage and began tuning my cello, swarms of bugs attacked me from all sides. I reached for my handkerchief and desperately tried waving them off, to the amusement of the audience. I realized that to get through this performance, I had to accept the bugs as my stand partners. I tried to tune, placed my bow on the strings, and TWANG, one of them broke. With a few chuckles from the audience, I walked backstage to change it quickly. I returned and started to play David Popper's *Tarantella.* After no more than thirty seconds, CRACK, this time much louder, and the neck of my cello, along with the fingerboard, separated from the body of the instrument. The audience burst into sidesplitting laughter watching me in obvious distress, clumsily collecting the scattered parts of my cello. I gathered all the pieces and, with a sigh, headed off the stage. My path was interrupted when I stepped on a rotten floorboard. It collapsed underneath me and my right leg disappeared almost to my knee. At this point the audience was standing and screaming in uproarious approval while I was ensnared helplessly in the middle of the stage, surrounded by what looked like the floating debris of a shipwreck. A couple of stagehands came to my rescue, pulled me up and dragged me off. Everyone applauded wildly and demanded more.

"Encore, encore!!"

They thought it was a musical comedy act. The next morning I received one of the best reviews of my life. The headline read, *THE FINEST YOUNG MUSICAL COMEDIAN OF OUR AGE IS BORN.*

In those dark, oppressive times everybody was looking for some comic relief. Alas, despite my critical acclaim, I never became a Polish Victor Borge.

The famed Russian cellist Mstislav Rostropovich came to the Academy at least twice a year to give master classes. He was tall and lumbering, but everything about his personality was exuberant.

He would tell us, "You must be fearless. Don't be afraid of technical challenges. Conquer the mountain from the top, not the bottom, and the rest of the journey will be easy!"

I idolized him and learned more from him than in all the years combined under Kowalski, my egomaniacal professor. Rostropovich's passion for music was infectious and it radiated to all of his students. In the months that passed between his visits, I worked very intensively, hoping to impress him upon his return.

At the very beginning of 1959, I asked Mr. Rostropovich to accept me as his student at the Tchaikovsky Conservatory in Moscow, hoping my ability to speak decent Russian would increase my chances. I knew that to maintain my sanity and improve my cello playing, I had to escape from the clutches of Professor Kowalski, make a bold move, and try to advance my musical career. A mere three weeks later, I received a letter inviting me to study in Moscow with the renowned master. Just about everybody understood the significance of this invitation and was very happy for me, full of praise and congratulations. But Mother and Father, with their intolerance for Russians, mocked me.

"What a ludicrous idea."

For them, nothing Russian could possibly be worthwhile.

Just prior to my imminent departure, my soon-to-be former professor, Kowalski, invited me to a rehearsal of the Warsaw National Philharmonic, considered the best orchestra in Poland. Kowalski asked me to bring my cello and I complied, even though it seemed a strange request. During intermission Witold Rowicki, the orchestra's music director and conductor, called me to his office and said he heard I was a talented cellist, knew I recently won a prestigious competition, and wanted to hear me play. Rowicki and Kowalski, along with several musicians, sat in the audience, and I was ushered with nervous excitement onto the stage of the beautiful concert hall. I played a movement from one of Bach's cello suites and the first movement of the Saint-Saëns Cello Concerto.

I couldn't figure out why this distinguished group would waste their time for such an impromptu recital. I was pleased, but puzzled, nonetheless. Kowalski was so vain, I figured that he simply wanted to show off his student. I should have known better; his deviousness soon revealed itself. When Kowalski learned about my future study with Rostropovich, he was angry and insulted, rather than proud. He conspired to do everything in his power to prevent me from going to Moscow, including arranging this "spontaneous" audition with the National Philharmonic.

When I finished playing, Maestro Rowicki called me into his office again and made a long speech about the greatness of his orchestra and his players, "They are the best in the country, the envy of Eastern Europe." He went on and on.

"I know you are only twenty years old, but you are very accomplished," he said.

Where is he headed, I wondered.

"Show up next Monday for rehearsal. During the first three weeks you will sit on the front stand with Kowalski for symphonic training. After that your permanent position will be on the last stand of the section. Welcome to my orchestra!"

He smiled and awaited my reply. I was dumbstruck.

When I regained my composure I said, "Maestro, please forgive me. I am young and still a student. Right now I am preparing to leave for Moscow on the invitation of Mr. Rostropovich, and will continue my studies with him. I am not interested in joining your orchestra."

Rowicki's pleasant demeanor faded as he pulled his chair closer to my own, scraping it across the floor.

With a slimy smirk he responded, "You should be very honored to play for me, and furthermore, to be invited to join the esteemed National Philharmonic. I will excuse your stupidity this time, but if you refuse my offer, you risk never playing the cello anywhere, under any circumstances, ever again."

His face was now a foot from mine and he was glaring, threateningly, into my eyes. I blinked and he patted my hand. *Will he break my fingers?* Chills ran through my body and I felt the blood drain from my face. I imagined being hauled off to prison like my father.

That night I drowned my sorrows in drink. On January 27, 1959, I officially became the youngest member of the Warsaw National Philharmonic.

10

An Italian Scheme

When the Warsaw Philharmonic was established in 1901, it quickly joined the elite circle of the finest ensembles in Europe. In the earliest days of World War II, however, its great hall was destroyed and half of its musicians—many of them Jewish—were killed. In 1955 a new concert hall opened. It was redesigned in an austere style and no longer resembled the magnificent Paris Opera House. The government, true to its socialistic posture, changed the orchestra's name to the Warsaw National Philharmonic of Poland, and Rowicki became music director and principal conductor.

Dutifully, but with bitterness, I attended my first rehearsal. Most of the players were older and wore suits and ties. I showed up in casual clothes and felt conspicuously out of place.

The orchestra manager, a prickly and impatient man, approached me and said in a serious voice, "*Panie* Zawistowski, you are now a member of the National Philharmonic—the most venerable musical organization in this country—and we expect you to comport yourself accordingly. I do not want to see you dressed this way tomorrow or any day after. You will conform to the dress code, which means wearing a suit and a tie like the rest of us."

The first piece we rehearsed was Camille Saint-Saëns' *Carnival of the Animals*. Its most popular movement, *Le Cygne* (*The Swan*), was written for solo cello, and Professor Kowalski, whose suit was pressed and hair slicked back, played it pretty badly. Despite his position as principal, Kowalski's sound was small and his interpretation very dull.

Maestro Rowicki was not satisfied and looked through the cello section. "Who else would like to play?" he asked.

I did not dare move even an eyebrow. The assistant principal raised his hand. His tone was much bigger than the professor's, but the playing was rough and without feeling. Rowicki scanned the cello section again. The tension among the twelve of us was palpable. I may have shivered slightly from nerves and the maestro's eyes locked onto mine.

He pointed his bony finger and said, "*Panie Leszku*, it is your turn."

I glanced at Kowalski, hoping for encouragement, but received nothing but an odious glare in return. He looked as if he wanted to see me fail. I lifted my bow and signaled to the maestro to begin. *The Swan* used to be one of my showpieces and, having Kowalski's wickedness on my mind, I played my heart out for the one hundred members of the orchestra. When I finished they applauded and Rowicki stepped down from his podium to shake my hand. Kowalski stood up and without a word, walked off the stage. I didn't feel sorry for him. He deserved that humiliation after preventing me from going to Moscow and studying with Rostropovich. The following day Kowalski called in sick, and I performed the solo for my first two concerts. After a week Rowicki moved me to the end of the cello section, near the harp and far away from the resentful eyes of the principal.

Even though the Philharmonic schedule was very intense, I still attended classes at the Music Academy. It was tempting to quit school, but I kept hearing Mother's voice in my head.

"The most important things in life are your health and your education. A good education can never be taken away from you."

I resolved to complete my Master's degree and enjoyed an unexpected bonus at the same time. I met a fellow student at the Academy, Urszula, a pianist with long, blond hair and elegant hands, and we started dating. She was confident, vibrant and very ambitious; we made perfect partners, intellectually and physically. Since I had my own apartment, she spent more and more time at my place, and soon we were living together. It was not just a casual relationship with some girl; for me it was a true love affair with a woman.

The Philharmonic, one of Communist Poland's most treasured cultural exports, was sent regularly to perform as emissaries throughout Western Europe. Our nation's top performing artists were a very powerful tool of

Communist propaganda and were widely used to promote the system's virtues. Hardly a proponent of the government's agenda, I was ecstatic, nonetheless, about the foreign tour to Italy planned for August of 1959. It would be my first venture outside Polish borders since I was seven years old.

We traveled by bus. As the newest and youngest member of the ensemble, I was seated at the very back. It was not until the start of the trip that my unfortunate problem with motion sickness revealed itself. We made several emergency stops and I christened every town we passed with my regurgitated lunch. Ultimately, the management moved me to the front row near the exit and next to the translator for the orchestra, a Polish gentleman named Zalewski, who lived in Rome and worked for the Polish bishops at the Vatican. He was about the same age as my father.

When I introduced myself he looked at me with curiosity. "Are you, by any chance, the son of Feliks Zawistowski?" he asked.

"Yes!" I answered enthusiastically.

And then, as if he were looking at a ghost, "Was he a POW at Ohrdruf?"

"Yes, my father was arrested and almost died in Ohrdruf after his participation in the Warsaw Uprising."

Zalewski burst into tears.

"Feliks was my companion in that death camp. We were both freed by U.S. soldiers and served in the army together until the end of the war. Oh my god, I can't believe you are sitting here next to me."

Zalewski had a difficult time controlling his emotions and peppered me with questions about my family, particularly about my father.

When we arrived in Rome he unearthed a photograph of himself with my father. They were in army uniforms with their arms slung across each other's shoulders, and I saw my dashing, heroic father after the war, an image that had all but faded from memory. There was so much feeling in this small picture I gently held in my hands. Both men had escaped death and in their faces I saw a rugged optimism.

I tried hard to avoid thinking about how little my father resembled the youthful idealist in the photograph. Zalewski, on the other hand, hadn't abandoned that contagious enthusiasm for life. He set out to show me the beauty of his adopted city whenever I had a break between rehearsals and performances. We visited the Coliseum, the Roman Forum, St. Peter's Basilica and the Sistine

Chapel. Walking through the sacred plaza facing the Basilica, we came across several prostitutes soliciting sex. One of them was visibly pregnant. In Poland prostitution was against the law.

Zalewski commented, "Italian women are free to make a living any way they see fit."

What kind of freedom does this symbolize, I asked myself.

For the remainder of the trip Zalewski treated me like his son. I seemed to have a predilection for accumulating substitute fathers. The two of us were inseparable. In Perugia the orchestra had a rare afternoon off. Zalewski and I drove to Assisi and roamed through vast fields of lavender and red poppies. We ate in a charming trattoria where I was introduced to delicious Italian wine. Over lunch I told him the dramatic tale of how I became a member of the Philharmonic. He was outraged and recalled his homeland with disgust.

"You cannot go back to Poland," he insisted. "You have an obligation to fulfill your parents' dream and escape from these Communists!"

Through his connections at the Vatican, Zalewski promised to arrange a scholarship for me to study with the great Italian cellist Enrico Mainardi, who was teaching in Rome at the Academy of Santa Cecilia.

"As a gift to your father, I will be your patron and take care of all your needs. You will move in with me as soon as the tour ends," he pronounced.

For the next two weeks Zalewski's proposal consumed me. I considered my father's decision to return to Warsaw instead of moving to the United States and the terrible mistake it had been. Then I deliberated over why he made such a choice. Youthful idealism was a luxury he couldn't afford, considering his obligations to his country and his family. For myself, I confronted only one major obstacle in deciding whether or not to defect. My sweetheart Urszula was waiting for me in Warsaw. As the end of the tour neared, I yearned to return to her and explained my feelings to Zalewski.

"You are a fool. Italian girls are much more beautiful than Polish ones, and besides, you are too young to be so serious. Don't commit yourself to only one girl. Have some fun. Experience many women."

I said goodbye to a very disappointed Zalewski and returned to Poland with the orchestra.

When we arrived back in Warsaw, I found my apartment empty of all of Urszula's belongings. She had left me for another man. When I confronted her she was not apologetic.

In a cold, matter-of-fact voice she said, "I already started cheating on you before you left for the tour."

I was devastated and angry, and felt incredibly naïve. Zalewski was right when he warned me about women, "*Cosi fan tutte!*"

I immersed myself in classes, rehearsals and performances, hoping music would help to ease the sting.

One of the orchestra concertmasters was Fryderyk Sadowski, who endured several years in Auschwitz. Beaten repeatedly by SS guards, his tall, lanky frame was misshapen; he wore a tight body corset and suffered from constant pain. His ticket to survival in the death camp was his violin. Although he never spoke of his ordeal, it was rumored he was concertmaster of the camp ensemble. Sadowski's orchestra greeted new transports with the last music most of them would ever hear. It was such twisted deception by the Nazis, sending so many of those arrivals straight to the gas chambers. Day after day, night after night, Sadowski played works by Richard Wagner, the favored composer of Hitler and the camp commandant. I tried to tell Sadowski the story of my brother Henryk, but Sadowski refused to discuss those years. The memory must have been unbearable. I wondered if he had been playing when my brother arrived at that vile place.

In September the Warsaw Philharmonic's oboist, Stefan Sutkowski, approached me with a very appealing offer. He organized a group of players from the orchestra to perform Renaissance and Baroque music and named it Musicae Antiquae Collegium Varsoviense. It was the first ensemble of its kind to be established in Poland, and Sutkowski invited me to be its cellist. The early repertoire brought back many good memories from my childhood when I was singing in the church boys' choir. Without hesitation, I agreed to join the group.

At the opposite end of the musical spectrum, Rowicki's Philharmonic announced the inauguration of a festival of contemporary music. It was called the Warsaw Autumn. For young orchestra members like me, the prospect of playing avant-garde music, some of it very experimental, was enticing. In a strict socialistic climate where totalitarian art reigned supreme, a festival like this was unheard of. Communist authorities scorned contemporary works, which they labeled "decadent," and as a result, nobody in Eastern Europe or Russia was ever exposed to such repertoire, let alone granted permission to perform it.

I felt like a window to the West had been opened, allowing some fresh air to permeate the stuffy dungeon that was Poland. Our orchestra was introduced to internationally recognized works by Bartok, Stravinsky, Schoenberg, Berg, daring new music by Ligeti, Stockhausen, Nono, Cage, and unknown pieces by Polish composers like Szymanowski, Lutosławski, Górecki and Penderecki. It was exhilarating to rehearse with many of the Polish composers who were in attendance. For the first time since being recruited, I actually felt proud to be a member of the Philharmonic, and I had to admit, Rowicki was a great pioneer and ambassador of new music.

In November the orchestra went on its first Russian tour to Moscow, Leningrad, Vilno and Riga. Traveling by train for days across vast expanses was painfully boring. Apart from reading, playing cards and drinking a lot of vodka, our only diversion was mindlessly staring out the train window at the passing countryside. No wonder neither Napoleon nor Hitler stood a chance of conquering this gigantic nation. After hundreds of miles, I noticed there were only women working along the tracks, not a single man. The women were peculiarly dressed and looked very poor, wearing many layers of clothes, sweaters upon dresses upon stockings, with multiple scarves on their heads, as if they carried all the clothes they possessed on their backs. It was miserably cold outside, so I speculated that this was how they shielded themselves from the elements.

At one of the stops I approached an older woman and asked her in Russian, "*Babushka,* where are all the men?"

She sized me up with distrust and, spitting on me, answered, "Where do you think?! They are in the army or working in the factories."

In Moscow we stayed at the colossal Hotel Ukraine, designed in Stalin's mandated gothic style, which looked like a freeze-dried wedding cake. It was a place with strange habits and rules. When I needed to use the bathroom, there was no toilet paper, so I exited the stall in search of the housekeeping staff. At the end of the spacious, carpeted corridor sat a plump, old woman who resembled a wrinkled Russian doll with a red-patterned scarf tied at the top of her disheveled, gray hair. Next to her on one side was another *babushka,* even older, and on the other side was a stack of toilet paper rolls.

I asked for a roll, but the two shook their heads firmly and said, "*Nyet!*"

The younger *babushka* ripped off one little sheet and asked for a *kopek,* the equivalent of a penny. Instead, I gave her five *kopeks* and received five little pieces of toilet paper. We played this game for a few minutes until finally I handed her a ruble in exchange for the whole roll, which I hid in my suitcase like a precious treasure.

Breakfast was even more bizarre. First thing in the morning, the hotel served me a bowl of piping hot Russian borscht with a layer of fat and a heaping mound of sour cream on top. It was accompanied by two thick slices of very dark bread and a small tin container of black caviar. A bottle of vodka completed the setting. After such a meal I was expected to play a rehearsal and a concert? I declined the vodka, asked for a cup of tea, ate my bread with butter, and could not resist some of the savory caviar.

Before the orchestra had departed for Russia, friends of my parents gave me a small package and asked that I deliver it to their relative who lived in Moscow. I was happy to do this favor for them and was curious to know what was inside the brown paper wrapping. On the only day without a rehearsal, with the secret parcel and an address in hand, I headed for the impressive Moscow subway trains. Descending the hundreds of steps into the underground system was like disappearing into a catacomb. The subways doubled as bomb shelters during the war and were extraordinary pieces of architecture. I boarded the train free of charge and got off at the right stop, but had no directions from there and got hopelessly lost. Spotting a policeman, I showed him the address written in Russian and asked for help. He glared at me very suspiciously, shrugged his shoulders and walked away, but I found a young woman willing to cooperate. She led me to my destination, which was, strangely, only a few feet from where the officer had been standing.

Entering the building I encountered a very odd scene. Each apartment door was open, as if there were no expectation of privacy. The mixture of human sounds and cooking smells wafting out of every living quarter was striking. I peered nonchalantly into a couple of the apartments. They were tiny and cramped and everything in them looked worn, including the photographs on the walls. I felt like I had stepped onto the stage of an unfolding drama and that at any moment, one of the actors would pull me in and I would be embroiled. Eventually, I found the tenant I was looking for. He was a small, shriveled Polish man, lined with age. In his room stood a bed, a table with two chairs and an armoire. That's it.

He was clearly shaken by my visit and, accepting the package discretely, in hushed tones he whispered, "Meet me at the nearest subway station. It could be dangerous for me if we talk in my place."

Before I left he motioned me to his armoire, and with the little strength he possessed, edged the heavy cabinet slightly away from the wall.

"I want to show you my icon," he said quickly, revealing a small, tin portrait of a saint, hanging at an angle.

The gesture was really peculiar and I didn't know how to respond, but speculated that the mystery package might contain a similar idol that was unavailable on the Russian market.

I met the old man on the subway platform and he treated me to some candy.

Apologetically, he explained, "My neighbors are nosy and distrustful. They would make trouble for me if I had a foreign visitor in my home."

The man was glad to receive word from his Polish relatives, but said he could never go back to his native country.

"I was a Polish Communist fighting in the Bolshevik Revolution. I wouldn't be welcome."

His beady eyes darted from left to right as he declared that Russians are poor and struggle so much in their daily lives because of reactionary American and Western forces determined to destroy the *true* people's society. I didn't ask him why he had that religious picture—as a Communist he was surely an atheist—but I did bring up the subject of toilet paper.

He answered, "It is in short supply in Russia, so most people use newsprint. After reading, they cut it into squares and put the stack in their bathrooms. The newspaper I like is *Pravda*," the official Communist Party publication, "because of the good quality of its paper."

I loved that. *There is no better way to treat Communist propaganda than to wipe your ass with it and flush it down the toilet!*

On the way back to the hotel, I was seized by the sudden realization that I am actually fortunate to live in Warsaw and work with the National Philharmonic. I even began to be grateful for the lost opportunity to study and live in Moscow. Kowalski's deception and the events of the previous year proved to be fortuitous after all.

Our last two concerts were in Leningrad and then Riga, the capital of the Republic of Latvia. I was relieved to leave ugly Moscow and discover the stunning city of Leningrad where I spent hours at the Hermitage Museum, basking in its magnificent collection of art. The program we played in Riga was Szymanowski's *Stabat Mater*, a requiem mass for orchestra, chorus and four solo voices. Performing it in one of the post-Stalinist Russian republics was significant. It was the first time the authorities allowed a piece of contemporary music with religious content to be heard publicly. I thought of the old man's religious icon hidden behind his armoire. *Maybe even Communists have to rely on a little bit of faith from time to time.*

The hall was packed with people cradling bouquets of flowers in their laps. There wasn't one empty seat. During the concert I noticed tearful expressions on the faces of some orchestra colleagues. The music was very profound and emotional, but we had played it many times in Warsaw, and though I had a deep appreciation for *Stabat Mater* I couldn't imagine crying on stage. Glancing at the chorus, I saw that half of the singers were also weepy as they sang. When there were a few measures rest, I turned to look over my shoulder at the public and choked up myself. Almost every person held their bouquets in front of their faces, with heads bowed, tears streaming down their cheeks. At the end, everyone, on stage and in the hall, sat motionless, suspended in silence for what seemed like an eternity. And then they erupted. With thunderous applause, they screamed and showered us with an avalanche of flowers, displaying the power that music has over the human spirit in all its intensity. For these people we were ambassadors of hope and guardians of their secret desire for rebellion against a system that had gripped them for too long.

My understanding of what it really means to live without freedom was coming into sharper focus. Two days later when the orchestra arrived back in Poland, I felt like dropping to my knees and kissing the soil of my Motherland.

11

April Fools

Rowicki was a good conductor, but not a great one. The iconoclastic Leopold Stokowski, on the other hand, was theatrical and impressive. Audiences loved Stokie—as he was called in musical circles—and so did I. His performance of Mussorgsky's *Pictures at an Exhibition* with us was a phenomenal success, and Rowicki was extremely jealous. *Pictures* was one of our director's personal showpieces and Stokie upstaged him. Two short months later, Rowicki reprogrammed the piece and conducted it himself. He ordered the stagehands to erect platforms in the middle of the orchestra for the percussion section, and doubled the normal battery of gongs and bells. This dramatic configuration was designed especially for the final movement, *The Great Gate of Kiev.*

We were subjected to a hellish week of rehearsals. The maestro loomed over us like a vulture. He reminded me of a Cossack, albeit a refined one; he was less scary-looking than the ones I encountered as a child, but crude, nonetheless. He was an arrogant narcissist and I lost patience with his antics. For fun, and a little revenge, on the day of our concert I bought a package of exquisitely sharp razor blades. About forty-five minutes before the performance when there was no one on stage, I discretely made my way to the ropes that held all the gongs and bells. Sweating, but with great care, I partially slit a few of the ropes. *Have I gone mad?* If I were caught my whole career would be in jeopardy. Even so, I completed the task and scurried off the stage.

When the performance began I could hardly concentrate on the music, in anticipation of what would happen when we reached *The Great Gate of Kiev*. Rowicki was thoroughly enjoying himself, basking in the attention. The critical moment finally arrived and the percussion players faced the audience, gripped their large mallets, and hit the bells with powerful strikes. The volume was immense. Rowicki encouraged them to produce more sound and they struck their bells even harder, reveling in the spotlight. Rowicki had an expression of triumph on his face until suddenly a rope snapped and bells began to fall to the floor, one after another. Then yet another rope broke, and metal upon metal clanged as they all tumbled down the platform toward Rowicki in a deafening cacophony. It was shocking. As the last of the bells rolled to Rowicki's feet like a discarded tin can, the orchestra and the audience dissolved into laughter. Our powerful maestro went pale, standing like a helpless fool barely able to move his arms. We finished the performance basically conductor-less. In the lively chatter after the concert, everybody agreed that the ropes must have been too old to withstand the weight, and that it was merely an accident. Of course, I said nothing.

I became very close friends with a double bass player in the orchestra, Wojtek Górecki, the sweetest man I ever met, even though he had a face like Frankenstein with a stiff crew cut to match. Whenever we were together I felt safe, knowing that with his looks nobody would give us trouble. The following May the Ministry of Culture sent me, Wojtek and a few other musicians for a week of social work at a youth gathering in the villages of Nieborów and Żelazowa Wola. Nieborów was home to an extraordinary seventeenth-century palace and not far from Żelazowa Wola, the birthplace of my country's most beloved composer, Fryderyk Chopin. The Chopin family manor house was surrounded by streams and wildlife, lushly landscaped, and miraculously survived World War II intact. That was ironic, considering the Nazis had banned Chopin's music.

In this rich historic and physically beautiful environment, the government imported international artists and held weekly seminars for young people from national art and music schools. Visiting performers, like Wojtek and myself, were assigned to play chamber music and give music appreciation courses to the students. As soon as I arrived I met an eighteen-year-old girl named Regina, a counselor at the camp. She insisted I teach her to play the cello. Although I was very occupied with my regular students, she persisted with sexy, coquettish looks until I could scarcely resist. From the first lesson it was clear a musical education was not what she was after. She was tone deaf, without talent, and simply not interested in music. Three days later Regina was in my bed. She was wildly uninhibited and wanted to make love at any time of the day or night. Wojtek encouraged me wholeheartedly. But, between rehearsals and concerts and having sex with Regina, after a week I felt like a dead rooster and couldn't wait to go home. I hadn't learned Regina's last name and didn't care to know. We had a strictly physical relationship. She never asked me about myself either.

That fall the Philharmonic played in the Warsaw Autumn Music Festival for the second time. At the beginning of one of the concerts, I looked out across the audience and noticed Regina sitting in the front row. She flirted ostentatiously with me throughout the performance. At the next concert she showed up again, sat in the same place and acted the same way.

When she found me backstage afterward, I told her in no uncertain terms, "Your behavior is very disruptive. This is not a game. I am here to perform for thousands of people and you are bothering me. Please leave me alone. I don't want to see you again."

During the Festival the orchestra was introduced to a new work, *Threnody to the Victims of Hiroshima*, written by the Polish composer, Krzysztof Penderecki, who was only five years older than I. We had already played a lot of contemporary music, but this piece was drastically different. Traditional musical notation was replaced by unique symbols, graphics really, accompanied by instructions on how the notations should be interpreted. We had to memorize Penderecki's symbols in order to produce his intended effects. The music was eerie, full of *glissandi*, quartertones and odd dissonances. I sat with my stand partner at the back of the cello section.

My colleague pointed to the music and balked, "What the hell do *these* symbols mean?"

Printed throughout the page were what looked to be various-sized open umbrellas. Before I explained what they mean, I jokingly told him he must bring an umbrella on stage.

"At this point the composer expects the audience to spit on us and throw things, so we will need to protect ourselves!" I snickered.

Behind us sitting quietly, undetected in the dark at the edge of the stage and observing the rehearsal, was the composer himself. Penderecki stormed from the rear directly to the conductor's podium and stopped the rehearsal with a wave of his hand and outrage in his voice. He told Rowicki what he overheard and demanded that the maestro throw us out. Rowicki called for a half hour break and ordered me to his office. I was sure he was going to fire me.

The maestro was furious. He spewed venom for a couple of minutes and then told me to sit down.

In his gruffest voice, Rowicki said, "For the first and the last time I will give you a lesson in professional behavior. You perform for the audience, not for yourself. When you walk on that stage, it is your responsibility to give your best, especially playing new works. Even if you think the music is a piece of garbage, your duty is to give it every chance for success and, for the sake of the public, play it as if it were the greatest masterpiece. This is the nature of our profession. Besides, you are paid for it."

Every word was appropriate. What's more, he did not fire me. I was extremely grateful for his generous, sound advice. We returned to the hall, and in front of the orchestra I apologized to Penderecki, Rowicki and my colleagues.

❧

After the Autumn Festival we went back to our standard classical repertoire. Gone were the contemporary and avant-garde. The status quo was what the Philharmonic's audiences loved to hear and there was no hope for change, except in the weather, and even that was turning grim and inhospitable. Imagine my surprise when the management announced one afternoon that they signed a contract with Sol Hurok, a well-known American impresario, for an orchestra tour to the United States in January of 1961.

My first reaction was they were treating us to a cruel joke, an early *prima aprilis*, April Fools. Such a trip could not be possible in the current political climate. Cold War tensions between Russia and the U.S. were at their peak. That same year a United States U-2 spy plane had been shot down over Russian territory. Khrushchev flew into a rage and used the incident to further Soviet accusations against the U.S. Would the government really send us into the den of the "imperialistic monster," the enemy of our "glorious" system? In this hostile environment, with relentless official state propaganda against the West in the press and on the radio, the news of our tour was difficult to believe.

Nonetheless, it was true, so I immediately went to see my parents with the exciting announcement. I could not call them because, like most Polish citizens, they didn't have a phone. A telephone in the home was granted by special permission and only to a few privileged individuals, most of them Communist Party officials. My parents were overjoyed. For at least a decade, they dreamed that a member of the family might actually be able to take advantage of the same opportunity Father had been given at the end of the war. I was the only potential Zawistowski who could fulfill this wish and travel to their imaginary land of milk and honey.

Father was particularly animated and relayed the story of his great uncle. In 1795 Poland was partitioned by Russia, Prussia and Austria, and for one hundred twenty-three years ceased to exist as an independent country. My grandparents' ancestral lands were absorbed into Czarist Russia during this time. The Polish people staged occasional uprisings against their occupiers, but by the end of the nineteenth-century the insurrections collapsed, and in retribution Czar Nicholas I banished thousands of leading Polish families to Siberia. For many years afterward, in an effort to weaken and eventually eliminate the Polish leadership, Russian authorities drafted all young men from the nobility for service into the army, which lasted no less than twenty years. My great grandfather was spared conscription as the head of an estate, but his younger brother, Bolesław, was to be drafted without question. Out of desperation, Bolesław fetched an axe from the barn, put the trigger finger from his right hand on a chopping block and amputated it with one swift blow. Writhing in pain, my great uncle collected the remains of his finger. He saved the bones in a leather pouch, which he wore around his neck.

Of course, the disability prevented Bolesław from being drafted, but the czarist police were not so easily duped. Rumor spread that he would be exiled to Siberia as punishment for his action. In order to avoid such a fate, Bolesław used his wealth to join a rank of exiles fleeing to North America. He eventually settled in the Cleveland area, married and had one son named Anthony, who in turn fathered two boys, Ted and Henry. Father told me that once a year, at Christmas time, he exchanged cards with cousins Ted and Henry, and that they very generously included a ten-dollar bill in the envelope each time. Father was convinced that if I were to contact them during my American tour they would be helpful.

A new vision for my future began to emerge. Exuberant, I left my parents that night after giving them a critical warning: "Do not breathe a word to anybody about our extended family in the U.S. If this information were to get out, the authorities would bar me from going on the tour. No cards to Ted or Henry until I am safely in New York. We leave in two months."

I luxuriated in an unusually optimistic frame of mind and actually found myself enjoying life. I bought a motorcycle and was feeling carefree on a frigid November evening while riding it to visit some friends. Maybe I was going a little too fast. It had been raining earlier in the day and my bike skidded and fell on the slick pavement, pinning me beneath it and dragging me for half a block before coming to a stop. I managed to extricate myself and didn't think I had broken an arm or a leg, but realized the left side of my body was severely injured, with piercing sharp pains shooting through my left shoulder and rib cage. A passerby stopped his car and asked if he could drive me to the nearest hospital. I refused, not wanting to step foot in a hospital again since my miserable days as a medical student scrubbing vomit and feces from the floor, but I was grateful to accept his offer to bring me home. We left the mangled motorcycle on the side of the road. By the following morning I could hardly lift my left arm. Struggling to breathe and in terrible pain, somehow I got myself to work. The rehearsal seemed endless, and as soon as it was over I went to my parents' apartment, afraid to be alone in this condition.

Mother prepared a very hot bath and then smothered my chest and arm with some smelly ointment. She arranged for a doctor from a local clinic to see me.

After a very cursory examination and no tests, he declared, "Leszek has early stage pneumonia, but since you are taking such good care of him at home, there is no reason for hospitalization."

Poland did have penicillin by this time, but he did not prescribe it.

I lay in bed with a high fever for days, motionless like an overheated zombie, steadily deteriorating into delirium. My parents became frantic with alarm. They defied the doctor's counsel and ordered an ambulance. Father had a client, an amateur violist, who was a military doctor in the finest government hospital in Warsaw, reserved for party operatives and other VIPs. I was admitted immediately. The doctors who examined me determined that as a result of the accident I broke a rib, and that broken bone, in turn, punctured the lining of my left lung, which collapsed. Not having been properly treated for so long, a liter of infected fluid accumulated in my chest cavity. In my semi-conscious state I didn't recognize the seriousness of the situation until the doctor inserted a long, thick syringe in between my ribs and drew out a sample of my internal fluids. The putrid stink from the fluid was worse than the outhouses I remembered from my childhood. Registering the expressions on the faces of the doctors and nurses, I sensed I was in grave trouble. The doctor in charge told me the internal infection was so serious he could not guarantee my survival. Forget about going to America. My daily fantasies about the trip ended abruptly.

Removing the toxic fluid from my lung all at once would cause permanent damage, so each morning the doctors gradually extracted a safe amount while simultaneously injecting powerful antibiotics. It was a painfully slow process. My parents visited me often, but Mother's behavior was anything but helpful. She always appeared in the doorway displaying a container of chicken soup and a strained smile, only to dissolve into sobs as if she were attending my funeral, rather than trying to bolster my spirits. I had little hope and slipped into a dark depression.

About ten days into my hospital stay and resigned to a premature death, I had an unexpected visitor. Regina from the music camp appeared in my doorway with an uncharacteristically somber countenance. She made a meager effort to be nice, offered a bit of false sorrow for my suffering, but wasted no time in getting to the point.

Reminding me that the doctors told her I would probably die, Regina declared with great urgency, "I am pregnant with your baby and I don't want it to grow up a bastard. You have to marry me immediately, or you'll rot in hell!"

I must be hallucinating again. My mind kept playing tricks on me during my infirmity. I had visions of rats gnawing tunnels into my rib cage, recurring dreams about manically sawing into my cello with my bow, panic attacks about falling into dark holes while explosions pounded the earth above, leaving me gasping for air. Regina's sudden appearance and dramatic announcement made sense in the tableau of these nightmares. In reality I had not been in contact with her for months and knew almost nothing about her. Our short relationship had been purely sexual. She could see my confusion, gripped my shoulders and urged me to fulfill my duty to her unborn child. In my helpless mental and physical condition, I agreed to marry her and accept the baby as my own. I would be dead soon anyway.

Later that evening Regina returned with a priest and two witnesses. The excited nurses tried to prop me up in bed as best they could, and the priest started to perform a wedding ceremony. In a daze, I could barely understand what he was saying, let alone the significance of the occasion. The priest whispered a string of incantations while waving the sign of the cross over my head several times, which I took to mean he was not only marrying us, but also giving me my last rights. In that hot, gloomy hospital room, with none of my family or friends in attendance, I wed Regina Madejak.

When the ceremony was over my new bride stayed for a few minutes, and perhaps out of some perfunctory sense of gratitude or a twisted attempt to consummate the marriage, she tried to give me a blowjob. A nurse came in and threw her out. That night I became hopelessly despondent. When the room emptied and the hospital fell silent, I struggled to pull myself out of bed and crawled to the window, intending to end my desperate situation. I didn't have enough strength to open the window and collapsed beneath it, unconscious. The following morning I woke up in a different room, in a bed with high side guards. Lying in the bed next to me was another patient who had a pleasant smile and a gleam in his eye.

The events of the previous day seemed like a distant nightmare. I actually found myself pleased to have a roommate. He was a cheerful gentleman my father's age, named Ziulkowski, a very bright and cultured man, hospitalized for the treatment of painful stomach ulcers. He was the director of the state-run meat-processing factory where all my favorite delicious Polish sausages came from. I was very impressed. As it turned out, Ziulkowski was a huge fan of classical music and had no interest whatever in talking about his sausages. He only wanted to hear about my musical career and the Philharmonic and our tours. It was such a relief to have a companion and no longer be miserable and alone.

My marriage the day before was a subject I didn't want to think about and chose not to mention to Ziulkowski. I spoke instead about the U.S. tour and my profound disappointment at not being able to make the trip. My roommate sat up in his bed and scolded me for my fatalistic attitude.

"If you really want to live and go to America, only you can make it happen. You are young and strong. Think positive!"

Every day he dragged me out of bed and forced me to take walks in the hospital corridor. He sat me by the window to gaze outside at the trees, the birds and the beautiful blue sky. Ziulkowski became my best nurse and therapist, a true friend. After three weeks the doctors told me I was out of danger. Not once during this time did my pregnant wife come to visit. Maybe she thought I was already dead. A week later I was released from the hospital. With renewed life churning through my system, and wanting so badly to join the orchestra on the tour to America, I went back to work immediately.

Still very weak and feeling quite a lot of discomfort, I rehearsed with my colleagues and pretended my health had returned to normal. In actuality, each time I took a deep breath, and with every movement of my bow, pain seared through my chest like a knife slicing through flesh. Eventually, I learned to breathe only in between phrases of the music, holding my breath while playing. In this condition my level of performance was not what it used to be, but I learned how to fake very well.

I had very little contact with Regina, except to provide her with money. She continued to live in the suburbs of Warsaw with her parents because I convinced her there was not enough room in my little apartment for both of us. She didn't complain. When I mustered the courage to tell my parents about the marriage and a grandchild on the way, Mother erupted and called Regina every name she could think of, *"Kurva, shiksa, suka!"* Predictably, she refused to meet her new daughter-in-law. Thank god my rehearsal schedule was extremely heavy in preparation for the tour, so I had little time to engage in this domestic drama. Wojtek thought I lost my mind marrying Regina and urged me to have the marriage legally dissolved, considering I was too sick and medicated to have been mentally alert on that fateful day. I was terrified that if I started legal proceedings against her, Regina might prevent me from going to America. I had only one thing on my mind: to be strong enough to go on that tour.

Even though discord plagued the relationship with my parents, when the Christmas holidays came I was overcome with nostalgia. This might be my last chance to be with the family. As was our tradition every Christmas Eve, Father, Mother, Uncle Stasio and his wife, Zdzisław and I gathered in my parents' apartment. Mother always cooked an array of dishes for the holidays—gefilte fish, fried carp, red beets with horseradish, chicken soup, *pierogi* stuffed with sauerkraut, delicious poppy seed cake—and served her specialties with great pride.

In Poland it was customary to show up unannounced since people didn't have phones, so Mother had no advance warning when I arrived with a very pregnant Regina. Uncle Stasio and his wife tried to be nice to her. Father and Zdzisław exchanged a few pleasant words, but Mother was like a stone. She spurned Regina's overtures and refused to speak to either of us, effectively ruining the evening for everyone.

January came at last and I was on my way to America, leaving my personal turmoil behind. The National Philharmonic flew to England first where the orchestra gave concerts in Bath, as well as in two smaller cities outside London. I had never been to Great Britain and should have been anxious to sightsee, but instead I could think of nothing other than crossing the ocean. After a long flight over the Atlantic, we finally arrived at Idlewild International Airport in New York City.

I stepped into the terminal and felt like I was walking on a different planet; it was crowded, noisy, gritty and chaotic, but I thought it was paradise. Driving over the East River from the Queensborough Bridge, I gaped at the city's panorama in utter amazement. It had the same magic as the image of the earth in Sputnik's orbit, and our busload of wide-eyed, excited Polish musicians gazed at it with our noses plastered to the windows.

We were booked at the Hotel Wellington, just one block from Carnegie Hall, in the very center of the city. The buildings were gigantic and the sheer number of people and cars buzzing about them were like a factory whose assembly line had gone haywire. In comparison, Warsaw was like a quiet, provincial town.

Before the first rehearsal I went to Carnegie Hall early in the hopes of finding a private room where I could practice. Approaching the backstage area I heard the rich sounds of an orchestra. I looked out onto the stage and saw the New York Philharmonic, with Leonard Bernstein on the podium, wrapping up its rehearsal. The orchestra sounded like a brilliant, cohesive group of virtuoso soloists. It had been drummed into my head for years that the Warsaw Philharmonic was one of the best orchestras in the world, but hearing the great New York Philharmonic was a revelation. Our orchestra didn't come close.

When it was our turn to rehearse, we sat on that famed stage where, for almost one hundred years before us, all of the greatest performers and orchestras from across the globe had delighted crowds of music lovers. The acoustics in the auditorium were the stuff of legend.

During intermission I went to explore the theater and encountered a short, skinny, middle-aged man with a dark complexion, Stanisław Arzewski, who introduced himself as Stasio. He explained in Polish that he is a pianist playing in a trio at the café in New York's famous Plaza Hotel and came to hear the preeminent orchestra from his ancestral homeland. After chatting briefly he invited me to visit his apartment when the rehearsal ended, and I felt privileged to oblige. When we arrived Stasio introduced me to his confident daughter Cecylia, who was about thirteen and a violinist. She played a solo for us and it was obvious she was a genuine talent. Stasio explained that she was a student at the Juilliard School of Music.

The Arzewskis were relative newcomers to America, having emigrated from Israel just four years earlier, in 1960. I asked for more details about his background, but Stasio resisted unearthing the past, and I knew well enough not to pressure anybody who survived those terrible years as a Jew in Poland. It was Cecylia who told me the story while Stasio looked away.

"My father came from a Jewish family and was twenty-two years old when he married my mother. Her name was Bronisława, but everybody called her Brenda. In 1938 they had their first child, my brother, Michael."

Cecylia went on to describe that the family enjoyed a modest, but comfortable life in Krakow where Stasio played the piano. Then came the German occupation of Poland and their daily existence became fraught with hardship and danger. For years, Stasio managed to earn a decent wage at a popular club until 1942 when the Nazis began their "Final Solution." He endured life in abject fear that it was only a matter of time before the family would be arrested.

They lived with Brenda's mother Stella, who had a job nearby. After work Stella always stopped at Stasio's club, so they could return home together. On a particular Friday night, two Nazi officers showed up at the club. One of them was very drunk and became abusive toward Stella. The other officer intervened, saving Stella from harm. The next night the friendlier officer returned to Stasio's club looking for Stella. He apologized profusely for his companion's behavior and handed her a box of chocolates, a true rarity in wartime Poland. Obviously, he had fallen for Stella and used his nasty friend as an excuse for an introduction.

His name was Max Nagler, an SS officer assigned to Krakow's postal service. Stella was a very alluring woman and, although she wasn't particularly young, with her blue eyes, beautiful blond hair and striking Aryan appearance, she captivated Max. After seeing each other for a few weeks, Max asked Stella to live with him and she agreed, with one caveat. She explained that her family was in danger of being deported to the death camps.

"If you want me, you have to take all of us," she demanded.

In the following days Stasio, with Brenda and four-year-old Michael, were quietly spirited into Max's apartment. Following them were Stella's sister Lola with her husband Frolek. The five were hidden in Max's tiny, low-ceilinged pantry in a building occupied exclusively by Nazi officers.

Stella lived with Max as his common-law wife. With her coloring, nobody suspected that she was Jewish. Her family, confined in this low space, couldn't wear shoes, only socks; they learned to tiptoe around on the floor covered with layers of carpets, and they could not talk openly, only whisper, which was particularly difficult for little Michael. They weren't even allowed to flush the toilet until Stella or Max returned to the apartment after work in the evening. The Arzewskis lived like caged animals for three, long years until the Soviet liberation of Krakow. In May of 1945, when they emerged from their hideaway for the first time, they were blinded by the daylight and couldn't stand up straight. Max singlehandedly saved their lives, and their gratitude was infinite. When the Soviets took over, the family did everything they could to protect Max. They burned all of his belongings, including his SS uniform, but it was in vain. The authorities tracked him down and showed no mercy, despite Stella's pleas for leniency.

"Max was sent to Siberia where he died," Cecylia finished the story, blinking with emotion.

On the way back to the Wellington, my new friend Stasio took me to the elegant Plaza Hotel to show me New York's celebrated Palm Court where he played every night. We made a powerful connection, Stasio and I—music had delivered us both onto American shores—and I hoped our friendship would endure as I was drawn further into the great metropolis.

On January 12, I had the honor of performing on the stage of Carnegie Hall. My physical strength was still compromised, but I played my best and furtively hoped it wouldn't be long before I would return. Concrete plans for a future in America hadn't yet taken shape in my mind, but I couldn't help indulging in a fantasy about one day becoming a member of the New York Philharmonic and making a life for myself in this electrifying city.

From New York we traveled to Washington D.C., Chicago, Detroit and Cleveland. Being in Chicago and Detroit, I felt like I never left Poland. So many people spoke my native language. Of course, I could hardly wait to meet my American family in Cleveland. Father told me one of his cousins was a medical doctor and the other a prominent businessman. I was so thirsty for freedom, to be free from Regina, from Rowicki, and from the Polish mono-lithic society. Without a doubt my cousins would help me.

As soon as we arrived in Cleveland, I excitedly phoned Ted first and then Henry, introducing myself and inviting them to attend the concert as my guests. They both spoke a little Polish and were polite, but each said they had no time to meet. Neither of them agreed to come to my hotel or to hear the performance. Henry explained he had some important social function at his club, and Ted promised to take his children to a baseball game. In blasé fashion, as if they received such calls from distant Eastern Bloc relatives regularly, they turned me away. I had not anticipated such a rejection and felt as if the earth swallowed me up.

My embryonic hopes of defecting vanished as quickly as they had sprung to life. Overcome by the power of this immense country, the United States of America, I knew I was unprepared and too scared to start on a new path in a new land, alone and like a wounded animal.

From the U.S. we flew back to the United Kingdom for a few concerts before returning to Poland. My playing was detached. When I thought about the dismal prospects awaiting me at home, the pain in my chest was even more severe than it had been when I lay dying in the hospital.

In the middle of February I was back in Warsaw, greeted by Regina and an infant son who was born on January 21, 1961, and named Piotr by his mother. I was happy to have an adorable baby to cuddle every night after work and not be stuck alone with Regina. We didn't have feelings for each other, but could shower the baby with our love. *Will I be a good father?* I would try my best to learn. My parents were disappointed in me yet again and this was a heavy burden to bear, but I refused to feel guilty and resolved not be worn down by these challenges. Instead, I was determined to focus on improving my physical condition and to develop and mature as a man. My grand illusions of freedom and a better future were, for the time being, to remain unrequited.

12

No More Practical Jokes

The coldness between Regina and me was of little consequence. I was trapped and accepted the moral and practical responsibilities that came with having a wife and baby son, which included finding a larger apartment for the three of us. Private landlords didn't exist in Poland; all housing belonged to the government. The majority of the Polish population waited years for new living quarters to be approved. But, as a cellist in the National Philharmonic, I was afforded many privileges. I approached the Philharmonic administration with my dilemma, hoping they would exert some influence on the proper authorities, and within days I had an appointment with the Minister of Culture.

The Minister offered me a two-bedroom apartment in a modern building smack in the heart of a park overlooking the banks of the Vistula River on one side and the National Museum of Art on the other. Most of the tenants were from the cultural elite, distinguished movie directors, writers, journalists and professors. Toward the end of the meeting, the Minister congratulated me on my success and reminded me of my good fortune.

Then he asked, "*Panie Leszku*, have you considered joining the Communist Party? You are college-educated, bright and ambitious. We need new blood, people like you," he said with an emphasis on the *new blood*.

He is trying to make a devil's bargain with me. I knew my living quarters were hanging in the balance and hoped the expression on my face didn't reveal my profound hatred for his breed of bureaucrats, people who gamble with the livelihood of others.

I tried to appear relaxed and cordial and answered, "Mr. Minister, I am very flattered and honored. However, you are probably aware of my intense professional workload. I am also trying to be a good husband and father. In my present circumstances, joining the great party would be selfish and irresponsible. It is not the right time. Nevertheless, I thank you for the offer."

He didn't pursue the subject further. I left his office perspiring, despite the coolness in the air. If my father were to learn his son was a member of the Communist Party, he would have killed me.

Within a month Regina, Piotr and I moved into our new, spacious apartment, but our co-habitation was heavy with conflict from the very beginning, our arguments growing in volume and frequency.

"You don't care about us," she said "us" as if Piotr shared her disdain. "It's spring, in case you haven't noticed, and we only have winter clothes. You want us to sweat to death?"

Finally, I decided to leave my cello at the Philharmonic and do my practicing in the theater to give poor Piotr some relief from the strident bickering. Regina didn't like classical music anyway. My wife was only interested in the money I provided to buy the fancy clothes she would show off to her friends, bragging that her husband is a member of the Warsaw Philharmonic. She never expressed a desire to attend even one performance, and that was fine with me.

I arrived at the concert hall after dawn one morning and heard the sound of a cello coming from the stage. Who the hell was there at this hour? I was sure all of my colleagues were still asleep at home. To my great surprise I saw my idol, Mstislav Rostropovich, his tails lying on the floor next to his fatigued body. He had played an unforgettable concert with us the night before.

"Losha, what are you doing here so early?" he greeted me, wearily.

"Good morning, Mr. Rostropovich. I come to practice before every rehearsal." Rostropovich beamed approvingly and with a wide smile said, "You are a smart young man!"

He told me that achieving perfection is the duty of every musician. This consummate artist had not been satisfied with his performance, and after the orchestra members left the hall he remained on stage to rework the piece. I was stunned. The standard I imposed on myself was nothing compared to the self-critical demon that had a hold of Rostropovich. For me, playing the cello was like trying to hold water in my palms and watching it flow through my fingers—though I was pleased with some performances, perfection inevitably slipped from my grasp.

At the Music Academy the staff treated me very differently from the other students. The professors were more interested in my juicy, slightly embellished Philharmonic gossip than their assignments, and gave me top grades whether I was prepared or not. Once or twice a week I went to Kowalski's home for a private lesson. His place was small, but very elegant, furnished in Polish and French antiques. The professor had soundproofed it hoping to avoid complaints from his neighbors by covering the walls with exquisite Oriental carpets. Our sessions usually lasted for over two hours and were exhausting, but no longer accompanied by tears. There was no childish weakness in me that my teacher could exploit any longer; we were now colleagues and equals.

At the end of each lesson, Kowalski rewarded me with a nice espresso, or sometimes even a shot of vodka. We grew accustomed to sitting together while he shared dramatic stories from his past.

Kowalski had nothing but contempt for Russians and didn't hesitate to speak of them in blatantly derogatory terms. In 1939 he lived in Krakow where he owned a small collection of old master paintings, fine Italian instruments and some antiques. As soon as he heard news of the Nazi invasion and the inevitable looting, he rushed to store all of his precious possessions in one of the two bathrooms in his apartment. He hired workers to brick up the entry to this bathroom and resurface its wall. After it was repainted he breathed easier, confident his treasures were secure. As long as the building was not bombed, he reasoned, everything would be safe.

Within the first few weeks of the occupation, a German officer appeared at Kowalski's door with an inventory of his paintings and instruments. Kowalski told him he had sold all of his valuables before the war in order to have money to survive the difficult period ahead. The officer, with the help of two soldiers, combed the apartment thoroughly and, not finding anything, they left. That was the last time he was confronted by the Reich.

When the war ended and the victorious Russian troops occupied Krakow, Kowalski once again had an unexpected visitor.

"A young Soviet officer entered my apartment with a similar list of my belongings. I told him that the Germans took everything. After a full inspection the officer apologized to me and vacated the premises. I heaved a sigh of relief, put on a recording of the Beethoven A major Cello Sonata, and poured myself a glass of liqueur. After a half hour in my tranquility, there was a violent pounding on my door. The Russian officer—he was raging with anger—came back with soldiers carrying big sledgehammers. After leaving me the first time, that clever Russian went to inspect the neighbors' units above and below mine and figured out there was a bathroom missing in my apartment. A few blows with their heavy hammers and the wall gave way, exposing my hidden treasures. They arrested me and threw me in jail. When I was released, I came home to find that they had taken everything, not only the valuables. My apartment was stripped bare, from floor to ceiling."

The proud professor left the next day and went to Warsaw to look for a new home. Being a man of great taste, over time he was able to recreate the elegant pied-à-terre of a gentleman, an old-world oasis in a tiny new space, but with only the barest luxuries afforded him under Communism.

❧

In May the Philharmonic went on a tour to Czechoslovakia to play in Prague's Spring Festival. The city was even more beautiful than Krakow, with medieval churches, palaces and monasteries all having survived the war without any damage. Despite that, the Czech people looked unhappier than the Poles. No one smiled. The only thing that seemed to lift their spirits was their wonderful beer—and they drank a lot of it. From Prague we traveled to Budapest. The Hungarians were bursting with energy, nothing like the Czechs. Still, when we returned to Poland I had to acknowledge that with all of the hardships we endured on our own soil, Polish people were still considerably better off than the Czechs, the Romanians, the Hungarians, the East Germans (who were now firmly behind the Berlin Wall) and especially the Russians.

Though we were more fortunate than our neighbors as a country, my personal life was in turmoil. The situation with Regina had deteriorated steadily. We could never agree about anything, in particular anything that concerned Piotr.

"He is sleepy, don't bother him!" she'd spit at me.

"I missed him all day. Let us play."

"Leave him alone."

My relationship with Mother also became increasingly intolerable. Like a stubborn mule, she refused to accept Regina or her grandchild as members of the family. I couldn't understand her attitude toward sweet Piotr, who was an adorable baby. It was wonderful to play with him and nuzzle up together. On Sundays, if I wasn't performing, I loved to walk him to the park in his carriage, his little arms and legs fluttering with excitement. But as soon as I got home, I felt like a visitor pretending to be a husband and a father. I really had no idea about parenting, and Mother certainly didn't offer any tips. If only she had volunteered to take Piotr for an afternoon from time to time, perhaps a bond could have developed between them, but that was not meant to be.

On the bright side were my occasional visits to Father's studio. He and I had established an unspoken, deep connection, and our time alone remained essentially a secret. Neither of us told Mother, knowing she would have thrown a jealous tantrum.

Ironically, I managed to turn work into a stress-reliever, devising practical jokes to play on my kind-hearted friend Wojtek. Lacking a sense of humor, he was a prime target. I knew there would be a perfect opportunity for some fun when Prokofiev's *Lieutenant Kije* Suite, with its well-known double bass solo, was included on one of our programs.

The night before the concert, on my way to the hall I stopped at a pet shop and bought a cute little white mouse, which came in a cute little white box. As soon as the intermission began the audience exited the hall to buy drinks and use the restrooms, and the musicians left the stage. I took the small package and inconspicuously approached Wojtek's instrument. Very carefully, I cracked the box open over the f-hole of his bass. Of course, the poor, scared mouse quickly disappeared into the vast dark space of the bass. I went for a cup of coffee and waited impatiently for the second half of the program.

The musicians filed back onto the stage and, out of the corner of my eye during tuning, I noticed Wojtek examining his instrument and looking very puzzled. The performance resumed and Wojtek's glorious solo began within minutes, in front of a thousand people. He played it beautifully, but with every stroke of the bow over the strings, Wojtek and the musicians sitting immediately to his right and left, heard a strange scratching noise. The sounds from his instrument were very mysterious, like a snare drum accompaniment to his solo. The vibrations of the bass must have driven the mouse crazy, and its tiny claws scratched wildly in pursuit of an escape route. It was a good thing I couldn't see Wojtek's face, or I would have burst out laughing. He rightfully suspected me as the perpetrator and got his revenge before the next concert by rubbing my bow with soap.

In the spring of 1962 the Philharmonic went on another tour. Our first stop was Innsbruck, Austria, where I stayed in a charming, Tyrolean-style inn with my colleague Emil, an oboist, also in his twenties. When we opened the door to our room, staring at us on the far wall was a portrait of Lenin perched above the beds. The hotel owner, in a gesture of supreme hospitality to the visiting Communist nationals, probably thought we would be comforted sleeping beneath an image of the hero of the Bolshevik Revolution. We took the offensive picture off the wall and hid it under one of our beds. When we returned later in the afternoon, hanging in the same place on the wall was a depiction of Jesus holding his heart in his hands. Emil was Jewish and I wasn't a believer, so if the proprietor suspected we were devout Catholics he was wrong. We took the Messiah off the wall and stored him under the other bed. After our evening concert, exhausted and ready to sleep, we found a third picture in the same spot, a mountain landscape kitsch, similar to my mother's scavenged tapestry. Emil and I fell into hysterical laughter. We were amused by our game and contemplated removing this painting as well, but discovered a fruit and cheese basket and a bottle of wine on an end table underneath the comical Tyrolean scene, and we chose to devour the late night snack instead.

The following morning the innkeeper asked, "Are you pleased with the new artwork in your room?"

"We are honored indeed to stay in your most comfortable lodgings," I answered politely.

With a smile that showed obvious satisfaction, he said, "I would be happy to sell my beautiful painting to you."

"Oh, no thanks. It belongs here," we responded, trying not to laugh.

During our long bus trips between cities, I passed the time daydreaming about destinations for defection. I had strong impressions of every nation I visited, from Western Europe to the United States. England was a possibility, but the British were aloof. Neither their weather nor their personalities were overly warm, and every time they spoke it sounded like they had just swallowed a cockroach. I enjoyed France very much, but the people seemed impatient and arrogant. Switzerland and Austria were aesthetically remarkable, their beauty unrivaled. But, somehow I didn't trust the Swiss, and couldn't erase from my mind Hitler's Austrian origins. Besides, they all put too much sugar on top of their cakes. I loved Italy, but the Italians' wild temperament and crazy lifestyle unnerved me. All of these countries were wonderful places to visit and perform in, but I had doubts about starting a new life alone as a foreigner in almost all of them. The only country that made me feel comfortable when I imagined disappearing within its borders was America. It was truly a country of immigrants. In Chicago, Detroit, Milwaukee, Buffalo, and even New York City, I could imagine functioning easily without knowing a single word of English.

In grade school we had learned about Polish immigration to the "New World," which started as far back as 1608 with the expedition of the Virginia Company of London under the command of Captain John Smith. It seems the British were a hapless bunch of settlers who, as outcasts, hadn't bothered to bring any experienced laborers to the colony. Jamestown was plagued by disease and ineptitude. Captain Smith, having received refuge in the Kingdom of Poland after his imprisonment by the Turks, sought out Polish carpenters and makers of pitch tar, turpentine, soap ash, glass and textiles. He brought them to Jamestown, and by 1619 the Poles had lifted it out of its dismal condition. But, they were denied the right to vote in the first election. "No vote. No work," the workers protested. Thus began the first successful strike on the North American continent. The ill-fated settlement wouldn't have lasted nearly as long as it did if not for the Polish immigrants who were, in the end, granted full rights as citizens.

In the following century, the great Polish heroes of the American Revolution—Pulaski and Kosciuszko supreme among them—made me very proud to be Polish. As a commander in the Continental Army, Kosciusko was a first hand witness to the treatment of slaves in the American South. He abhorred the existence of slavery and serfdom and asked his friend and the executor of his will, Thomas Jefferson, to use the ample proceeds of the commander's Revolutionary War pay to purchase freedom, education, land and livestock for his own and Jefferson's slaves. It was an unprecedented abolitionist act that far overshadowed any effort made by Jefferson, and one that, unfortunately,

Jefferson did not honor. Kosciusko died in 1817 and Jefferson failed to execute his wishes. He eventually sold one hundred of those slaves at auction to pay for his own personal debts. Kosciusko's vision of emancipation predated President Lincoln's Proclamation by sixty years. He was a true American hero and I decided my future was in the great nation where his legacy survives.

None of my family members or closest friends knew of my intense desire to defect. Nor did they imagine the Philharmonic would perform in America again. I knew, however, that after our initial success it was only a matter of time before we would be invited back.

In the beginning of 1963, my hopes were realized when Sol Hurok engaged the orchestra for another concert tour to the U.S. scheduled for October of 1964. Of course, I was ecstatic. The timing could not have been better since I would finish my graduate studies a few months before our departure. I asked for a two-month leave of absence from the Philharmonic and the Musicae Antiquae in order to prepare for my Master's performances at the end of October. My concerts were very well-received. Even Mother was proud. On December 14, 1963, Warsaw University's State Higher School of Music awarded me a Master of Fine Arts degree. My years of juggling between the life of a professional and the very different life of a student were over.

Some of the older members of the Philharmonic teased me about pursuing a university degree.

"Will that scrap of paper help you to play better?" they would ask.

I thought the diploma might prove to be my meal ticket in the U.S.

As soon as 1964 began I vowed to behave more carefully than ever in my life. My terrible accident before the '61 tour never veered far from my consciousness, and I couldn't take any chances. No more practical jokes. At home I tried my best to be a compliant husband. I didn't trust Regina for a second. She was very shrewd and if she had even the slightest inkling I might defect, she would not have hesitated to notify the authorities, and they would assuredly stop me from going on the tour. Living under such a cloud of paranoia, I didn't dare try to take any English language classes. That would have waved a red flag of suspicion, both at home and at work.

Months before leaving, every member of the Philharmonic needed to fill out endless pages of questionnaires for the Polish passport office. Many of the questions were essentially the same, re-written in a slightly different way to catch the responder in a lie or an inconsistency. If the authorities didn't like one's answers, he or she could be subjected to extremely unpleasant interrogations. This was to be avoided at all costs.

As our departure drew near, my excitement was dampened by news of my friend from the hospital, Ziulkowski, the director of the meat-processing factory. The whole city was talking about him. Reminiscent of my experience in Moscow, purchasing toilet paper in Warsaw had become almost impossible. Toilet paper was our most sought-after commodity. At the moment of delivery to the market, Poles formed long lines and within minutes, cleared out the shelves down to the last roll.

"Where is all the toilet paper?" the press probed.

The public demanded an answer. Some courageous investigative reporters pursued the story and uncovered the source of the problem.

The paper factory was functioning normally, producing thousands upon thousands of rolls, but most of it never arrived at its destination. The investigators followed the delivery trucks and discovered that the toilet paper was diverted to my friend's meat factory. There, it was finely shredded and mixed in with the meat. Toilet paper was heavier and cheaper than meat, and it conveniently absorbed the flavors. Adding a portion of the paper into our delicious, famous Polish sausages yielded fantastic profits. From this operation, Ziulkowski and his co-conspirator, the director of the paper factory, skimmed a fortune off the top and stashed it away in Swiss banks. For almost four years, my friend used to send me gift packages of Polish sausages. Unwittingly, millions of Poles, myself included, and diners across Europe, happily ate their way through Ziulkowski's recipe of sausage mixed with toilet paper.

My friend was arrested for industrial sabotage and found guilty. His sentence was death by hanging. For me the news was devastating. I would never forget how he nursed me out of my suicidal depression with such care at the hospital, and I would always remember him with great affection and gratitude. Soon after the authorities took his life, everybody in Poland was once again able to enjoy their toilet paper and their delicious sausages, separately and in abundance. In Ziulkowski's memory, for the time being I stopped eating Polish sausage.

On our first trip to the U.S., I remembered being shocked to see so many cars on the roads. It seemed as if everybody were driving, and I fell under the spell of the American automobile culture. During my summer vacation from the Philharmonic, I enrolled in driving school. Regina was pleased—for a change—because she presumed we would buy a car. In Poland, in order to be accepted into driving school you had to either own a car or apply for a permit to buy one. There were only three choices—Polish, Czech or Russian—and the Polish cars were typically even worse versions of unreliable Russian models. In fact, when the first Polish-designed automobiles were assembled under Soviet rule after World War II, they had no reverse gear.

The official explanation was, "We don't need reverse. Communism only moves forward!"

I paid a small deposit, knowing the permit and actual delivery of the car would take between six months and a year. In the meantime, I studied the manuals and attended driving courses in order to obtain a license before our flight to the U.S. Even though I hardly ever got behind the wheel, a road test was mandatory. Having nothing but a theoretical understanding of what to do with this powerful machine didn't help me to actually drive it.

I arrived at the appointed time on the day of the test and hoped I wouldn't embarrass myself. After starting the engine with trepidation, I turned onto a Warsaw street, lost control, and drove smack onto the sidewalk, barely missing a tree in my path. A few blocks later, I struggled to hit the brakes and almost ran over a group of senior citizens hobbling across the street. While I was happy not to have killed anyone, there was no doubt in my mind that I failed the test. Always an optimist, I slipped an unusually large bribe into the instructor's palm when I handed him my paperwork.

On August 21, not only did I receive my license in the mail, the instructor, in a gesture of high-octane irony, approved me for a professional chauffeur's license. I was probably the worst driver in the whole of Warsaw, but I could legally drive taxis and operate commercial buses and trucks.

One month later, on Friday, October 2, I said my goodbyes. It broke my heart to leave little Piotr, my sweet son, behind. But I was convinced that, *He will be better off without the battles at home.*

The orchestra boarded a Swiss Air plane for Zurich. From there we flew to the great city of New York. At the age of twenty-six, I left my past in Poland.

Michalina Ruzik (center),
Warsaw, 1929

Leshek at one year old,
Warsaw, 1939

Zdzisław, Michalina and Leshek (in the days before the boys were sent to a village for adoption), 1942

General Konstantin Rokossovsky

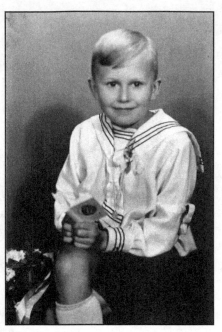

Leshek in his church choirboys' uniform, 1946

Professor Tadeusz Kowalski

Leshek playing cello in the park, 1948

National cello competition, 1958

Music school graduation recital, 1956

Leshek (far right) with the Musicae Antiquae Collegium Varsoviense, 1960

Leshek (front row, second from right) with Warsaw Philharmonic colleagues at the Moulin Rouge in Paris (Wojtek Górecki front row, second from left wearing sunglasses), 1961

Leshek's National Philharmonic ID card, 1959

Leshek's driver's license (the year of his defection), 1964

13

In Search of a Savior

Flying across the Atlantic, my colleagues in the National Philharmonic and I were treated royally and shown superb Swiss efficiency and service. Delicious Italian wines flowed as the airline indulged us in splendid European culinary pleasures. Succulent steaks, warm breadbaskets accompanied by the finest cheeses and, of course, unrivaled chocolates delighted the long-neglected palates of everyone in the orchestra. Compared to Warsaw's cuisine—which consisted mainly of cabbage, potatoes and pork swimming in grease—this was the height of delectable gastronomy. During the first few hours in flight, my colleagues acted like a bunch of parolees tasting their first real meal in years and embellishing stories about the free world that awaited us.

I, on the other hand, sat quietly with closed eyes, pretending to be unwell. I was terrified that if I joined in their high spirits, I would have a drink, or two, and blurt out my intentions to defect. My secret weighed so heavily in the pit of my stomach that I couldn't enjoy any food. The allure of freedom drew me like the tide to the moon, but the risk of discovery inhibited my every move. It was safer to remain detached and wait to be delivered onto American shores, four thousand miles from Warsaw and into an unknown future.

Slipping deep into thought, I reviewed everything that led up to our departure from Warsaw's International Airport. The steps I took to prepare for a new life in the West endowed me with a naïve confidence. Despite the uncertainty that diluted my plan, I was armed with youthful determination to succeed as a musician in America. I was invincible, or so I thought, and presumed my university diploma and bogus chauffeur's license—both of which I packed in my suitcase carefully pressed between some clothes—would be key. When we first came to the U.S. in 1961, I found it remarkable that there were so many good symphony orchestras throughout the country. It never occurred to me that the competition would be stiff for a job in any of them. As a cellist I was very self-assured and had no doubt somebody would hire me. My laughable, almost non-existent English didn't matter. I would communicate through music.

Before leaving Poland we were stripped of all our identity documents. No Polish citizen was ever in possession of his or her passport at home. The government handed them to us at the gate of the international airport and confiscated them as soon as we arrived back in Warsaw. Attached to our passports were visas, so-called H-1, valid only for the duration of our stay overseas. To be approved for the visa, every orchestra member was forced to sign an American Embassy paper stating, *On the day following the final performance of the Warsaw National Philharmonic in the United States, the undersigned will depart with the ensemble and return to Poland.* I paid very little attention to this agreement, and I wasn't the only one. The rate of Poles defecting to the West was an increasing problem for the government, and everyone knew it. At the time people joked,

> *What makes up a Polish string quartet?*
> *An orchestra returning from a tour to the West!*

Throughout our almost full day of air travel, I struggled to keep my nerves under control. Finally, on Friday, October 2, 1964, at three o'clock in the afternoon our plane touched American soil. I was shaking with excitement. *I will live like an American, speak, think, dress like an American.* I made this promise to myself with delusional optimism, presuming our six-week tour would give me enough time to learn all there was to know about the American way of life. After a lengthy customs process the orchestra boarded motor coaches for the five-hour drive from the airport in New York to Washington D.C., where our first concert would be performed. Midway through this endless bus ride jet lag began to set in and, by the time we arrived late in the evening, I was too exhausted and punchy to even think.

The next day—our only free Saturday afternoon—we were escorted on a sightseeing tour of the city and welcomed at a reception in the Polish Embassy, an ornate structure that looked like a nineteenth-century French manor house with a few striking interior touches from the English Renaissance. In 1919 at the close of World War I, the first Polish ambassador to the United States, Prince Kazimierz Lubomirski, bought the mansion and gifted it to the Polish government. The opulent rooms with crystal chandeliers, marble fireplaces, and a wonderful collection of Polish master oil paintings and sculptures, were awe-inspiring to say the least. I couldn't help wondering how these supposedly austere Communist Party bureaucrats could live the high life in such aristo-cratic surroundings. Prince Lubomirski was probably turning over in his grave.

On Sunday we played our first concert. From that moment on, the schedule, organized for us by Sol Hurok Attractions, was insane. In forty days we would perform four different concert programs in twenty-nine U.S. cities covering most of the Northeast, and two Canadian cities, Toronto and Montreal, for good measure. To make matters worse, we would travel exclu-sively by bus. My insides roiled at the thought of weeks and weeks of motion sickness.

In every city I made a conscious effort to meet as many Polish people as possible, and would write their contact information in a little notebook I kept in my breast pocket. At our rehearsal in Hamtramck, Michigan—a small town swallowed by greater Detroit and attached to "Poletown," named for the thou-sands of Poles who emigrated there—I was introduced to Frank Grabowski, the gregarious music director of the Hamtramck Philharmonic. He was a kind fellow with a casual manner and a keen intuition about people. He invited me to his home after our concert, and must have sensed that I was thinking about a life in the U.S because he offered me a job with his symphony. How easy it would have been to say, "I accept!" Nonetheless, I thanked Maestro Grabowski and resisted telling him about my plans, playing off his proposal as flattering, but unrealistic.

On November 10 we arrived in Cleveland, and once again I called my cousins. I reached Ted and got the same cold reception. He said he was very busy and couldn't come to my concert or even meet me at the hotel for a quick cup of coffee. *Why in the world did my cousins refuse to see me? They are treating me as if I have some contagious foreigner's disease.*

I resolved that neither Detroit nor Cleveland was appealing anyway. Regardless of their large Polish populations, I had no desire to live in either.

One of my favorite American jokes was,

What's the difference between Cleveland and the Titanic?

No difference, except that Cleveland has a better orchestra.

As we made our way around the country, my paltry list of acquaintances grew. In Minneapolis I became friendly with Maestro Stanisław Skrowaczewski; in Montreal, Henry Stern, an uncle of my good friend Emil; and in Buffalo, Alicia and Edward Posłuszny, who were the owners of a New York meat-processing factory that made Polish kielbasa. Alicia and Edward had me over for dinner and, as a parting gift, presented me with a huge box of savory sausages. I hoped they didn't use toilet paper in their product—like my dearly departed sausage-producing friend from Warsaw—to enhance its flavors and their profits. On our way to Toronto I distributed the assortment of smoked meats among my colleagues. Everybody loved them, and loved me for sharing. I wanted to be remembered by the orchestra members as a decent, generous guy.

After our concert in Philadelphia, my closest colleague from the Warsaw Music Academy, Tomasz Michalak, who was studying conducting at Philadelphia's prestigious Curtis Institute of Music, joined me for a drink and we talked until the early hours of the morning. Tomasz drank heavily and bragged with a drunkard's ostentation that he had no intention of returning to Poland when his visa expired. In a booming, unsteady voice that could be heard all over the bar, he urged me to defect as well.

Tomasz pounded his fist on the table, "You must apply to Juilliard in New York. It is a perfect place for world-class cellists, and you will thrive in that city!"

After so many weeks of touring the States and holding my tongue, I was dying to be honest with my old friend. But again, I kept quiet.

His final words of wisdom were, "New York is crawling with Immigration officers. If you take my advice, I implore you," at this he lowered his voice, "do not tell a soul."

As if I didn't know.

At the end of almost six grueling weeks, we arrived in New York City, our final destination. Hurok put us up at the auspiciously named Hotel Bristol, on Forty-seventh Street between Sixth and Seventh Avenues, a third rate joint in a very seedy part of Manhattan. The area was overrun with hustlers, dealers, prostitutes, pimps, panhandlers, and sex clubs like The Venus, Harem and the notorious Mine Shaft. That evening and the next we would perform further uptown in Carnegie Hall. These two concerts would be my last with the National Philharmonic, and unlike three years before, this time I would not give in to my fears. Sunday, November 15 would signal the beginning of my new life as a free man. The ideals I was raised with led me to this place, and as I sought courage I reminded myself that Poland and the harrowing memories of oppression belonged to my past.

Although I had made some contacts, as the tour wound down I realized all I really had was a pocket full of crumbs. Even though we were in New York, I didn't care what or how I would play because the essential pieces of my defection plan were still missing, and my anxieties were operating at a fever pitch. I couldn't sleep, couldn't eat and felt terribly unsettled. I hadn't figured out what I would do come Sunday morning, where I would go, who I would call. My search for a lifeboat continued.

During our first rehearsal in Carnegie Hall, I noticed a few people scattered about in the audience. I presumed they were managers from the Hurok office, or perhaps officials from the Polish consulate. In an attempt to focus and relax my nerves, I closed my eyes. When I opened them I noticed a man sitting in the last row of the auditorium. It was quite a distance, but I could see he was wearing the unmistakable collar of a Catholic priest. What was a priest doing there? I guessed that he was Polish, and must love music. As soon as the orchestra broke for intermission, I headed straight to the back of the hall and introduced myself.

The gentle-looking priest, with thinning, sandy-colored hair and a large frame, stood, shook my hand and in perfect Polish said, "My name is Father Henryk d'Anjou. I am pleased to meet you."

I whispered, "Please sit down. I have something very important to say to you and little time to talk."

In a hushed voice I told Father d'Anjou that I wanted to make a confession, and it had to be held sacrosanct between us, according to God's law. He fixed his gaze intently upon me and probably thought I was a little crazy demanding a speedy confession in such an unconventional setting.

"This is a matter of life and death. Please do not refuse me." He realized I was serious.

The priest made a discreet sign of the cross, and in the name of Jesus Christ asked me to confess my sins.

"Father," I said, "at this moment I have only one sin and it is not against God. It is against my country. After tomorrow's concert I will not return to Poland. Nothing will change my mind, but I am very frightened. If the Polish authorities find out about my intentions, they could kill me. You are the only person I am entrusting my secret to. I did not even tell my parents before I left Warsaw."

D'Anjou sat unwavering in his seat and listened without judgment.

"When the orchestra goes home I do not have a place to stay, and don't know what to do or how to proceed with my defection. I desperately need your help. As a priest I imagine you work in a New York parish. Please, can you arrange with some of your parishioners to give me shelter for a few days? I have a Warsaw University diploma, I am a very good cellist, I promise you, I won't be a burden to anybody and I will repay your kindness." I continued breathlessly, "My father is Catholic and, although my mother is Jewish, I was raised in the church and my mentor and closest friend is a Silesian priest. Can you help me?"

After I finished my plea the priest leaned in and with a very soft and loving voice said, "My son, do not be afraid. You are in God's hands. We are all children of Abraham. Be proud of your Jewish heritage. Jesus was Jewish. That makes us all Jewish, does it not?"

I was stunned. All my life I hid my Jewish heritage in anti-Semitic Poland, and because I was blond and had blue eyes, nobody bothered me. But in America even Catholic priests call themselves Jewish!

Having just met Father d'Anjou, I didn't know about his commitment to humanitarian values and his standing as a well-respected and outspoken critic of Marxism and anti-Semitism, which turned out to be a reflection of his own horrific experiences during and after World War II. In German-occupied Warsaw in 1943, he was studying at the underground Warsaw University and pursuing a degree in medicine when he was captured and sent to Majdanek in Central Poland, one of the most notorious death camps. Days later he was among six thousand men taken from the camp to labor on the construction of a highway connecting Berlin to Moscow. D'Anjou had been subjected to three months of captivity, his hands raw and bloody from excruciating work, when one day a sympathetic guard gave him permission to rinse them under cold water at a nearby pump. Gambling with his life, he took advantage of the chaos that erupted with the arrival of a soup train, dashed undetected through the forest to the next railroad station, and jumped onto an approaching train.

When the war ended, d'Anjou agonized over all the prisoners he left behind who faced certain death, and decided to abandon his medical studies and join the priesthood to provide aid and comfort to those in need. He received doctoral degrees in Jewish history and theology and was ordained in 1948, at the same time that the Polish KGB began a systematic infiltration of the church hierarchy. Even after he came to the United States, d'Anjou received letters and phone calls threatening his life if he continued to sermonize against Communism, anti-Semitism and racism. The warnings did nothing to deter his defense of the Jewish community. This modest priest, who had wandered into our rehearsal, committed his life to a kind of altruism I had never known.

An impish smile crossed his face and he said to me, "Play your absolute best this evening because I will be in the audience. I promise to make immediate arrangements for your shelter. Do not worry. Tomorrow, before your final Carnegie Hall rehearsal, I will bring detailed information."

Out of thin air I found a safe harbor and a place to throw my anchor overboard.

That night I played with all my heart for the priest. On my walk to the hotel after the concert, everything around me looked gilded and beautiful. Even the pimps and the whores around Times Square took on a special glow. *In a couple of days I will be liberated, with no need to hide my past.*

I awoke on Saturday in eager anticipation of what lay ahead and arrived very early for our rehearsal. Aside from a crew of stagehands who were still setting up chairs and stands, the hall was empty. I waited for Father d'Anjou in the very same seat as the day before. The rehearsal was scheduled to begin at ten o'clock. At nine-fifty I was still sitting there patiently, but d'Anjou hadn't appeared, so I got up reluctantly, went to the dressing room, retrieved my cello and took my chair on the stage. Without even tuning I started to rehearse the first work on the program, written by Witold Lutosławski, a prominent contemporary Polish composer, and eerily titled *Funeral Music*. The sounds that emerged from the orchestra penetrated my very being, and the hope and euphoria from the previous day evaporated. Had d'Anjou betrayed me? I was crushed and suddenly felt orphaned for the second time.

We moved on to Chopin's Piano Concerto. Its nostalgic beauty was painful to hear. The notes cascaded across the pages and I felt as if in suspended animation. I smelled Polish soil, recalled the medieval castles of my homeland, the storied mountains and ancient forests, and saw flocks of storks flying away for the winter, their reflections on the surface of the Vistula River. I thought about how the decision to leave Poland tortured our country's most cherished composer. With tears in my eyes and despair in my heart, I searched longingly for my trusted priest. Seconds later Father d'Anjou appeared accompanied by another priest, and I was no longer overcome by the melancholy of Chopin. Instead, I wanted to sing the finale from Handel's *Messiah* out loud. *Hallelujah! Hallelujah!! Hallelujah!!!*

The moment we broke for intermission, feigning nonchalance, but with great inner excitement, I made my way toward the priests sitting at the back of the hall. D'Anjou introduced me to Doctor Arthur Slomka—a Silesian priest from New Jersey who, coincidentally, knew my old mentor from Poland, Father Kochanski—and then very discretely put an envelope in my hand with instructions for the following day.

"You will be picked up by an elderly Polish couple, Josef and Maria Mikrut, members of a friend's parish, who will drive you to Brooklyn where they will give you a small room in their apartment to stay for a few days," d'Anjou whispered. "You can call them from Woolworth's at the corner of Forty-seventh Street and Seventh Avenue. Mr. Mikrut promised to be there within an hour of your call."

After I told the priests that the orchestra was scheduled to depart for the airport at five o'clock sharp, they suggested, "Late in the afternoon your colleagues will probably be busy with last minute packing for the trip home. You should leave the hotel at about three-thirty, so you can slip out undetected. Spend the time before with your orchestra friends, casually exploring your new city."

When d'Anjou and Slomka got to the bottom of the detailed list they compiled for me, which included telephone numbers for them and the Mikruts, it was time to part ways. During the few minutes I spent with these two special men, an unfamiliar feeling of relief washed over me. It was as if I had come out the other side of a nearly impassable maze. Expressing my profuse thanks, I wanted to hug them both, but held back. Our time together may have already raised suspicions.

Strolling happily to the stage through the foyer on one side of the hall, gazing at photograph after photograph of world-famous performers, an older gentleman stopped me. He looked very patrician in a fashionable suit, had perfectly combed gray hair and a distinctive, wide face, and introduced himself in Polish as Marek Mayevski. I tried to appear relaxed and told him my name. With a fatherly smile, peering straight into my eyes he handed me his calling card and asked that I phone him. I agreed, but was unsure of what this man's motives were and fearful that he sensed my intention to defect.

Mayevski put his hand on my shoulder and said, "I look forward to seeing you again . . . at the performance tonight, of course. Call me. Goodbye."

On my way to the hotel after the rehearsal, a bombshell hit me and I stopped dead in my tracks. *How will I take my cello with me after the concert? If I can't keep my cello, I might as well get on the plane and go back to Poland. What the hell am I going to do?* The cello was my essential tool for survival, like a dancer's legs or a singer's vocal chords. I broke into a cold sweat.

So many unresolved questions had been churning in my consciousness for months, some of them major, and others, trivial. This was one of the most important of all, and it never popped into my head.

The majority of the orchestra musicians carry their own instruments, but because the cellos and double basses are so large, the Philharmonic technical staff always brings them from hall to hall in shipping cases. And when each tour ends, all of our instruments are immediately loaded onto trucks by the stagehands and driven straight to the airport for final shipment back to Warsaw. If I were to take my own cello to the hotel after the concert, everybody would know I decided to remain in the U.S.

I struggled with this unthinkable predicament until I came up with what I hoped would be a foolproof plan: I would go back to Carnegie Hall immediately, pick up my performance clothing, and bring it to the hotel. On most nights I dressed for the concert in the orchestra dressing room with everybody else. Not tonight. I would put on my tails at the Bristol, cover up in my long overcoat, and walk to the hall. After the performance, when my colleagues went straight to the dressing rooms to change out of their formal wear, I would bolt to the stage door with my cello under my arm, and as fast as I could, get to the hotel before anybody else.

We began our concert with the Lutosławski *Funeral Music*, which served to bury my past. The Chopin that followed symbolized my heritage and identity. After intermission we played Brahms Symphony No. 4. His monumental music filled me with strength and hope for a better future. Performing it I was once again transported to the land of my birth. I imagined my proud father in his Polish officers uniform and my strong mother clad simply and wearing her indispensible leather pumps. I was overcome by memories of their incredible suffering, their fortitude and their perseverance. Through the music I saw brave General Pulaski on his white horse charging to victory and death against the Redcoats in the Battle of Savannah; I saw General Kosciuszko—who had willed his property in America to purchase the freedom of slaves—fight until his dying days to secure political justice and dignity for the downtrodden; and I saw Ignacy Paderewski proudly playing Chopin for President Wilson in the White House.

The concert ended to tumultuous applause. I was psychologically and physically drained, with perspiration pouring down my face, but still tried to find Father d'Anjou in the audience. All I saw was a blur. The orchestra members rose for their final bows and rushed off stage to the dressing rooms. Having rehearsed it over and over in my head, I made a hasty dash for the exit, tightly gripping my uncovered cello. I didn't look at anybody and kept my gaze fixed on the stage door. From Fifty-sixth to Forty-seventh Streets I ran down Seventh Avenue like a madman, oblivious to what was going on around me.

The working girls tried to block my way, yelling, "Stop maestro, play for us!"

It was after ten o'clock at night in the middle of November, and the New York air was frigid. I left my coat behind in the dressing room and the sweaty shirt was practically stuck frozen to my body.

I made it to the hotel undeterred and ran to the elevator, shadowed by the puzzled looks of the doorman and receptionist. Their expressions seemed to say, *'Another crazy musician!'* Safe in my room, I slid the cello under the bed and quickly took off my tails and wet clothes and jumped into a hot shower. I felt thoroughly cleansed, washing off the perspiration, the tension and the past.

But my night was horrendous. I couldn't sleep for a moment. The incessant traffic, frenzied human sounds, millions of lights outside the window, all appeared to me like the nightmarish stories from the fairy tales Mother read to me as a child. Those memories and the time I was sent for adoption were so present in that tiny hotel room. In the disorder of my thoughts I envisioned the twisted branches of willow trees, bare of foliage, reaching for me like witches in a wicked dance. Through their long, tyrannical fingers I saw thousands of eyes with brilliant colors, all from different creatures. My ears exploded amidst the frightening noises. And then suddenly, the lights went out. They disappeared. And it was quiet. It was seven o'clock in the morning on a Sunday. Even Times Square needed a rest.

Despite the early morning chill it seemed like the weather would be nice. After shaving, showering again and donning my custom-tailored, elegant suit—on my last tour to London I bought some good quality English wool and had a tailor in Warsaw make me the best outfit I'd ever owned—at eight o'clock I was ready to call the Mikruts. But it was too early and I resisted the temptation. Father d'Anjou specifically told me to call them at three-thirty, and anyway, they were most likely good Catholics attending Sunday Mass. Since my friends at the hotel were still asleep after a late night, I ventured out on my own to learn a little more about the city that would become my home.

Woolworth's counter had just opened, so I went inside and ordered a cup of coffee. When it was served I dumped five spoons of sugar into the cup and filled it with cream. After every few sips I added more cream and sugar to the weak American brew, and the waitress kept refilling my cup, no charge. With such dark rings under my eyes, she probably thought I was hung over. By the time I got back to the hotel, I had downed at least ten spoons of sugar and a pitcher of cream. With a burst of energy I forgot about my sleepless night and rang the room of my best friend, Wojtek.

When he opened the door, Wojtek looked at me and asked, cocking his square, Frankenstein head and looking befuddled, "Why are you dressed up?"

"This is Sunday," I said. "Everybody—at least in Poland—dresses better on Sunday. And besides, we just finished a slave labor tour with great success, and I want to show the American people that not all Poles are peasants!"

Wojtek thought my explanation made sense and enthusiastically changed into his best attire as well. He even put on a tie.

We walked down Fifth Avenue to St. Patrick's Cathedral and Rockefeller

Center's skating rink, and from there, all the way to the Empire State Building. My first visit to this world-famous landmark was in 1961 and, after paying the entry fee, they gave me a miniature, painted tin replica of the building to attach to my clothing. Written on it were the words, "*I'VE BEEN TO THE TOP.*" For the three years since, I carried this tiny souvenir in my wallet, like an amulet, for good luck. I showed it to Wojtek, but when I saw the bewildered expression on his face, I changed the subject.

At two o'clock we were back at the hotel, and I asked Wojtek to stop in my room for a moment. After closing the door, I reached into my pocket and took out all the paper dollar bills that I saved from our per diems and handed him the stack. I knew this amount of money would be sufficient for Regina and Piotr to live on for at least two months. I trusted my friend implicitly and asked him to bring the money to Poland and give it to my wife.

"I am staying in America," I announced, surprised to hear these words spill out of my mouth after all the months of discretion.

Wojtek was speechless. The poor man turned ashen, obviously shaken. He embraced me in a bear hug for a long time, and neither of us spoke. Wojtek didn't try to persuade me to reconsider; he just turned and left the room with my money and my big secret.

At three-thirty I pulled my cello from under the bed, covered it with a hotel bath towel, put it under my left arm, and with my suitcase in my right hand, walked out into the street. D'Anjou and Slomka were right—I didn't run into anybody from the orchestra. When I got to Woolworth's again, I quickly ducked inside to call the Mikruts. Digging for change, I realized how foolish it had been to give all my savings to Wojtek. Only seventy-five cents was left. I lifted the receiver off the pay phone, but it was out of order. I found another phone booth down the street and tried again. This time I lost my dime. On the second try I dialed very carefully, 212-SO8-2777. The phone rang and a man answered.

With butterflies fluttering in my stomach I said in Polish, "Hello, Mr. Mikrut? This is Leszek."

I described where I was waiting and the stranger asked me to please be patient. "I am not the best driver, and we are coming all the way from Brooklyn. Don't worry, my wife and I will find you," he assured me.

I leaned against the telephone booth, awkwardly trying to balance my bare cello and my suitcase, and waited for the Mikruts. At five o'clock the buses carrying the Warsaw Philharmonic Orchestra members to the airport stopped at the red light across the street. Some of my colleagues waved when they saw me, stunned. Others turned away and refused to look, as if they were afraid of being implicated. When the traffic light changed and the buses disappeared from my sight, I knew I was really alone in the middle of that crazy, wonderful city.

My watch read six o'clock and I was still waiting. By seven my body was numb from the cold, and I felt helpless. But I continued to wait. On the corner of Seventh Avenue, across the street from Woolworth's, was a sprawling topless sex club that drew a lot of perverted activity to its storefront. The prostitutes kept beckoning me to go with them. Some were pleasant enough, even sweet, but others were obnoxious. I tried not to pay attention to their taunts. I just wanted to be rescued.

At around seven-thirty a beaten-up, rusty American guzzler clawed its way to the curb in front of me. I was surprised to see Mrs. Mikrut behind the wheel. Josef opened the passenger side door and ushered me into the back of their car with great haste, his eyes darting up and down the block. They both apologized for the long delay, explaining that they had never been to Manhattan and got lost.

"How long have you lived in Brooklyn?" I asked.

"Twenty years," they replied.

I was astonished. For the Mikruts, crossing the East River was terrifying. In their minds Manhattan was nothing but an island of sin, inhabited by god-less street cretins who were best avoided. And delivering me into the backseat of their old sedan from the pit of the Times Square sex trade, their fears were most likely justified.

I could tell by Mrs. Mikrut's death grip on the steering wheel and Josef's furrowed brow, these people were genuinely worried about their safety and sacrificed a lot to help me. As we drove across the city, I began to feel very light-headed and small in the dark, cavernous back seat, as if I were floating off into space and heading toward the moon. The bravado that had always been my strong suit was stripped from me, and I had no choice but to submit to whatever my new world had in store. On Sunday, November 15, 1964, I waded into the unknown.

14

The Mikruts

I was freezing cold and more than a little scared waiting on that street corner for my rescuers. As soon as I climbed into their humongous car, my stiff legs melted into the vinyl seats and my shaking body and chattering teeth quieted. I tried to introduce myself properly, but Mrs. Mikrut shushed me.

"Leszek, don't talk. You are like an icicle. Josef, turn up the heat so the poor boy doesn't catch pneumonia. Too bad we didn't bring any vodka," she said.

"*Pan i Pani* Mikrut," I began to thank them, but again she stopped me.

"In America people call each other by their first names. I am Maria and my husband is Josef. Most people wouldn't be able to pronounce *Zawistowski* anyway," she laughed. "So you will be Leszek. Brooklyn, where we live, is like a big pot of *bigos*," referring to our native hunting stew full of every sort of ingredient. "There are people from all over the world with very strange last names. Just like yours."

Josef stared curiously at my cello. He pointed to it and said, "I've never seen such a big violin. Or is it some kind of guitar?"

"It is like a large violin," I explained, "but it's called a *cello*, and to play you sit down and hold it between your legs."

The Mikruts were amused, and intrigued, by the strange oversized possession that accompanied me all the way from Poland.

"I will play for you when we arrive," I promised.

The trip down Broadway took such a long time. Maria drove slowly and navigated their big car with great caution through hostile traffic. As soon as we pulled onto the bridge over the East River and left the borough of Manhattan, the tension in her posture eased. She settled into casual banter and told me about her background. Born to Polish immigrants in the United States at the turn of the century, life was extremely harsh for her rural parents who sought work in one or another American city, barely scraping together a living when the Depression struck. Maria's mother and father longed for the Polish countryside and their childhood village, and the family found its way back to Poland. When she was forty Maria met Josef, and they married. Taking advantage of her American citizenship, they moved back to the States, escaping the German occupation. They settled in Brooklyn, and for over twenty years lived in an ethnically diverse neighborhood with a large Polish population. *Pierogi* were available at practically every corner deli.

When we arrived at No. 60 on Sixteenth Street, I stepped onto the curb and saw that their block looked like a long corridor of identical houses. Each one was built of brown stone with a few steps leading to the front door. They all butted up against each other, like rows of encyclopedias neatly ordered on a shelf, contrary to Polish city houses, which always had spaces in between— narrow alleys that could be useful as escape routes, if necessary. The area also looked very different from Manhattan, no big skyscrapers or crazy traffic. I mounted the steps to the Mikrut's building and turned around to look at Josef's immense 1950s Ford. It was as long as the entire width of No. 60.

Josef and Maria were both short and squat with strong, broad shoulders. Their faces bore the imprints of hard work and premature aging. Josef took my suitcase, and I carried my cello up the stairs to the third floor. The Mikrut's apartment was so characteristically Polish, I almost felt as if I were stepping back into Warsaw. The table was covered with an intricately hand-embroidered linen cloth—the kind Mother made—and hanging on the faded beige walls were images of Jesus Christ, the Polish black Madonna from Częstochowa, colorful paper cutouts and other popular folk art.

The moment we entered, Maria headed straight to the kitchen and came back quickly with a plate of bread and salt to welcome me in traditional Polish style. Josef poured vodka into three small glasses and we drank it bottoms-up, toasting to one hundred years of good health. The bread was very tasty; nothing like the spongy and tasteless white American loaves I had been eating for the last six weeks. With it, Maria served delicious marinated herring, pickled wild mushrooms, a variety of sausages and ham.

I had been so consumed by the drama of the day that, since the over-sugared and creamed coffee in the morning, I hadn't thought about food, let alone eaten any, and was overcome by intense pangs of hunger. I devoured the Polish delicacies like a starved puppy. In between mouthfuls of food and glasses of vodka, I told the Mikruts about myself, my parents, and why I defected.

Josef asked, "What is your profession?"

"I play the cello," I answered.

"No, I mean what do you do to make a living?"

I tried to explain that good classical musicians are well paid, not only in Poland, but in the States as well.

"Every major American city has a symphony orchestra that engages instrumentalists like me to perform throughout the year with guaranteed employment. As soon as I get my first job, I'm going to repay you ten times over for your generosity," I said with supreme confidence. "Don't worry, I promise I will be earning an excellent salary soon."

Maria and Josef looked very skeptical.

The three of us drank more vodka. "*Sto lat!*" echoed repeatedly as the time passed. Midway through the evening I took out my cello and started to play. Since Christmas was just around the corner, the piece I chose was Poland's most cherished Christmas carol, *Lulai że Jezuniu* (*Go to sleep my little Jesus*). Maria and Josef were mesmerized. They asked me to play it again and again and we all sang together. We were drunk not only with spirits, but with nostalgia for our homeland. Chopin incorporated this beautiful carol into one of his famous *Ballades* for piano and it rang in my ears as Maria finally showed me to my room late into the night. I didn't realize how exhausted I was, and sleep came immediately.

I woke up the next day with a terrible hangover and was disoriented until I splashed cold water on my face. In the morning light I could see that the apartment had a long, narrow hallway running through it, like an intestinal canal, and off of it sprang a few slender rooms. My mother would have called it a *kishka*, a sausage. The place was simple, relatively poor and impeccably clean.

Maria was waiting for me with a hot breakfast, but Josef had already gone to the paper factory where he was a manual laborer. Maria told me she cleaned houses for several middle class families who lived in the area around Prospect Park and would have to go to work soon.

Before leaving she gave me a set of spare keys for the apartment and the front door of the building, and then she put ten single dollars into my hand, cautioning, "Only pay with small bills because merchants always try to take advantage of newcomers."

On this second morning as an immigrant on American soil, I confronted the reality that, other than the Mikrut's warm bed and tasty food, I had no idea how to proceed. I began by calling Father d'Anjou, who was happy to hear my voice and asked how my hosts and I were doing. He was amused that it took the Mikruts four hours to find me in Times Square, but not surprised.

"Many immigrants in New York live for years in their own communities," explaining that they work very hard and are usually too preoccupied by their struggle for survival to stray from the boundaries of their safe ethnic havens.

"Now, let's talk about your immediate future, my son. You cannot just decide to live in America. You need to have immigration papers and should request political asylum as soon as possible. Write this down. Contact an attorney named Lydia Savoyka from the National Catholic Conference in the Department of Immigration. She's the best in New York and I already spoke to her about you. Her telephone number is BO9-2494 and address, 20 West Broadway, fourteenth floor, Department of Social Services. Please call me with any news. Good luck, and God bless you, my son."

I thanked him profusely and was encouraged to know that I would have an official advocate working on my behalf.

I phoned Miss Savoyka and the first thing she asked was, "What type of visa do you have?"

When I told her it was an H-1, there was an ominous silence before she spoke again.

"*Panie Leszku*, you are in trouble. The American authorities will try to deport you back to Poland. Tomorrow morning, please come to my office so we can begin the process of applying for political asylum."

This was not what I expected to hear. I never thought about the possibility of legal obstacles blocking my path. My presumption was, anybody escaping a Soviet-controlled Communist country would be welcomed with open arms in the United States. This development left me shaken and confused. My mind wandered back three years to the Polish pianist, Stasio Arzewski, whom I met when we toured the U.S. in 1961. I remembered that he played in the Plaza Hotel's Palm Court and that his daughter, Cecylia, was a violin student at Juilliard. At the time it had occurred to me that the connection might prove to be valuable one day, so I wrote his number on a piece of paper and kept it in my pocket notebook all this time. I called Stasio for advice and he was very surprised to hear from me.

"Where are you? You didn't go back to Poland?" he asked.

I told him I defected and was living with a Polish couple in Brooklyn.

"*Oy vey!* You brave boy. *Odważny boychik!*" Stasio shouted on the phone. "This is fantastic! *Oy.* I cannot wait to tell Cecylia. *Mazel tov, mazel tov,*" he continued mixing Yiddish with Polish. "Tell me, when can I see you?"

I told Stasio that first I needed to see my immigration lawyer to apply for political asylum.

"They could deport me back to Poland."

He chuckled on the other end of the line and called me, like my mother very often did, *meshuggah.*

"What are you talking about? With your talent and qualifications, America is going to grab you up. Anyway, if your Catholic lawyer gives you a hard time, I will take you to a Jewish organization specializing in immigration. For sure they will fix your papers. This is so exciting. *Mazel tov!*"

My last call of the morning was to Marek Mayevski, the well-mannered Polish gentleman who approached me in the wings of Carnegie Hall.

"I did not return to Poland with the orchestra," I told him.

Unlike Stasio, his response was unemotional. He matter-of-factly explained that when he saw me speaking to the priest, he had no doubt I was planning to defect.

"That is why I gave you my card."

After listening to my account of the last twenty-four hours, Mayevski suggested I get on a subway that very afternoon so we could meet in his apartment. The thought made me uneasy, but he assured me that moving around New York City by subway was fast and not complicated.

"Very close to the apartment where you are staying is the R train. Take it to Fifty-seventh Street and Central Park South in Manhattan. From the subway station exit, walk along the big park to Columbus Circle and continue to Sixty-seventh Street. My address is 2 West Sixty-seventh Street, the first building on the corner and across from the restaurant *Café des Artistes*. The doorman will direct you to the fourteenth floor and I live in 14G, like Gregory. Simple."

I was slightly familiar with that area of the city having performed in Carnegie Hall, so I accepted his invitation and left a note for the Mikruts. *I am taking a subway to Manhattan,* I wrote.

The ride took much longer than I anticipated, but it was a fascinating experience. At every stop I saw a kaleidoscope of colors, cultures, styles, personalities, flowing in and out, not like in Warsaw where almost everyone was Polish and looked more or less alike. I felt like a passenger from Jules Verne's novel, *Around the World in 80 Days.* In fact, New York City had just played host to the 1964 World's Fair and I wondered if all the foreigners decided to stay and ride the subway. Sitting in the midst of this extraordinary cross-section of humanity gave me hope that my decision to choose the United States as my new home was the right one.

With the help of a tourist street map, I found Mayevski's imposing apartment building with its huge windows spanning three floors. I couldn't imagine being surrounded by such enormous glass walls that overlooked one of the most beautiful landscaped wonders of the world, Central Park, and calling it "home." Mayevski, who was very aristocratic and stylish, opened the door to their apartment and the first thing I saw at the far end of the foyer was a carved stone fireplace mantel so tall, I could have stepped inside it. There were paintings by Picasso, Chagall, Miró, Scurat, Dubuffet and Appel taking up every inch of wall space, such that a few others had to stand along the floor. The place was exploding with art.

Mayevski introduced his wife Julia, an unpretentious and soft-spoken woman, and invited me to join him for some fine French cognac, which he sipped from a glass the same shape as his wide face. He came from a wealthy noble family from the Krakow region of Southern Poland—my grandparents were probably paupers compared to his—and he fell in love with art early on. When the Nazis invaded Poland, the Mayevskis fled to Paris and eventually emigrated to New York. Mayevski had met so many of the great artists of the era personally—like Picasso and Chagall—that several prominent art galleries, auction houses and museums took advantage of his expertise and connections, and hired him as an art consultant.

I told Mayevski about my looming appointment with the immigration lawyer the following day, and he insisted on going with me.

"I can help you find the address in that tricky part of lower Manhattan," he said, "and also be there to give you some moral support," claiming Immigration officers were nasty and my case could be more difficult than I expected. "Keep a very low profile and don't trust anybody. No interviews to the press or the radio."

I placed a lot of faith in my new friend and appreciated his wisdom and advice. As afternoon turned into evening, Julia asked me to stay for dinner. I phoned the Mikruts so they wouldn't worry, but nobody answered. I settled into Julia's meal of red beet soup and very long Viennese hot dogs with over-cooked asparagus and tasteless potatoes. I wouldn't forget this menu because Julia served it every time I ate with them.

At seven-thirty I boarded the R train back to Brooklyn and didn't arrive at Maria and Josef's place until almost nine o'clock. I opened the door and saw the two of them hunched over in their chairs at opposite ends of the kitchen table, praying. On the table was a little statue of Jesus and a burning candle. The poor couple was convinced something terrible had happened to me and paid the priest to perform a mass for my soul and my safe return. But a miracle happened—I came back!

The three of us embraced each other and cried like babies. At first I didn't know whether I was crying out of guilt for having scared them, or out of fear for my future. I was deeply thankful for the people who showered me with such care in my new country, but there was a dreadful emptiness in the pit of my stomach. The offerings of meals and comfort hadn't answered the questions about what lay ahead.

15

Lifeboat

aria was up at first light the next morning. She sat at the kitchen table in her bathrobe with her hands clenched around a cup of coffee as tightly as the curlers in her hair. She looked as if she hadn't slept a wink. Like most immigrants, she had a deep-seeded, and well-founded fear of the authorities. She asked that I go to church with her to pray before my meeting at Immigration.

The National Catholic Church of the Resurrection on Leonard Street was walking distance from No. 60. It had a modest white façade, much like the little church in the village from many years ago. As we approached, I felt very vulnerable. But, the interior was warm and inviting, the altar bright with candles and framed by porcelain angels, and I was happy to be there. During the service my thoughts were in Poland with little Piotr and my parents. I asked God to protect them, and me, and not abandon us in the days ahead. No matter that I didn't believe in a higher power, this hour of spirituality and reflection gave me renewed strength, and I left the church, with Maria's arm tucked in mine, feeling calmer.

Mayevski and I met at the Fifty-seventh Street subway station, changed trains and headed downtown toward city hall. Navigating Battery Park was much more confusing than midtown Manhattan and I was glad he had come along. As soon as we entered the Immigration building, I was stricken by a terrible case of the jitters.

Sensing my unsteadiness, Mayevski put his hand on my shoulder and said in a hushed voice, "Do not be afraid, *Panie Leszku*. We all had to go through this."

The cramped reception area was swarming with foreigners. Mayevski asked for Lydia Savoyka because I was too nervous to speak. She emerged from her office full of life, a young woman barely older than I, and introduced herself. At thirty-two years old to my twenty-six, Savoyka was extremely attractive, with lovely light brown hair, penetrating eyes and very high cheekbones, typical of Slavic people from the southeastern region of the Ukraine. She was nothing like the menacing image of an immigration attorney I anticipated. She moved with the energy of a news reporter chasing a story, and abruptly asked to see my passport and visa. When she saw that the visa was indeed an H-1, she grimaced.

"Very bad, very bad," she repeated in her rapid-fire manner of speaking while flipping through the document. "*Panie Leszku*, I don't know if I will be able to spare you from deportation. This is a temporary working visa, the worst! Before leaving Poland you signed an agreement at the American Embassy in Warsaw that you would not attempt to stay in New York after your visa expires, did you not?" Without waiting for my answer she said, "This is terrible," shaking her head pessimistically. "In any case, I will do everything I can to save you. We will apply for political asylum."

I thought the floor would drop from under me.

"Now, tell me all about yourself," Savoyka asked.

She was particularly interested in the story of my father's persecution by the Russians and his fervent anti-Communist posture, and hoped his wartime record might be compelling enough to grant me asylum. With no small measure of bitterness, she told us that her father, a very prominent Ukrainian attorney who lived in Krakow, was not so lucky. After the war the Soviets arrested and killed him.

During our conversation the phone rang constantly, and almost every time she grabbed the receiver a different language came tumbling out of her mouth. Mayevski could not contain his curiosity.

"How many languages do you speak?" he asked.

Laughing, she responded, "I speak eleven, but I would like to learn a few more."

After two hours of intensive questioning and endless paperwork, Savoyka made two pronouncements.

The first, "Keep silent and don't breathe a word about your defection to anybody. The press might pick up the story and it would make news. It is imperative we postpone this inevitability for as long as possible."

And second, because I was young and educated, it occurred to her that I could attend an American graduate school and be granted a temporary student visa. I told her about my friend Stasio, whose daughter was studying at Juilliard, and suggested that I could ask him to arrange an audition for me. At this, Savoyka's mood changed drastically, her cheekbones rising with delight.

"Leszek, I will fight for your asylum, but at the same time you have to go to Juilliard tomorrow and apply for admission. Let there be no delay. The timing is critical because their second semester begins in January, which gives us only six weeks to work."

She gave me her home telephone number and urged me to call anytime if something unforeseen happens. The complex legalities she laid out were overwhelming. I tried to thank her with the utmost sincerity, but couldn't hide my fear.

I called Stasio Arzewski from a public phone booth and asked him, with urgency, to arrange a meeting at Juilliard for me. He enthusiastically agreed to make an appointment for the next day.

In the early hours of Wednesday, November 18, I left the Mikrut's Brooklyn apartment for Manhattan once again, carefully following Stasio's instructions to take the No. 9 train from the Columbus Circle station to 116th Street by Columbia University. From there I walked up Broadway to 122nd Street and found Juilliard on Claremont Avenue, just around the corner. When I exited the station the street was teeming with students. Many of them had long hair and were dressed like gypsies. In Warsaw we only saw such fashions in newspaper reports about the hippies in the Capitalist West. No one in Poland dressed that way. Neither the authorities nor the public at large would have tolerated it.

I spotted Stasio, who was extremely short and thin, only when the hippie crowd parted. We proceeded straight to the office of Dean Gideon Waldrop. I showed him my diploma from the Warsaw Music Academy, told him about the master classes with Rostropovich and my most notable experiences as a professional cellist.

Mr. Waldrop looked puzzled and asked, "With your qualifications, why do you want to go back to school?"

My illegal immigrant status was lurking in the back of my mind and I replied, "I think Juilliard will be the ideal place to improve my playing."

Since I already had a Master's degree, Waldrop suggested I apply for post-graduate study and scheduled an audition for me on November 30. I could not believe how swiftly he moved in my favor. I was beginning to think New Yorkers moved at a different pace from the rest of the world.

On our way out Waldrop asked, "Do you know Halina Rodzinski? She is a personal friend of mine. I'm sure you know of her late husband, Artur Rodzinski, the famous Polish conductor and music director of the New York Philharmonic. You must get in touch with her," he insisted.

"I heard the name, but haven't had a chance to meet her yet. I just arrived in New York a few days ago," I answered.

Scribbling her number on a piece of paper, Waldrop said, "Good luck with your audition. I hope to welcome you as the only Polish student at our school."

When we left Juilliard, Stasio invited me to his apartment for a typical Polish lunch of *pierogi* stuffed with farmer cheese and a salad of shredded carrots and apples. Cecylia asked me to please bring my cello the next time I visited, so we could play some duets together, or maybe a trio with Michael. Her question served as an important reminder that I could not take my cello anywhere, let alone all the way uptown. I didn't have a carrying case for it and couldn't lug a bare cello on a New York subway to my audition at Juilliard. Stasio suggested we go to the Rembert Wurlitzer Company, the largest musical instrument dealer and repair shop in New York. He was sure they would lend me something.

Returning to Brooklyn, and alone in the Mikrut's apartment, the first thing I did was pick up my cello. I hadn't had a moment to practice for three days and was in no shape to take an audition at Juilliard in less than two weeks. I practiced scales and technical exercises, and it felt good getting my fingers back in the groove. By the time Maria came home it was already nightfall, and she found me sweating in the unlit apartment, bent over my instrument and deep into the music. I was oblivious to the darkness in the room.

"*Synku!*"—she called me 'son'—"Are you all right? Why are the lights off?" She hurried to the light switch. "You look ill!"

That night I called Savoyka and Father d'Anjou to tell them the good news about my audition.

The priest said, "I will call my friend Halina Rodzinski right away. She could be helpful."

How coincidental, I thought. The dean of the Juilliard School of Music and a Polish priest, who had most likely never met each other, both gave me the same advice to call the same person on the same day.

When my conversation with d'Anjou ended, I saw that Maria and Josef had been watching me and were smiling from ear to ear. They made no attempt to hide their pride that this esteemed priest had become my friend.

As soon as the Mikruts left for work in the morning, I launched into hours of intense practice, with a time-out only to write to my parents and the administration of the Warsaw Philharmonic. Knowing the Polish censors would open the letters, I claimed, prematurely, *I am staying behind in New York because the Juilliard School of Music has accepted me for post-graduate study. It is an opportunity I cannot pass up.* Of course, Mother, with her profound superstitions, would probably have thought I jinxed my chances by lying, but I was extremely concerned about my family, and feared the authorities would make an example of me by punishing them. In my letter to Regina, I promised that every month she would receive U.S. dollars equal to at least what I was paid by the Philharmonic. *You will have more than enough money to take good care of Piotr and to live very comfortably.* That was not a lie. *Please tell Piotr I love him,* I wrote.

As the days wore on I became more and more conflicted about political asylum. I knew it wouldn't go over well in Warsaw and might result in more extreme retaliation against my family. I wished we had just stuck to applying for a student visa, but it was already too late. According to Father d'Anjou, news of my defection was already broadcast on *Voice of America* and there was no turning back.

※

I was happy to see the Mikruts off to work every day, cherishing my solitude in their apartment, undisturbed in that tiny space. The Juilliard audition loomed as my biggest immediate challenge, and I tried to clear my head and think about nothing but practicing. I did, however, have to face not having a cello case.

When Stasio and I appeared at Wurlitzer's shop one afternoon, on display, like exotic birds, was an array of superb Italian violins, violas and cellos. I felt like a kid in a candy shop, salivating at the rows of endless treats. Most Polish musicians played on essentially cheap instruments, the ones the Germans and Russians thought weren't worth looting. In the music world these crude relics were known as "cigar boxes."

Mr. Wurlitzer's gracious daughter Marianne was there to greet us.

"Would you like to try one of these cellos?"

She handed me a magnificent Stradivarius and encouraged me to play. With my heart palpitating like a lovesick schoolboy, I started to play a Bach suite and was transfixed. My father would have been beside himself with joy. The head of the shop, Simone Sacconi, emerged during my revelry and Marianne introduced us. I told him my father was a luthier in Warsaw, not knowing Sacconi was reputed to be the most pre-eminent luthier in the world.

Stasio explained my need for a cello case and Marianne brought out a heavy, old, black plywood case that looked like a coffin and handed it to me.

"This is yours to keep . . . free of charge," and she gave me two sets of expensive new strings and a cake of rosin, along with the case.

Sacconi wished me luck and gestured toward his magnificent collection. "Work hard and maybe some day you will be able to afford one of these beauties."

During the subway ride back to Brooklyn, with my weighty wooden case taking up the space of two people, I caught myself thinking about an obvious difference between Americans and Poles. In Warsaw people were edgy, distrustful and frequently hostile. The kind of generosity I was shown by New Yorkers was nonexistent. Everyone in Poland really had to stand alone, for survival.

Over dinner I told the Mikruts about my experience at Wurlitzer's.

"I am so relieved and grateful to have a case for my cello. Now I can take it anywhere!"

Maria's eyes filled with apprehension. "*Jesus Maria, Leszku,* please don't do anything crazy."

To be considerate, I surprised Maria the next morning and went to Mass with her, hoping to meet the organist and arrange to play in honor of the Mikruts at church during the upcoming Sunday service. Since I couldn't repay them for their hospitality in dollars, a performance during Mass would be my gift for now.

When Maria and Josef approached the altar to receive the Sacrament of Communion, I played Gounod's *Ave Maria*, my old standard, and they were moved to tears. Afterward, much to the Mikrut's great delight, the priest invited us to his private quarters for tea, and when we left he shook my hand with a ten-dollar bill in his palm. I wouldn't have to ask Maria for subway fare for a while.

On our way home we stopped at the Mikrut's favorite Polish grocery. The storeowner had gone to church that morning and was pleased to meet me.

"I liked the way you played that big violin. Maybe someday Radio City Music Hall will hire you. They are the best, you know!" he proclaimed.

Then he, too, stuck a few dollars in my jacket pocket. It had only been one week since I stood, helpless and shivering, on the corner of Forty-seventh Street. Now, in the true Polish-American spirit, I was meeting people every day who were stuffing my pockets with cash. *How will I return the favors? I must somehow get my papers and a job as soon as possible.* That night Maria made delicious *naleśniki* and, downing a bottle of vodka, Josef and I toasted each other over and over, "*Sto lat, sto lat!*" The truth was, I didn't give a shit about a hundred years. I just wanted to get through the week.

I practiced countless hours every day for the next seven days and chose my audition repertoire: a Bach cello suite, a Brahms sonata, and movements from the Haydn, Saint-Saëns and Schumann Concertos. I had performed these works for my Academy graduation and could still play them from memory.

Rostropovich's advice echoed in my mind, "Losha, when you prepare for a performance, you must never practice for your ears only. Explore all the possibilities of your instrument and take the music apart, phrase-by-phrase. You will make great discoveries beneath the surface of every piece and then, when you walk on stage you will play for each person in the audience. And remember, never be satisfied!"

I stayed away from Manhattan, holed up in the Mikrut's apartment with my cello, and still felt uncomfortable about calling Halina Rodzinski out of the blue. If Juilliard accepted me, I would contact her. But not until then. The week flew past like a hurricane. I stopped drinking, could barely eat Maria's dinners, and even though I was thoroughly exhausted, had trouble sleeping.

On Monday, November 30, with my cello and music in hand, I was on the subway headed for Juilliard. Stasio, my loyal interpreter, and I were led to a large, ordinary classroom where Dean Waldrop and the rest of the jury—two cello professors, Zara Nelsova and Maurice Eisenberg, violin professor Dorothy DeLay, and the violist from the world-renowned Juilliard String Quartet, Raphael Hillyer—were seated. By the time I began I wasn't really nervous. After all, I convinced myself, it was an audition for a school, not the Philharmonic. I didn't feel intimidated and actually rather enjoyed showing off.

When I finished, Professor Eisenberg approached me with a warm smile and an exuberant handshake. Hillyer complimented me in Russian, and since my English skills were less developed than those of a four-year-old, Stasio translated the positive comments from the rest of the jury. Waldrop took me to his office to answer a few technical questions about scholarships, and by three o'clock I was officially informed that the jury voted to accept me as a student of Professor Eisenberg in their post-graduate study program. Of course, I called Savoyka with the exciting news and she asked me to come to see her immediately.

I felt giddy. I loved New York, loved America, loved everything and everybody around me. I announced to Stasio, "I will walk to Savoyka's office in lower Manhattan! I am free and I don't feel like being cooped up on a train!"

Stasio laughed at my preposterous idea, reminding me of the kilos of wood I was carrying. At 125th Street he put me on a subway going in the direction of the Immigration Office. I grinned broadly at all the passengers and would have hugged some of them if they hadn't been looking at me like I was a weirdo. Even though the train was loud and dissonant, clanging against its rails and hurtling ungracefully through the tunnel, in my head I heard nothing but beautiful music. I thought, how marvelous it was that music kept saving me; it was my bright light in a gloomy childhood, my only hope when Mother kicked me out, my ticket to America, and now my escape from deportation.

When I arrived in Savoyka's office, she led me into a private room and closed the door behind us. With a very serious look on her face, she said stiffly, "Congratulations on your acceptance into Juilliard. But, I have bad news. United States Immigration denied your application for political asylum. They consider you a part of the Polish Communist cultural propaganda machine. And, because you didn't belong to any anti-government organization and were never persecuted by the Polish authorities, in their judgment you cannot be classified as a political refugee."

Savoyka had known about their decision for days, but waited to tell me until after my audition. At first, a part of me was secretly relieved because I thought my family might be spared severe punishment in Poland as a result.

Then Savoyka said, "Please understand, you can be arrested at any time and face deportation as an illegal alien. We will begin your student visa application process today, but it will take several weeks. The result of this race against time is beyond my control."

I couldn't breathe.

Seeing my reaction, she tried to soften the blow by saying, "You might still have a chance. Congress and the American press were highly critical recently about the treatment of a Lithuanian sailor who jumped overboard from a Russian fishing boat and swam to shore. The U.S. authorities picked him up and sent him back to his ship. Russian security killed him immediately. The United States was responsible for sending that courageous man to his death, and it unleashed cries of protest across the West. This outrage might help the timing of your case."

I was in no shape to be consoled. In such a short period of time, my emotions had swung from one extreme to the other. A few hours earlier I was dancing on heavenly clouds in solidarity with my new home country; now I felt like I was drowning. Awful childhood memories of fear and capture shot through me, and I trembled uncontrollably. Savoyka put her loving arms around me and I lost myself. Burying my head in her chest like a child, I burst into convulsive sobs.

16

Halina

Back in the apartment and thoroughly drained, I dragged my weary body down the narrow passage toward my room, wishing I didn't have to face the Mikruts on the way. I couldn't hide my physical and emotional exhaustion and they stopped me, visibly concerned.

"What has happened?" Maria asked, clasping her hands over her heart.

I told them the audition went well and I was accepted to Juilliard.

"Don't worry, I just have a post-performance let down."

They had no idea what I was talking about, but since Savoyka advised me to say nothing about the bad news from Immigration, I managed a strained smile and walked on.

I tossed and turned all through the night. With every noise from the street below, every dog bark and gruff male voice reverberating from down the block, I was afraid agents were coming to arrest me. My recurring childhood nightmare reared its ugly head. I was trapped in the Polish countryside with the grotesque, twisted branches of those dreadful willow trees undulating wildly as they tried to snatch me. Black crows circled overhead, their shrieks becoming more deafening as they closed in, threatening to scare me awake until I saw my father, with blood streaming down his face, KGB thugs dragging him from his bed, and it was then that the line between dream and reality softened, crossed from one side to the other. Those who wanted me captured were as close as the chill I felt on my neck from a crack in the windowpane, I was sure of it.

Why the hell was I hiding like a fugitive in Brooklyn? I had had a successful and moderately comfortable life in Warsaw. Curled up in the corner of my Sixteenth Street mattress, I speculated that if I had only lowered my head and held my breath a little longer in Poland, perhaps I would have gained some wisdom about such foolhardy ambitions. Instead, now I was in deep trouble in a foreign land. There had to be a way out.

The next morning, as soon as Maria left for work, I called Father d'Anjou. He understood my anxiety, despite the good news about Juilliard, and he tried to comfort me.

"Lydia will never abandon you. She is a member of the National Advisory Council on Immigration and is highly respected by many important friends in Washington. You mustn't lose hope."

He had kept his promise to phone Halina Rodzinski on my behalf and asked that now I call her personally.

"Like Savoyka, Rodzinski is very involved in helping people and is influential in a multitude of Polish charitable organizations in New York. She is very anxious to meet you."

After our conversation I felt somewhat better and finally telephoned Mrs. Rodzinski.

When a woman's voice answered I asked, "Madame Rodzinski?"

She was amused by my old-fashioned aristocratic Polish etiquette and called me *synku* with a laugh.

"What has taken you so long? Please come for dinner tonight so we can become acquainted."

After shaving, showering, polishing my shoes and making myself as presentable as possible, I made my way to 200 East End Avenue. On the way I stopped at a florist and purchased a single red rose. It was a Polish custom to bring flowers to a lady, and one stem was all I could afford. When Mrs. Rodzinski opened the door I was struck by her glistening eyes and strikingly pretty face, framed by pure white hair that was set at the base of her neck in graceful waves. Her features were slender, like Katherine Hepburn's. She greeted me with an affectionate, dazzling smile.

The apartment was very elegant and well-appointed, with magnificent paintings adorning its walls and floor-to-ceiling books and records filling its shelves. The view from the east windows was stunning and included Gracie

Mansion, home to the mayor of New York City. Dean Waldrop had already informed Rodzinski about my acceptance to Juilliard as the only Polish student in the school. Like all the other Poles I encountered in these first weeks, she, too, insisted I call her by her first name, Halina. We had an instant affinity for each other that was cemented further when she learned my mother had studied painting at the Academy of Fine Arts in Warsaw and I received my degree from Warsaw University, both of which she also attended. Halina was born in 1904, just a few years before my mother, and we wondered if she and Michalina might have been classmates many decades ago.

Just before dinner Halina's son Richard, endearingly known as Riki, arrived. He was a handsome nineteen-year-old who swept into the living room wearing a long fur coat, looking as dashing as a young Polish aristocrat from a bygone era. I introduced myself and described my troubles with Immigration and his mother quickly dismissed my concerns.

Halina shook her head and said, "You did not come to this country to clean houses or work in factories. You are a very desirable immigrant. And besides, you are represented by the best attorney in the city, Lydia Savoyka."

After dessert I listened to her dispense some practical advice for my near future. "First," she insisted, "you should apply for financial help from the many Polish charitable organizations in New York."

I hadn't thought of that and didn't know where to begin. Halina stood by my side and coached me while I wrote letters asking for grants from Polish Mutual Assistance and from the Kosciuszko Foundation. She also gave me the names and telephone numbers of two Polish-born acquaintances with the Metropolitan Opera, who still spoke in our native language: Felix Eyle, the Met's orchestra manager, and Henry Kaston, a violinist and known jewelry artist.

Her last pronouncement was, "You have to move. Once the Juilliard semester begins, the commute from Brooklyn with your cello will be too difficult. I will try to find you a home on the right side of the river."

The evening with Halina changed my outlook. Her confident, encouraging words counteracted the anxiety that had been choking me for weeks. That night I slept like a log. With renewed energy, the next morning I called Felix Eyle. He answered in a typically formal, European manner, but after hearing that Madame Rodzinski suggested we speak, Eyle invited me to his office at the Metropolitan Opera. The "Old Met," as it would soon be called, occupied an entire city block between Thirty-ninth and Fortieth Streets on Broadway. I heard many stories about this legendary building and its historic grand theater. The most famous Polish singers, Marcella Sembrich-Kochanska, brothers Jan and Edouard de Reszke, and Jan Kiepura had great success on its stage. I arrived on time and was navigated along the unexpectedly narrow and shabby hallways of the Met on the way to Eyle's office. Even though it was built in 1883, the Met looked as if nothing had been done to modernize the backstage area since the previous century. There was barely any room to maneuver amidst the remnants of past productions stockpiled haphazardly, like discarded parts in an abandoned hangar.

Eyle began by praising Artur Rodzinski. He reminisced about his years as the assistant concertmaster of the Cleveland Orchestra when Rodzinski was its music director. But I steered the conversation toward my desire to play in the Met Orchestra some day. Eyle laughed.

"That is impossible. I would like to hear you play, but first, get a real visa. A student visa doesn't count. And you must apply for union membership. Then, perhaps we can arrange an audition. At this point it would be illegal for me to listen to you."

There I was, back to square one.

A rehearsal break was called and Eyle led me to the orchestra pit to introduce the principal cellist Yves Chardon, concertmaster Raymond Gniewek and violinist Henry Kaston, Halina's friend, who asked me to wait for him until the end of the rehearsal, "So we can get to know each other."

Sitting in the opulent auditorium and listening to world-class singers and the Met Orchestra, I was dying to jump into the pit and play.

After the rehearsal Kaston took me to a coffee shop on Broadway. He was a balding little man in his mid-fifties who looked like a baby bird with big ears. It turned out he didn't really want to hear about me at all, but prattled on about his own background and exploits. He was a war refugee who had escaped Europe via the underground railroad and crossed the Atlantic to the U.S. on a Portuguese rescue ship. On board with him were artists Marc Chagall and Max Ernst, but noticeably absent was their colleague Pablo Picasso, who opted to remain in France. Apart from playing the violin, Kaston was a successful jeweler, premiere bow maker and inventor. He boasted about fabricating

Salvador Dali's unique jewelry designs and making a violin bow for Jascha Heifetz. We walked to Forty-seventh Street between Fifth and Sixth Avenues, New York's famous jewelry district. The street sparkled and was flush with customers. I wondered where New Yorkers got the money to buy all those glittery treasures. Kaston introduced me to one of his dealers and showed off a few of his own striking creations. Despite his obnoxious bragging, I was impressed. We made our way along Sixth Avenue and when we passed Radio City Music Hall, Kaston asked if I would be interested in playing a few shows there. I was confused. Only two hours earlier, Eyle said that I could not work without union papers.

Kaston smirked, "Don't worry. I can fix that minor problem. And before Christmas you can make some money!"

As we parted company, with a sly twinkle in his eye, Kaston took a thick wad of money out of his pocket. I never saw so many bills in anyone's hands.

Registering my shock, he said nonchalantly, "I won it at the race track." Then he pulled out fifty dollars and handed it to me. "Send the money to your kid so he can enjoy the holidays."

I gratefully accepted his gift.

Back in Brooklyn I headed straight to the Polish grocery store I visited with Maria and told the jovial owner, Mr. Baber, that I was asked to play a Christmas show at Radio City.

He was so proud of his prediction from the week before and said, "When you played that bass violin in church, everybody liked it. You must really be good if Radio City hired you to play in their great orchestra!"

I didn't know anything about the quality of the Radio City orchestra, but I wanted to believe him. Baber's store was an authorized PKO dealership—the official agency for currency transfers between the United States and Poland—so I asked him to please wire fifty dollars (twenty-five to my parents and another twenty-five to Regina and Piotr). It felt wonderful to send them money, especially before Christmas.

The following day, a Thursday, Kaston called and asked me to play two shows on Saturday at Radio City.

"How can I do it without a union card?"

Kaston answered, "Don't worry, you will substitute for a friend of mine. Nobody will ask you any questions, and my friend will pay you in cash."

I accepted, but told him I didn't have a tuxedo. Kaston assured me I could borrow his friend's, which he keeps in the locker room at the hall.

"He's a bit bigger and heavier than you, but that doesn't matter. I'm sure you can manage. I hope you will not embarrass me," he chuckled. "Good luck."

On Saturday afternoon I arrived at Radio City, which was excessively decorated with Christmas baubles, and was greeted by a middle-aged Polish man named Jan, who was a violinist in the orchestra.

"This is the hardest job in town, especially around the holidays," he moaned. "We play so many shows a day, from time to time every musician needs some relief and finds a substitute. Otherwise, we would go crazy."

Jan took me to the locker room to change and presented me with a tuxedo. The jacket hung down to my knees and I had to roll up half the sleeves in order to expose my hands. Charlie Chaplin's Little Tramp was more fashionable in comparison. I was horrified.

"I am like a clown," I said, my face turning red. Jan laughed hysterically, but convinced me nobody would notice my comical appearance because I would be sitting in the rear of the orchestra and out of view.

The interior of the Music Hall was cavernous, the biggest venue I ever played in. Its Art Deco design was stunning, and my nerves quickly gave way to excitement. I had to sight-read the music, but did it without any problem and was able to truly enjoy the spectacle that was The Christmas Show, especially the gorgeous dancers who were called "Rockettes." They reminded me of the sultry performers at the *Moulin Rouge* in Paris. Their long, perfectly sculpted, sexy legs moving and kicking in unison to the music was hypnotizing. I had not been with a woman in a long time and fantasized about being in love with all of them.

The next morning I accompanied Maria and Josef to church once again and was surrounded by dozens of parishioners who wanted to shake my hand and congratulate me. Word spread about my performance at Radio City, and for them I became an overnight star. For the first time since I arrived in this cautious Polish community, the Mikruts and their neighbors could stop worrying about me and about how I would make a living. In their admiring eyes I was on the road to success.

17

The Gatekeeper

Since early childhood my life had been fraught with extreme danger and uncertainty, but none so sudden and stark as on that chilly Sunday morning when I was arrested. I stood on a slab of unsteady, cracked sidewalk in front of the Mikrut's apartment building and, confronted moments earlier by two Immigration officers, I begged Maria to call Savoyka. I was handcuffed like a common thug while Maria sobbed like a baby, driven across the East River in a car that looked like a hearse, and thrown into a concrete cage.

Savoyka had warned me, "Please do not forget, you could be arrested at any time."

I heard her words, but didn't pay enough attention. And now, the morning after performing the spectacular Christmas show at Radio City Music Hall and reveling in the adulation showered upon me by Brooklyn's Polish community, deportation and probable death were staring at me from the other side of those prison walls. Locked in that cold cell, darkness cast its long shadow. I was crippled with fear and could not control the violent eruptions in my gut.

After several hours the guards called my name. They escorted me to a small room where a translator told me to wait for my lawyer.

When Savoyka walked through the door, she must have registered the sheer terror on my face and said in a firm, but quiet voice, "Leszek, relax, don't be frightened. Everything is going to be all right. Remember, Juilliard accepted you. That is in your favor. Stay calm." And then, "Tell me everything that has happened since we spoke."

I began by recounting my experience playing at Radio City the night before. Savoyka was horrified.

"Oh my god! *Jesus Maria*. You did what?!? You are not allowed to work at all, let alone on a union job. This was the stupidest thing you could have done, and totally illegal. That Kaston fellow could have created serious trouble for you with Immigration and the union. Please don't utter a word about that job to anyone."

She took a deep breath.

"Immigration refuses to release you from detention until the deportation hearing before a judge. Tomorrow morning I will pick up the official letter from Juilliard and bring it to the hearing. Your appearance is scheduled for tomorrow afternoon. They will try to deport you directly to Poland, or at least to Switzerland since you flew to the U.S. on Swiss Air. Of course, if they send you to Zurich, the Swiss authorities will put you on a Polish plane bound for Warsaw. Switzerland doesn't want any new immigrants."

She continued, "When you stand in front of that judge you have to stage the finest, most dramatic performance of your life. If we lose, our last resort will be getting you over the border to Canada. I know how you feel about being detained, but try to rest your mind and sleep tonight. You need to be strong and very alert tomorrow. I will help as much as I can, but you are the actor here and you must outdo yourself."

Savoyka left and I was moved to a different section of the jail, housing a couple of dozen detainees, all men. I was the only one wearing a suit and tie, and probably the youngest. Nobody spoke. They glanced around furtively, like trapped rabbits. Sitting on a hard, wooden bench I tried to assess the reality of my situation. *What should I say to the judge? Will he even give me a chance to plead my case? What will they do to me in the meantime?* Unlike the agents who arrested me, the prison guards were rough and intimidating, and couldn't refrain from shouting orders and pushing us around. I didn't understand most of what they barked and didn't want to understand. I wanted to yell, '*Fuck off and leave me alone!*'

Shortly before nightfall they brought in cots with thin blankets and set down plates of slop for all of us. I hadn't eaten since the night before, so I managed to swallow a few bites of food, awful as it was. Savoyka asked me to try to have a good night's sleep, but that was an impossible request. I couldn't believe the Americans were on the verge of effectively signing my death warrant. In the past three weeks I met many good people who were welcoming and generous. I was so stupid to have forgotten my lifelong fear of the police, only to find myself in their clutches, locked up with no consideration for my human rights. The American system was as Kafkaesque as the Polish and Russian—efficient, senselessly bureaucratic and dehumanizing.

At two o'clock the following day, sick with fatigue and fright, I was escorted to an unventilated room that looked like a bunker. If Savoyka hadn't already been sitting there, I would have thought they had taken me to a torture chamber. Then I saw an imposing desk with the American flag hanging behind it at the far end of the room. In front of it sat an official translator, a stenographer and a security guard. They were all staring at me.

Savoyka leaned over and said, "When the judge starts the proceedings I will be beside you taking notes, but I won't be allowed to speak on your behalf. Your defense will be in your own hands."

After a few tense minutes, a judge entered the chamber. He was a skinny old man who showed hardly any signs of life, and certainly no emotion. We rose from our seats and the proceeding began.

In Polish the interpreter instructed, "State your name, age, nationality, and swear to tell the whole truth and nothing but the truth."

Looking down through narrow glasses sternly perched on the tip of his nose, the judge informed me in a monotone that I broke U.S. immigration law by staying in the country after my visa expired. He knew I applied for political asylum and was denied because I had no proof of involvement in any anti-Communist activities in Poland.

"In fact," he pronounced, "the contrary is true. As a dutiful member of the National Philharmonic, you are a contributor to the cultural propaganda of the Polish government."

The case for the judge was done and dusted, and he saw no reason why I should remain inside American borders for a moment longer.

When he finished his cold declaration of the facts as he saw them, he asked me with rhetorical boredom, "Do you have anything to say?"

The stenographer's fingers were poised a breath above her keys, and the translator was prepared to relay a brief, futile litany of pleas.

"Your honor, may I tell you about my background?" I asked.

He mumbled something that sounded like "proceed," expending no visible energy. Savoyka gave me an encouraging glance and I stood up, trying to find inner strength somewhere deep within the dread that gripped me.

"Your honor, I was only a small boy during the Nazi occupation. My family went into hiding and we were separated from each other for years. Imagine, a four-year-old child away from his mother trying to survive as an orphan in a strange village."

The intimate details of my family's past came flooding out.

"My oldest brother was murdered by the Nazis in Auschwitz, and my father barely got through the war alive. He was an officer in the Polish Army under the command of General Sikorski in London. Father took no orders from the Soviet leadership in Moscow. He was arrested after the Warsaw Uprising and, like my brother, was sent to a Nazi death camp. General Patton's units rescued him and he proudly served with the U.S. Army until the war was over. In gratitude, *your* military granted him residence in America. Our entire family was granted American visas. But my father made the terrible mistake of turning down that offer and returning to us in Warsaw instead, as a show of solidarity with our struggling countrymen. It was a decision that resulted in his brutal arrest by the KGB and three years of confinement in a Soviet gulag. My family lost all their property to the Russians, and lived with the constant fear and hatred of the Communists that exists among my people to this day. We fantasized about a place where human rights and dignity were the rule of law. Throughout my youth my family and I listened in secret to *Voice of America* and *Radio Free Europe*, risking arrest while imagining a better life. As a cellist I was forced to join the Philharmonic. I had no choice. It is fiction that I took part in Communist propaganda.

"Your honor, standing here before you, my dream and the dream of my parents is within reach. You are the gatekeeper to Paradise, and I humbly ask you to allow me to become a member of this great democracy instead of committing me to hell. From the day I learned about General Pulaski having spilled his blood and died for this country so that you, your honor, could call yourself a free American, I have struggled to earn the same privilege.

"I am asking you not to send me to my death. You must know what the Communist authorities will do to me if I am sent back. Remember, the color of blood is the symbol of Communism. You falsely accuse me of supporting the Communists when it is *you*, sir, who will be a Communist collaborator if you deport me. If you sign that paper you will never, never, for the rest of your life, be able to wash the stains of my blood off your hands. If you return me to Poland, the authorities will execute me like a criminal. Let me be clear, before I accept such a fate I will kill myself, and there is nobody who can stop me, including your agent who escorts me. If in the confrontation I hurt him, you will have his and my blood on your conscience. The first genocide of the war was perpetrated by the Soviets when they murdered thousands of Polish officers in the forests of Katyn. Your honor, do not add to those numbers; do not make me another victim.

"I love your country. It is now my home; America is my destiny. If you allow me to join your society, I promise you, someday you will hear me play on the stage of Carnegie Hall. I will perform with all my heart, a proud citizen of America playing my best for you!"

I slumped down into my chair, exhausted and dazed. My translator was breathless and sweating, but the judge did not move from his vulture-like position and exhibited no reaction. I saw that he and Savoyka had some sort of exchange, but I was in a fog and felt like I was slipping into deep water. When the judge rose to leave the room, I was asked to stand. The security guard helped me to my feet, and for that I was grateful. He brought me to yet another windowless room where I was left alone for several hours. Fearing the worst, I closed my mind off from thought. I reached the end of the line, and in this airless, white space I experienced a transcendental calm like the thrown arrow that does not move in mid-air, but is suspended as the earth orbits underneath. I was this arrow, unencumbered and gliding.

Just before five o'clock the same guard fetched me again, and we floated down a dark corridor together until he delivered me in front of Savoyka, who was standing with tears filling her eyes.

She embraced me and whispered into my ear, "You are free! Leszek, you will not be deported. You did it. I am so proud of you. The judge did not have the guts to send you to Poland. Thank god! Now you will go to Juilliard and we will have enough time to work on your official immigration papers. You were crazy to speak that way to the judge. He must have hated being called a Communist collaborator. Let's go." With uncontained excitement, she kept repeating, "You are free, free, free!"

Part of me did not want to be yanked from the euphoric space I had found. I was still in shock and couldn't really grasp that the nightmare was over. Savoyka's elation and non-stop chatter eventually brought me back down to earth.

Practically skipping out of the Immigration building she said, "Don't call me 'Pani Savoyka, Pani Savoyka' all the time. From now on, I am Lydia. Come, I will take you to meet my sister Vera, and we will celebrate together."

She hailed a taxi and we went straight to her apartment. Even behind her closed door, I couldn't tame my raw nerves.

"Leszek, you are a mess. Cheer up. It is over. You are safe. The threat is gone. Believe me."

Vera opened a bottle of champagne and we toasted to my future. All through supper Lydia kept referring to the speech I made to the judge.

"Leszek practically accused him of being a Communist!" She couldn't get over my audacity.

Lydia didn't want me to return to Brooklyn that evening because she knew I hadn't slept and was more than a little tipsy from the champagne. Before she showed me to her guest room, I called the Mikruts and Father d'Anjou to tell them the amazing news. Of course, they were overjoyed. Josef and Maria both said they thought we would never see each other again. I hadn't thought so either.

Did I really win my freedom in America? It still hadn't sunk in when I drifted off to sleep.

18

An American Christmas

I knew how hard Josef and Maria worked to earn a meager living and began to feel uncomfortable accepting their hospitality any longer. I was not a kid after all, and though they didn't utter a reproachful word, they must have wanted me to make my own way.

Over dinner I disclosed the details of my detention and deportation hearing to the Mikruts. With their spoons suspended in midair above their *flaki* and their eyes wide open, I recited the speech I made to save my life.

"I warned the judge that if he deports me, he would be no different from a Communist collaborator!"

Maria fondled her napkin like a rosary and said in a shaky voice, "*Jesus Maria, Jesus Maria.*"

She looked skyward, appealing to the Holy Mother for reassurance.

"Are you crazy?" she whispered, afraid that the apartment might be bugged.

Maria kept turning toward the door as if J. Edgar Hoover were going to march in and charge her with subversion. She was an Eastern European in America in the post-McCarthy era, and knew that attaching the Communist label to anyone was the worst of all possible accusations; it certainly wasn't the kind of insult an illegal alien should hurl at an Immigration judge. *"Jesus Maria.* You were so lucky!"

Josef countered with stunned admiration, "The boy was right."

This seemed an opportune time to tell the Mikruts that Mrs. Rodzinski was looking for new accommodations for me in Manhattan.

"She knows a lot of people and can find me a place closer to school," I announced, thinking they would be relieved.

On the contrary. Both Maria's and Josef's faces fell. They were surprisingly unhappy to hear this news.

After dinner I quietly retired to my room and the Mikruts to theirs. Now that the immediate danger of deportation was behind me, I could start on a path toward independence by connecting with some of the Poles in my miniature pocket notebook. I wrote letters to Maestro Skrowaczewski, Henry Stern, and my wonderful new sausage-making friends from upstate New York, Alicia and Edward. I also dropped a short note to Alicia's father—Frank Wardynski of Wardynski's Meats—who was the renowned Kielbasa King of Buffalo. His company motto, "Don't give me that baloney! Give me Wardynski's!" is still a household slogan in New York State. I refused to write to my cousins in Cleveland, remembering with bitterness how they had treated me; I was dependent on the generosity of my short list of contacts, but I still had my pride.

The following afternoon, with a look of suspicion on her face, Maria handed me an envelope from Polish Mutual Assistance. I opened it to find a check for $300 with a very nice note expressing their hope that the money would help during my difficult period of transition. *We wish you success at Juilliard and all the best during your first year in America,* it said. In 1964, $300 was enough for me to live on for several weeks in New York City and to send more money to Regina. I skimmed over the list of the Polish Mutual Assistance board of directors and saw Arthur Rubinstein's name as an honorary chairman. I presumed Halina was behind the grant.

The timing of the check could not have been better. Marek Mayevski invited me to the swanky annual Christmas party at the Kosciuszko Foundation, a center for Polish high culture in New York, and I would now be able to rent my own damned tuxedo and not have to borrow somebody else's clown suit.

A few paces down from the wealthy Astor residence and next door to the city's central synagogue, Temple Emanu-El, was the beautiful limestone Kosciuszko mansion, its ballroom and art galleries packed with the crème-de-la-crème of Polish society. When Marek—who looked suave and primed for schmoozing—and I entered, I spotted Halina chatting with Father d'Anjou. Although Marek was pleased to meet them both, he was obviously distracted by a very alluring brunette at the opposite end of the room and insisted on dragging me into the ritzy crowd, elbowing his way through a doting group of partygoers who were surrounding her. She was Basia Hammerstein—daughter-in-law of Oscar Hammerstein II, the acclaimed writer and lyricist of the most famous Broadway musicals—a young, glamorous Polish lady with sparkling hazel eyes, wearing an off-the-shoulder black cocktail dress. Before Basia married Hammerstein's son James, she was a Broadway actress and singer. Apparently, with her intellect, looks and vivacious personality, Basia was always the center of attention at any social gathering. This evening was no different. Marek was bewitched and looked at her—somewhat salaciously, I thought—with lust in his aging eyes.

He introduced me to Basia as a cellist and a recent immigrant from Poland, and she was intrigued, having left the country with her family just before the war broke out. She longed for stories from her homeland and certainly preferred them to the thinly veiled advances from Mayevski. Some time later Halina joined us and wasted no time in asking Basia if there were any chance I could stay with her for a few weeks until my studies began at Juilliard. Basia explained politely that having a strange man living in her apartment would be impossible since she was going through a nasty divorce from James that included a fight for custody of their son. She did offer to make inquiries among her friends and hoped to come up with an alternate solution. I left the party feeling encouraged.

Sure enough, Basia phoned me the next afternoon.

"Leszek, good news, pack your things. I will pick you up in an hour and take you to my neighbor's home; he is a dear friend who will give you a place to stay."

Her announcement was so sudden. I hardly had time for tearful good-byes with the Mikruts. They understood the move was necessary, but didn't expect to lose me so soon.

Maria held me in an embrace for a long time repeating, "God be with you," over and over.

Basia pulled up behind Josef's clunky station wagon in her rugged military Jeep, with an adventurous twinkle in her eye. When I climbed into her passenger seat, it occurred to me that I was trading the sanctuary provided me by two loving people, for the unpredictability of a stranger whom I had met only hours earlier. But Basia never seemed like a stranger. From our first handshake, I felt as comfortable with her as if we had been friends for years. We took off for Manhattan. She lived at 124 West Seventy-ninth Street in a handsome old building just a half block from the Museum of Natural History and the New York Planetarium. Helping me with my few belongings, we went up to her apartment where I met her good-looking, ten-year-old son Andy. Basia introduced him with great flair as Oscar Andrew Hammerstein III. She sat me down in her cozy living room, made a cup of tea for each of us and described my new benefactors.

Their names were Luther and Stephanie Henderson. Luther was an African-American pianist and composer, his wife the daughter of Romanian immigrants, and they had a seven-year-old girl named Melanie. Luther was a very successful arranger of Broadway shows and had worked with Oscar Hammerstein and Richard Rodgers on *Flower Drum Song* and with Jule Styne and Bob Merrill on *Funny Girl*. He also arranged music for Duke Ellington and other world-famous performers.

Basia said that there were two conditions in exchange for my room and board. First, whenever Luther had a composing or arranging deadline, I would help copy his new music.

"No problem." I told Basia. "It will be an honor."

And second, the couple wanted me to act as a companion, a baby-sitter essentially, for little Melanie. I would walk her to school, play with her when she came home, supervise her piano practice and keep her company when her parents were busy. I didn't know how to respond to this second condition. Coming from all-white, monolithic Poland, I had never even met a black person, and now an African-American man was opening his home to me, trusting me with his little girl. I was going to live in his mixed-race household and serve as their nanny. Such a thing could only happen in the United States, I thought.

After dinner Basia escorted me to the Henderson's apartment. Luther was forty-five years old, tall and dashing, with warm eyes and a dignified, generous smile. Stephanie, whom Luther affectionately called "Steffi," was the same age as her husband, but looked very young. She was blond and extremely attractive, with strong Transylvanian features and a personality to match. I sensed immediately she was a formidable lady of the house. And then there was pretty Melanie, who took the best from both of her parents. At first she was shy and studied me intently with her big dark eyes. I couldn't have seemed a very likely playmate. But after a few minutes of attempting silliness in my funny foreign accent, she relaxed and was ready to have some fun. She showed me to my room, which had been the maid's room off the kitchen. It was small, but away from the family bedrooms, which afforded me privacy.

Melanie was very curious about my cello and begged me to play something. The instrument was almost twice her height, and when I sat down next to Luther at the piano, Melanie stood so close I barely had room to move my bow across the strings. Her father and I played a couple of light pieces we hoped would amuse her, and by the time she went to bed in the evening, we all felt comfortable with our unconventional arrangement.

The first time Luther asked for my help copying music was the night after my arrival. We worked until three o'clock in the morning so that he could have the score and parts ready for his opening of the original musical comedy *I Had a Ball* on Broadway. Music was Luther's passion. He told me that when he was eight years old and living in Harlem, his mother Florence paid fifty cents to take him to a classical music concert at Lewisohn Stadium on 136th Street. The night Luther went with his mother, the New York Philharmonic performed with none other than Ignacy Paderewski as piano soloist. Luther was so captivated by Paderewski's virtuoso playing he decided, then and there, that he wanted to become a pianist himself. His parents supported Luther's talent and ambition, and in 1942 he graduated from Juilliard and went on to receive his Master of Music degree from New York University in 1947. When I tried to tell Luther that Paderewski was also my musical inspiration, I stumbled over the English, but I am sure he understood how moved I was by his story.

Luther worked tirelessly to maintain his perch at the top of the music industry, sometimes up to twenty hours a day. On many nights I stayed up with him until the wee hours as he wrote feverishly while I copied his music, and over time I got used to his frenetic schedule. Luther introduced me to real American jazz and on a whim asked me to improvise with him. As much as I loved jazz, I had no talent for improvisation and knew it was an innate ability that couldn't be learned. Luther's versatility was extraordinary and I was in awe being in his company.

Since I had set foot on American soil, most of my time was spent worrying about finding a safe place to lay my head at night, seeking advice, overcoming legal hurdles and constantly feeling scared. Living with the Hendersons stood in stark contrast. I revered Luther, found Steffi incredibly dynamic, and adored their little daughter. Every morning after walking Melanie to school, I practiced for a few hours before I came to fetch her at the end of the day. Steffi bought a large English-Polish dictionary to help all of us communicate, at least on a basic level. She also arranged for me to take English as a Second Language courses in the evenings. The classes were held far downtown in the East Village near St. Marks Place where the environment was pretty intimidating, especially at night. The streets were overrun with people who seemed to have no regard for traffic or order. They wore crazy clothing, had wild hair and populated the sidewalks in large clusters playing alternative music on their guitars. While my English was slowly improving, I was learning a lot about the underbelly of the city and American youth culture at the time. What struck me most was the abundant freedom of expression.

A week before Christmas Steffi came home with a beautiful tree, and Melanie shrieked in delight. The three of us had a wonderful time trimming it while Melanie's puppy, a large mischievous poodle, pranced around threatening to escape with the ornaments. We adorned the living room with extravagant seasonal decorations, and by the time night fell the apartment was transformed into a festive wonderland. Colorful strings of lights outlined every window and doorway, reindeer and Santa Clauses populated the tables and shelves, and without restraint we strew tinsel everywhere. The following weekend Steffi threw a lavish party for all of their illustrious Broadway friends. When the guests arrived, Luther called me over to meet the legendary Duke Ellington and his son Mercer, Lena Horne, and the most gorgeous man alive, Harry Belafonte, whom I idolized as a performer when I was still living in Warsaw.

I had no news from my parents or Regina. Under the circumstances their silence was understandable, but I was anxious to know how they were doing. I hoped Piotr was thriving and that his mother was treating him well. He was in my thoughts every day as my first Christmas in New York City approached. For me, the joyful lights reflecting across the city, the frenzy of shoppers and the festive atmosphere were bittersweet, coming from Poland where indulgences in holiday sparkle didn't exist. Basia invited the Hendersons and me for Christmas dinner and served a traditional Polish meal with *bigos*, *pierogi*, fried fish, carp, and a poppy seed cake that transported me back to my mother's living room. At the end of the evening she presented me with a beautifully wrapped woolen scarf, and Melanie, grinning from ear to ear, handed me a second package with a pair of leather gloves inside.

"I hope they will keep your precious hands warm," Steffi said with a smile.

I could only give them my appreciation in return.

On New Year's Eve the Hendersons went to a party and left me at home to watch over Melanie. After putting her to bed I turned on the television, and for the first time, watched the ball drop in Times Square as the clock struck midnight. I was so relieved to see the end of 1964. I reflected on the past twelve months and began to daydream about the next twelve. Sitting alone in the Henderson's cozy living room, surrounded by evidence of their proud roots and their thriving family, I felt safe and calm. Their household was full of love and warmth, and having their sweet girl around me was extremely comforting, especially during the holidays. I missed Piotr.

Luther and Steffi must have found me asleep in front of the television when they came home. The next morning I woke up sprawled across the couch, a soft pillow under my head and a fuzzy blanket covering my body. Opening my eyes, I felt a world away from Poland, and from the little immigrant community across the East River in Brooklyn. Living with the Hendersons gave me hope for a better future. After all, a better future was the reason I left my country.

19

Murray Hill

T he first week of 1965 came with an abundance of snow and an unexpected flurry of money. I received letters from the Stern and Posłuszny families that included best wishes for my new life in America and checks for fifty dollars in each envelope. My seventy-five cents from just a few weeks ago had grown amazingly to over $400.

The next two letters that arrived were from my mother. In the first she expressed thanks for my generous Christmas gift, but informed me that both Father and Zdzisław lost their government jobs after aggressive interrogations by the Warsaw police. It didn't matter that they had no inkling about my plans to defect; they were fired anyway. In a confident tone Mother wrote, *I am not worried. You will send us plenty of money for our living expenses now that you are rich in America.* Enclosed in her second letter was a notification from the administrative director of the Warsaw Philharmonic, informing me that on December 31, 1964, I was officially dismissed from the orchestra.

The news about my family's persecution triggered alarms of guilt. What I feared most had become a reality. Immediately, I composed a carefully worded diplomatic letter to the Warsaw Philharmonic management explaining that my stay in New York would only last for the duration of my studies. *Upon my timely return to Poland,* I lied, *you will be very proud of me. My advanced education will be of great benefit to the National Philharmonic, to which I am so devoted.* Of course it was all bullshit, but I thought it might help protect my parents and brother for a time. An official reply from the orchestra arrived soon after and began, *To: Citizen Leszek Zawistowski, The Philharmonic will accept Citizen again if Citizen shows up for work by the fifteenth day of August, year 1965.* Citizen this and citizen that. At least they didn't call me *comrade.* They threw a pack of lies right back at me, but I hoped the target was now on my back and my family would be left alone.

In the meantime, Central Park served as a winter paradise for Melanie and me. We went sledding and made snowmen almost every afternoon. Before I knew it, registration day at Juilliard had arrived. Michael Arzewski came to the school with me on the first morning of the semester to help with English translation and any necessary paperwork. The narrow corridors inside the drab building were crammed with students. I was hoping to see some dancers, but Michael explained, to my dismay, that they were in a separate part of the school. We found the registration office and retrieved my pile of documents. When Michael read the cover page, a broad smile spread across his face. *The Juilliard scholarship committee has granted student Leszek Zawistowski full tuition*, it said.

I began to think Mother was right—in America money grows on trees.

My school schedule was packed: cello lessons once a week with Professor Eisenberg, six hours of Juilliard Concert Orchestra rehearsals, three hours of string quartet coaching and another three with a piano trio. Rehearsal time with the chamber music ensembles and my own private practice hours weren't spelled out, of course. I realized it would be impossible to take care of Melanie and couldn't expect the Hendersons to accommodate me and receive nothing in return. I went to Halina for advice. She made a couple of phone calls on the spot to see about new living arrangements for me. We jumped into a taxi to meet her friend, Wanda Roehr, a Polish ex-pat who lived at 23 East Thirty-seventh Street, just around the corner from Madison Avenue, in a residence that occupied an entire four-story townhouse.

Mrs. Roehr's uniformed maid greeted us with a delicate curtsy, ushered us into the formal living room, and served tea and cookies on fine china. Dominating the room was a massive oil painting depicting Mrs. Roehr in extravagant grande dame style, without even the barest glimmer of a smile. In person, however, she exhibited no affluence, looking instead like a grieving Italian widow wearing an oversized, dowdy and shapeless black garment, her thick ankles shoved into plain black pumps. I would soon learn it was one of only two outfits she wore; that one for daytime and another, of slightly dressier material but no more shapely, with shinier shoes, for evenings and parties.

I felt uncomfortable, intimidated even, in the company of this prickly, eccentric Polish matriarch, and uncharacteristically, I kept my mouth shut. After a few minutes of small talk between the ladies, Halina got right down to business. She described me as a courageous young cellist from the Warsaw Philharmonic, her protégé, and presently the only Polish student at Juilliard.

"Is that so?" Mrs. Roehr asked, turning to me and expecting a reply.

I wasn't sure how to respond, but launched into a biography of sorts and recited the story of my family ancestry. I bragged about my father's background, expressed respect for the lost culture and traditions of old Poland, and ended with enthusiastic praise for her paintings. It was a scattered attempt at legitimizing myself in her eyes and the old lady seemed satisfied.

Halina asked if the Wanda Roehr Foundation would be willing to provide me with a room for the upcoming semester.

Looking directly at me, Mrs. Roehr replied, "Better yet, the fourth floor apartment of my townhouse happens to be vacant. I will allow you to occupy it if you agree to help my maid mix and serve drinks when I entertain from time to time."

I nearly dropped to my knees at her feet in gratitude, but chose to kiss her plump Polish hand instead. I was worried that there must be a catch. A rent-free apartment in such a wealthy area was too good to be true.

That evening, my heart full of remorse, I sat down with Steffi and explained in halting English that my intense schedule at Juilliard would make it impossible for me to continue taking care of Melanie. Apologetically, I expressed my profound appreciation for their hospitality, but said I would be leaving the following week. Steffi seemed surprised by the sudden announcement, but she was forgiving.

The day I left, Melanie looked so sad when I took her to school for the last time. I was sad, too. On the way back I stopped at the florist to buy a thank-you bouquet for Steffi, packed my things and took a taxi to Thirty-seventh Street.

I moved into Mrs. Roehr's Murray Hill apartment and once again kissed her hand in traditional European fashion, repeating my thanks for her generosity. By then she had shed her formality, and with a hearty, folksy laugh said, "Such a nice boy."

My new home had a foyer, a small kitchen and bath, and a large living room-bedroom combination. It had impressive views of Madison Avenue and the back of the J.P. Morgan Library. When my colleagues at Juilliard asked where I lived, they were surprised to hear my answer. They probably thought I was rich, but pretended to be poor. The décor of the apartment was posh by my standards and had nothing in common with any place I ever lived in before. A large Oriental rug graced the center of the living room, and seated romantically beneath a crystal chandelier, was a table and chairs. There were two handsome paintings hanging on the wall above a comfortable leather sofa, and next to the sofa was a fancy old desk with a telephone seductively perched on it, like a sleek lounge singer atop a Steinway. *Would I really have my own phone?* It was difficult to believe. Mrs. Roehr explained that I could use the telephone freely to call anybody in the city.

"But, if you want to make a long distance call, you need to ask for permission. Anyway," she said with an old-fashioned air, "I rarely phone people outside New York. Isn't it much nicer to write a personal note?"

She invited me for dinner that evening, and after our tasty meal she settled comfortably in her armchair, sipping liqueur from a beautiful crystal glass while I played the cello for her. Within a half hour her eyes closed and she fell asleep. As quietly as possible, her ever-present maid escorted me from the room and bid me goodnight.

Lying in my luxurious new bed and listening to the remarkable quiet outside my window, I was comfortable, but not sleepy. The events of the past few weeks rushed through my head and kept me restless and alert. I had deserted little Piotr in Warsaw, brought scrutiny to my family by defecting, and abandoned sweet Melanie as well. I lived with the Hendersons for a short time, but it still pained me that I left so abruptly. With every twinge of excitement I felt about my future, I was rattled by conflict. *Have I let my ambitions divert me too far from my obligations? What and how much do I owe, and to whom? And how will I figure all this out while resting between soft sheets under a dazzling crystal chandelier with a magnificent telephone silhouetted in the window by the New York City moonlight?* I couldn't come up with any answers that night.

Despite having an apartment in Mrs. Roehr's townhouse just two stories from her own quarters, she maintained the utmost respect for my privacy. As soon as my studies at Juilliard began, I needed a lot of time to practice, and Mrs. Roehr only knocked on my door twice throughout the entire semester. Halina, on the other hand, showed no restraint. She appeared unannounced at least once a month, sweeping into my living room with a devilish smile brightening her lovely face. Every time she came I was in the middle of practicing, and was sweaty and disheveled.

"*Synku*, I just want to see how you are doing. It seems you are very well."

I didn't mind her visits because she was like a doting mother, and I found myself wanting to please her more than I ever wanted to please my own mother. Halina never caught me in the midst of romancing a girl, or idly passing the time with cigarettes and drink, like so many young men my age might have been doing. I never lost focus on trying to build a life for myself in America. And this made Halina swell with pride.

Though clothing meant nothing to Mrs. Roehr, she did cherish luxury items. Parked under the building in a private garage was a fifteen-foot, black, chauffeur-driven Cadillac, her pride and joy. Every Saturday morning she and I were taken downtown to First Avenue near Seventh Street where we pulled up to a famous Polish-Ukrainian butcher shop called Kurowycky Meat Products. Kurowycky's was famous for its curing process, which dated back to pre-war Ukraine, and for its Lower East Side smokehouse. The owners had fled the Nazis and then the Communists, and arrived on the shores of New York with nothing but a mastery of butchering pigs. Across the street from Kurowycky's were two other Polish merchants, a bakery and a little shop which sold only fresh butter, lard, goose fat and organic eggs, just like Mother's description of Polish stores "in the good old days." The volume of delicacies Mrs. Roehr bought each week occupied the entire front passenger seat of her town car, and I was the beneficiary of samples all the way home. They were far more delicious than the toilet paper-filled sausages from my past.

About a month after I moved in, Mrs. Roehr summoned me for a "serious talk." I was afraid I had done something wrong.

"My poor chauffeur is very, very sick," she said when I entered the room.

I felt sorry about the chauffeur, but breathed a sigh of relief that I wasn't going to be evicted.

Then she announced with satisfaction, "Until he recovers, I need you to drive my car. He told me you are licensed as a chauffeur, too. What luck!"

In a panic, I tried to explain that I never owned a car in Poland, hadn't been behind the wheel since driving school, and had bribed my instructor for the license.

"I told the chauffeur this story to laugh about the idiocy of Polish bureaucracy. I cannot possibly navigate a limousine on New York City streets," I balked.

She refused to listen and hastily ordered me to go to the garage and pick up her Cadillac. Scared to death, I obeyed her command.

When my role switched from passenger to driver, that humungous black beast looked ten times longer and seemed too tightly wedged into its parking space underground. It took a long time for me to get up the courage to turn on the ignition and exit the garage with its labyrinthine corners. I drove around the neighborhood to get a sense of the bustling Manhattan traffic around me. It was like joining the Running of the Bulls. The worst menaces were the taxi drivers. They were like swarms of yellow bees coming at me, blowing their horns, showing me dirty gestures through their windows, and cursing in a multitude of foreign languages. When I got back to our building, Mrs. Roehr looked annoyed.

"What took you so long? I've been waiting for almost an hour! Leszek, drive me down to First Avenue," she ordered.

If only she knew how terrified I was. Sitting in the back seat, Wanda Roehr was an impulsive, unrelenting navigator.

At one point we were in the far left lane on Park Avenue, about to plunge into the Murray Hill Tunnel, when she screamed at me from behind, "Leszek, turn right at the next corner. Turn right! Do you hear me!?! RIGHT!"

I jerked the steering wheel to the right and prayed for clear passage, cutting off dozens of angry drivers who threatened retribution. Adrenaline pulsing through my veins, I was relieved not to have created the most monumental pileup the city of New York had ever seen. This feeling was repeated almost every time we hit the streets. It was a miracle we survived and the Cadillac emerged without a scratch. I soon became grateful for every chance I had to escape—via subway—to the sanctity of Juilliard.

20

The Vaghy Quartet

Being a full scholarship student, what I dreaded most was the requirement that I play in the concert orchestra. With my professional experience, I was sure it would be a waste of time. Not so. Many of the musicians were much younger than I and, amused by my accent, they exposed me to some idiomatic English like, "we had a gas," "don't have a cow," and "do you dig it?" *Dig what?!?* It was like deciphering Penderecki's musical notation. The orchestra rehearsed in a room that was barely large enough to accommodate everyone. The first violins were as close to the wall as possible, giving them just enough space to move their bows, and the imperious conductor, Jean Morel, a paranoid, insecure old Frenchman, stood on a podium that was practically in the doorway. Directly to my right sat the fabulous sixteen-year-old violinist Pinchas Zukerman, who was not only a virtuoso, but an expert prankster as well, like I had been years ago. He understood a few choice words in broken Polish—his parents had emigrated to Israel from Poland—and loved to try them out on me whenever he could. During one of my first rehearsals with the orchestra, a huge cockroach suddenly emerged from the f-hole of my cello.

Pinchas screamed in Polish, "Look, a *karaluch!* The *karaluch* has an apartment in Leszek's cello. Ha, ha, ha!"

When the big, brown bug dropped to the floor, all the kids around me stopped playing and began to chase it around the cramped room. The entire orchestra was laughing. Morel called for order at the top of his lungs, but nobody paid attention. This embarrassing incident, which had surely been devised by Pinchas, was an uncomfortable reminder of my past in Warsaw when I humiliated my colleagues in the Philharmonic. It was much more fun to be the perpetrator than the victim.

Before enrolling in Juilliard I rarely had the opportunity to play in a string quartet, the most revered of all chamber music ensembles, and was very happy for the chance. Our coach was Dorothy DeLay, one of the world's most highly respected teachers and an absolute favorite of mine. She was like a mother hen caring for all her students, her chicks. The quartet I was assigned to included two refugee brothers from Hungary, the Vaghys, who left their homeland after the revolution of 1956—Dezso, first violin and Tibor, viola. The second violinist, Ron Erickson, was a lanky, young accomplished American musician from Los Angeles. The Vaghys were skilled and extremely ambitious. After working together for a month, they encouraged us to formalize the group, which we did, calling ourselves the Vaghy String Quartet in compliance with the brothers' insatiable appetite for recognition.

The very nature of string quartet playing is intense and demanding. Dezso, Tibor, Ron and I rehearsed for countless hours—four soloists with very dissimilar personalities and backgrounds, trying to agree on a unified interpretation of each piece. It was nearly impossible. We cursed at each other in three different languages and, thank god, didn't understand the insults most of the time. When we reached a consensus musically, the results were impressive and word of our quartet spread quickly.

Four years before, a woman by the name of Susan Wadsworth—who happened to be a close family friend of Halina Rodzinski—founded the Young Concert Artists management company. Susan was slight in stature, but tireless, with lively, sparkling eyes. Her mission was, "To help in discovering and launching the careers of extraordinary young musicians." She was very concerned about the woeful deficiency of music in the city's classrooms and arranged a series of concerts for our Vaghy Quartet in and around New York City, frequently in public schools.

"Many students never hear classical music before they encounter our Young Concert Artists," Susan lamented every chance she got.

One spring morning we arrived for our first performance at a high school. We took our seats on stage in a rundown auditorium and were ready to inspire, but the sea of students in the audience was out of control. They shouted, pushed and threw things at each other, ran from the teachers, and tested the limits of misbehavior in every possible way. The principal, through his bullhorn, yelled at the adolescent mob to stop, without any effect. Teachers marched up and down the aisles like kabuki actors, pointing, waving fists, with hands on their hips and cross expressions on their faces. Under these hostile conditions, the four of us, with our pressed suits and fragile instruments, pondered what to do. As musicians we never encountered a less welcoming crowd. Had I behaved that way in Poland, or Dezso and Tibor in Hungary, we would have been sent to a gulag. Nonetheless, we started to play a movement from Bartok's String Quartet No. 6 and after a few measures, the wild energy that possessed these high-strung teenagers started to release its grip. Bartok was our pied piper and his music blew across the hall like a soothing wind. The students fell silent. Within a couple of minutes they sat in rapt attention. When we finished, Ron spoke to the kids in a normal voice, without using a bullhorn. He thanked them for listening, said a few words about the music we played, and invited some onto the stage. They were fascinated by our instruments, wanted to pluck the strings, feel their weight, run their hands along the smooth wood, and I could see them imagining—like Luther Henderson had when he was a boy—playing themselves one day. Their reaction was Susan's whole point, of course.

Susan's glowing reports about me prompted Halina to arrange an audition with one of history's most famous conductors, Leopold Stokowski. She knew full well that a student visa would only get me so far; a work permit and union card were my real tickets to freedom.

On March 16, 1965, at five o'clock in the afternoon, with Lydia by my side, I appeared at Stokowski's apartment, 1067 Fifth Avenue. I was beyond nervous. When we entered the maestro's studio, furnished floor-to-ceiling with recordings, I was struck by his stunning looks. Standing only a handshake away, he seemed taller and more debonair than I remembered from his days as a guest conductor in Warsaw, with his long, fluffy, aristocratic white hair and his hands extending toward mine like a magician's.

On top of his Steinway grand piano sat an immense Persian cat, who regarded me with disdain. The maestro inquired about my prior experience and was pleased to hear I had been a member of the Warsaw Philharmonic when he conducted Mussorgsky's *Pictures at an Exhibition*.

"What are you going to play for me?" he asked with interest.

"Maestro, I have prepared the Schumann Concerto, a Bach suite and a sonata by Beethoven."

"Beethoven!" He cut me off and his hair seemed to poof in exclamation. "Ah, tell me," he turned to his overstuffed cat, scratched under its scornful chin and demanded, "Who is your favorite pianist?"

The cat responded with a guttural meow that sounded like "ARRROUW, ARRROUW, ARRROUW."

Laughing, Stokowski declared with a mischievous grin, "His favorite pianist is Claudio Arrau! No Beethoven this afternoon because, you know, Arrau is playing an all-Beethoven program at Carnegie Hall tonight, and anyway, my cat doesn't really like Beethoven!"

Such strange behavior unnerved me even more and I began to wonder if the audition could be some kind of joke.

I played the opening of the Schumann Concerto, some Bach, and finally the Bacewicz Concerto I had played for my Music Academy graduation. Then the maestro pulled out some music from his vast collection and asked me to sight-read a few orchestral excerpts—the overture to Mozart's opera, *The Magic Flute*, a page of Prokofiev's *Classical* Symphony, and the opening of Beethoven's Symphony No. 5, which he handed to me with a wink. Stokowski was very impressed. Without a word, he went to his desk and typed a short note.

> *Mr. Leszek Zawistowski is a well-schooled cellist and sensitive artist. I can recommend him with confidence for symphonic and chamber music repertoire.*
> *Leopold Stokowski*

He handed the note to Lydia and said, "I hope Mr. Zawistowski will agree to be the co-principal cellist of my orchestra in Carnegie Hall, the American Symphony."

Clasping Stokowski's venerable hands in mine, I wanted to hug him and his unfriendly cat, but the cat bristled and lowered his ears, so I thought better of it and gave Lydia a big squeeze instead.

Lydia asked me to wait for a few minutes while she and Stokowski discuss the legal aspects of my engagement. The two of them walked to the other end of the room and left me alone with the Persian monster. Lydia explained that while very honored by his offer, I did not have a union card, and under these circumstances I could not legally be employed in an orchestra. The maestro wasted no time in picking up the phone and calling the union president, Max Arons.

When he got off the phone he said, "All is arranged. Go to the Musicians' Union office tomorrow, pay your dues, and they will give you a membership card right away."

When we left Stokowski's apartment Lydia was jumpy with excitement. She met this famous conductor in his own home, heard me play for the first time, and succeeded in arranging my union membership before I was even a legal resident of the United States.

"Your worst problems with Immigration are over!" she cried. "No more nightmares about being deported. We are on the fast track toward your legal residency in America." She did warn me to be very careful with the union president. "Don't dare engage in conversation with him. The less you say the better. Just get the card and get out."

When I called Halina to share the news, she was ecstatic, praising God to the sky. She invited Lydia and me to come to her apartment immediately. We were greeted at the door with the joyful, teary eyes of my Polish-American mother, triumphantly waving a chilled bottle of Dom Perignon Champagne waiting to be uncorked. In my enthusiasm about being engaged by the American Symphony, I blurted out impulsively that I would quit Juilliard.

"No, no, no," the ladies cried in unison.

They insisted Juilliard was my legal insurance policy and also the best way for me to integrate into American society.

"Anyway, your English skills are sorely in need of improvement!" Lydia remarked with a laugh.

I hoped that some day I would be released from the grip of the double life of student and professional, but obviously this was not yet the time.

I arrived at Local 802 the next day and a clerk ushered me into Max Arons' office. There he sat, a short, stocky man behind his desk, glaring at me suspiciously.

"So you are that Polack Stokowski wants. I only agreed to do this as a favor for him. You are a lucky boy. Here is your card. Behave yourself and don't brag about it to anybody."

Intimidated, I made a hasty exit, headed straight to a corner bar and ordered a vodka. I needed to cleanse myself of the creepy feeling I had from the union office and to celebrate the precious possession in my wallet. I signed my American Symphony contract in Carnegie Hall a few days later, and at the bottom of the last page, confirming that this was actually not a joke, was the unmistakable, child-like signature of Leopold Stokowski.

My colleagues at Juilliard and in the quartet were impressed. The first cellist of the Juilliard Orchestra, who never even said "hello" to me, suddenly became friendly. Some people might have been a little envious. But, my new job didn't start until October, six months hence, and my present money situation was anything but enviable. In the hopes of finding some financial support, I wrote to various Polish organizations and called the Kosciuszko Foundation to make an appointment with its president, Dr. Stefan Mizwa.

Joining Dr. Mizwa for the meeting was another Polish man, in charge of student scholarships. In a confident voice I presented my case for a grant—not mentioning my future job with the American Symphony—and explained that being new to the country and the only Polish student at Juilliard, I needed help. They listened skeptically and then asked me how old I was.

"Almost twenty-seven," I answered, and they both laughed in my face.

"Mr. Zawistowski," Mizwa said after catching his breath, "You are a grown man, not a kid. You have to roll up your sleeves and find work. This is not a place for freeloaders." He stopped laughing, looking at me with condescension and said, "What do you think . . . money grows on trees?"

I heard my mother's stern voice warning me, "If you want to be a musician, you will be no better than a thief!"

These two men from Poland humiliated me like no one had since I arrived in America, not even the Immigration judge. I left the foundation, my face crimson with disgrace. I thought of all the generous handouts I received over the past several months and felt ashamed. *Have I grown spoiled and accustomed to charity?* The further I walked, the angrier I felt. I was not a freeloader. I was just trying to survive.

Throughout the spring of 1965, the Vaghy String Quartet engagements were my only source of income and I had to be exceptionally careful with every penny. Susan Wadsworth attended many of our performances, and after one of them she unexpectedly informed us that the quartet was chosen to play for two months in the summer with the Aspen Music Festival, as part of the Young Artists of Aspen program. Each member of the quartet was granted a full scholarship for tuition, room and board. Hearing Susan's pronouncement, I briefly felt the sting of Dr. Mizwa's rebuke, but snapped out of it. There was no question I devoted every ounce of myself toward playing the cello, and the honor of performing in such a world-class festival was deservedly ours.

It was April and the spring blossoms were bursting open. Basia had bought a house in Pearl River, fifteen miles outside New York City, and on weekends she would pick me up in her Jeep and we would flee the city, driving up the beautiful Pacific Palisades Parkway, awash in pink-budded cherry trees gracing both sides of the road. Basia's house needed a lot of work, especially a new coat of paint. The property also cried out for more foliage and a vegetable garden, Basia's dream. I brazenly offered my services as painter and gardener, despite having no experience with either. I did whatever she asked of me, secretly hoping to receive some modest compensation in return to ease my unstable finances. The neighbors probably thought we were a married couple setting up house. The truth was, while Basia was exceedingly attractive, for me she was like an older sister, and I provided her comfort and companionship while she tried to recover from her bitter divorce. Together we painted the interior of the whole house, planted dozens of trees and shrubs, and created a therapeutic space for peace and reflection. She genuinely loved that place and so did I. From time to time Basia did pay me for my labors, which helped replenish my empty pockets.

In the weeks leading up to our departure for Aspen, I indulged in leisure time and had some relief from legal worries. I practiced very diligently, but became increasingly dissatisfied with the sound of my cello. Unlike the prized sonority and richness of legendary Italian instruments, mine sounded thin and dry. Of course, I was emotionally attached to it since it had accompanied me on my dramatic journey from Poland to the States and was originally found for me by my father. The cello was the work of Jacob Stainer, a well-known seventeenth-century German maker. It was golden-brown, quite large with a high-arched belly and a beautifully carved scroll depicting a lady's head, its most distinctive feature. With sadness though, I had to admit that my cello was more pleasurable to look at than to play.

I knew fine string instruments carried very high price tags, in the many thousands of dollars. Nevertheless, before leaving for Aspen I went to the Wurlitzer shop once again, hoping they might take my cello in trade for a better one. Sure enough, Marianne Wurlitzer presented me with a magnificent specimen, circa 1880, made by Stefano Scarampella from Mantua, Italy. As soon as I played a few notes I fell in love with its sound. Seizing on my excitement, Sacconi, with his shrewd business instinct, offered me a deal I could not refuse.

"You keep the Scarampella. We will take your Stainer and issue you a loan for $3,000, which you can pay off over time," he said, with too broad a smile for someone who was fronting me such a large sum of money.

I hesitated, but they agreed to wait until I got a steady job before beginning the monthly payments. I knew I would use that cello with pride for the rest of my professional life and eagerly accepted their offer.

In the meantime, the quartet was to leave soon for Colorado and I hadn't made transportation arrangements.

Basia said, "Leszek, this is your new country; you should explore it. Buy yourself a Greyhound bus ticket for ninety-nine dollars and you can travel anywhere in the United States for ninety-nine days. Go to Aspen first, and when the festival is over you can visit Las Vegas, San Francisco, Los Angeles, anywhere you want, and then back to New York. You will see how big and beautiful your America is."

I decided to take Basia's advice. The Vaghys, who were driving their Volkswagen Beetle to Aspen, agreed to take my cello, and I, with a small suitcase, ginger root for nausea, and the hope for an exciting adventure, boarded a Greyhound "Silversides" bus heading west.

I chose a mid-country route through West Virginia, Kentucky, Missouri and Kansas, different states from the ones we drove through on the Warsaw Philharmonic tours. It was summertime and since Americans were enamored of their expansive highway system and their automobiles, most of the passengers on the bus were vacationing Europeans with oversized sunglasses and Kodak "Brownies" snapping photos relentlessly; or they were indigent travelers, the elderly, African-Americans and Native American Indians. Driving from state to state, I was mesmerized by the colors of the changing landscape and by the kaleidoscope of humanity stepping on and off the bus. I heard about the historic role Greyhound played only four years earlier when the Freedom Riders boarded the bus lines with a much greater purpose than my own, and I began to get a sense of the deep social divisions in America, so different from the single class Communist state I grew up in.

Basia was right to suggest I meet my new country. The trip was long, but unforgettable for a newcomer like me. After more than three days of travel, with few stops and little rest, we finally arrived in Aspen. I was ready for a long shower and a comfortable bed.

21

Aspen

Ifound my way to the Aspen Music Festival registration office where I was given a key and meal vouchers and told that Ron Erickson would be my roommate, with Dezso and Tibor in an adjoining room. What luck, I thought. After greeting the three of them and quickly gobbling down some food, I took a much-needed shower and conked out.

The next morning Ron shook me out of a deep slumber. "Wake up, Leszek, or you'll miss breakfast."

Stretching after such a delicious sleep, I poked my head through the curtains and saw the most beautiful natural paradise, clear blue skies, majestic meadowed hills spotted with quaint mountain dwellings and ski chalets. The morning sun glistened off my window, beckoning me outside, and a hummingbird stopped in his travels to bid me welcome. It was breathtaking. I straightened my back and yawned deeply. And then it hit me, like a kick in the gut. My nostrils filled with the most nauseating smell. It could only be described as death. The odor transported me back a decade to my medical school days and those horrible autopsies. The stench was exactly that, a room full of corpses oozing with bile.

"Ron," I asked choking back a gag, "what that terrible stink is?"

He shrugged his shoulders and replied, "I don't smell anything."

I thought it must be coming from our lodgings and stepped outside the room to catch my breath. The fresh air revived me.

Gordon Hardy, the dean of the Aspen Music Festival—and Juilliard—

announced that the Juilliard faculty, in charge of choosing the most talented, mature musicians as the Young Artists of Aspen, named our quartet as recipients of the honor for that summer. The Amadeus Quartet would coach us. We discussed schedule and repertoire, which included playing the Shostakovich String Quartet No. 8 in C minor (Opus 110) on the July 12 evening concert at the Wheeler Opera House.

Smack in the center of town, the opera house boasted of seats in lush Moroccan leather, a periwinkle ceiling bespeckled with silver stars, and a dazzling, thirty-six-light chandelier, exceptional in the days of gaslights and only possible because Aspen had been the first Western city wired for electricity. Four short years after the Wheeler Opera House opened in 1889, like the town itself, it fell into decades-long abandonment and disrepair until the mid-1950s when the old theater was elaborately refurbished. Its stage would be a highly unusual setting for our Aspen debut, particularly since we would be performing an edgy, contemporary quartet by Shostakovich.

We were taken to meet the members of the esteemed Amadeus Quartet. They were extremely friendly and after exchanging names, introduced us to their precious instruments, which included two Stradivariuses, a Guarneri del Gesu and a rare seventeenth-century Gasparo da Salo. When I complimented Norbert Brainin, the group's first violinist, on the exquisite sound of his violin, he said with a wink and a smile, "A good instrument helps, but in the end, it depends on how you use the thing."

I was not looking forward to retiring to our nauseating motel room after such an eventful day, but when we walked in the door the odor had dissipated. I took a refreshing shower and when I emerged, I saw Ron standing in the room wiping his naked body with a soaking wet towel. And there it was again, that disgusting smell. Ron kept re-wetting his towel with what looked like gasoline and vigorously scrubbing his six-foot frame.

"What that *is*?" I asked, holding my nose.

"It's Listerine," he explained, "the best way to get rid of germs and bacteria. I never go to bed without it."

The odor made me ill, but I had to get used to it since that would be my goodnight fragrance for the rest of the summer.

As tempting as it was to explore our surroundings, we rehearsed like crazy instead, hoping to live up to expectations and impress everyone. In fact, we were in a kind of unspoken competition with another string quartet. The leader of that group was a member of the Jascha Heifetz master class, a beautiful and brilliant young violinist from Los Angeles, Toni Rapport. We considered ourselves to be rivals and childishly didn't attend each other's quartet performances. I did hear her in a wonderful chamber music concert in Aspen's unique "hall"— which was an enormous tent—playing Francis Poulenc's septet, *Le Bal Masqué*, with James Levine at the piano.

My first encounter with the other festival musicians was during an orchestra rehearsal. There were several terrific players in the cello section: my colleague from Juilliard, André Emelianoff, Paul Katz, who later became the cellist of the Cleveland Quartet, and Robert Gardner, principal cellist of the New York City Opera. Bobby was also the cellist in Toni Rapport's quartet and an eccentric fellow, well-known for riding an old, battered bicycle on Aspen's dirt roads with his cello case strapped to his back.

The orchestra rehearsal took place on the picturesque Castle Creek campus, in a space large enough to accommodate the whole ensemble. During the break a group of us went outside to admire the serene little lake surrounded by mountains. It was a very hazy day, fog hovering delicately over the surface of the water. Wanting to be friendly, I attempted to make a smart comment to my colleagues. I took out my trusty Polish-English dictionary from inside my coat pocket and flipped to the word "fog."

Standing in the middle of all the musicians, I opened my big mouth shamelessly, breaking the stillness in the air, and exclaimed in my heavily-accented English, "Very fucky day!" No answer. So, I repeated, "Fucky day."

Everybody looked at me in astonishment. With a self-satisfied smile on my face, I looked from one side to the other for a response, but they just stared at me, puzzled. I glanced nonchalantly at the dictionary entry once again. Maybe I had said the wrong word. No, there it was, phonetically written, fôg, or foˇg. Then everyone burst into hysterics. The young women covered their mouths and shyly tried to hide their enjoyment of the moment. The men chortled aloud, their guffaws echoing across the lake and disrupting the gossamer fôg before us. The principal cellist Leopold Teraspulsky, of Eastern European background himself, walked over to me.

"Mr. Zawistowski," he laughed, "the words "fog" and "fuck" are very different. Fog you get when you boil water. Fog is what you are seeing in front of you."

And he gestured with his hands, steam rising, fog floating, making sure I understood.

"But, 'fuck' means 'sex,'" moving his fingers in a crude manner. "When you lie on top of a woman and stick your endpin between her legs," he poked and poked, "that means 'fuck!'"

I was so embarrassed.

"Sorry, sorry, please forgive. So sorry," I repeated.

This was my introduction to my colleagues in Aspen.

We played quartet concerts in Aspen, Denver and Greeley. The Greeley Concert Association presented our final performance of the summer at the College Center. Since it was over one hundred miles from Aspen, we were the overnight guests at a ranch outside of town belonging to Warren Monfort, the largest employer in Greeley. Warren drove us to the most impressive cattle farm I had ever seen, populated by thousands upon thousands of cows. We rode for at least a half hour between throngs of animals elbowing each other for space, cows mooing as far as the ear could hear. The stench of shit in the air was even stronger than Ron's Listerine. Our host was very proud.

"When the wind blows toward Greeley, the whole town smells like my herd!"

The following week the Director of Young Artists posed a question that gave us a thrill.

"Will you record Mozart's *Dissonance* and the Shostakovich quartets for our Aspen label?"

Of course, we accepted and spent most of the next week in the Walter Paepke Memorial Auditorium practicing and recording. This LP was the only one issued by the Young Artists of Aspen.

Toward the end of the summer I was rewarded with some spare time to enjoy Aspen's outstanding beauty. I explored the mountains and took the chair lift to the summit, which felt like being on top of the world. Standing at the high altitude and filling my lungs with pure mountain air, a strange feeling came over me. It was as if my two divergent lives briefly intersected. I was in Poland visiting Zakopane, the most famous resort town in the Tatry Mountains, vacationing with my mother, father and brother, picking wild mushrooms and wading in a stream, and at the same time I was in America, the so-called land of the free, on a new path.

Even after such an exhilarating two months, September was fast approaching and I was ready to move on. Ron, who didn't like long trips in the car alone, asked me to drive back to New York with him. He planned to visit his parents in Los Angeles first, which was fine with me. My journey would not have been complete if I hadn't made it to the West Coast. A few days before our departure, each member of the Vaghy Quartet received one hundred dollars from the Wanda Roehr Foundation. Mrs. Roehr heard about our success in Aspen and wanted to surprise us before the trip home. On Sunday, August 22, with the first rays of the sun, Ron and I piled into his VW bug and headed for California.

We decided to take our time getting from Aspen to Los Angeles because there was so much to see en route, ancient Native American villages and the miraculous natural rock formations of the region. In Utah Ron exited the highway for a detour to Arches National Park with its remarkable prehistoric petroglyphs, and then we made our way to the glorious Bryce and Zion National Parks. When we drove through a small Indian village the next morning, our windows rolled down because it was hot and Ron had no air-conditioning, I was shocked to see so many poor people, especially the beautiful little children running barefoot over the rocky terrain in threadbare clothes. As a young orphan child I was in tatters and had no shoes, but that was during the war. I couldn't understand how such poverty was possible in this rich country, particularly in a time of peace. After passing through Indian reservation country we drove toward Las Vegas. The landscape became more and more forbidding, without any evidence of life—no structures, no tourist stops, few signs, and only crooked Joshua trees to guide our journey. We were in the middle of a vast, empty, cracked desert and the temperature was creeping up over one hundred degrees. There was no relief from the heat, nor was there much conversation between us. We just wanted to make it to Las Vegas.

Shortly before noon our car suddenly started to sputter and the engine died. Ron and I were petrified. He wiped the perspiration from his brow and looked at the gas gauge. The needle was at the very bottom; the tank was empty. In the excruciating heat we waved at passing cars for assistance, but nobody even slowed down. We were stranded. With no water in the car and very dehydrated, we pushed the poor Bug down the road in search of help, drenched in sweat, our faces scorched by the sun, and the steel body of the car burning our hands. We felt on the verge of death when in the distance, like a mirage, Ron and I saw a tiny run-down service station. It was the first sign of civilization for miles. We abandoned the car on the side of the road and tried to run on our wobbly legs.

Nearly delirious, I heard myself, like a stranger's distant voice, yelling, "*Woda, woda . . .* please!!!"

It turned out that Las Vegas was only a mile from where we broke down. We poured water down our throats, splashed our parched faces, used the restrooms, got gas and fled. After the sumptuous natural beauty we encountered during the first part of the trip, Vegas seemed like a hallucination. Neither of us had any interest in exploring it, or its casinos. We were desperate to get out of this sin city and the Mojave Desert, which was like driving on the surface of the moon. Before sundown we left the arid, hostile landscape and were greeted by the lush foliage of San Bernardino County and Los Angeles. What a relief. Everyone looked happy, driving their clean, shiny cars along the palm tree-lined streets. We arrived at Ron's parent's house just before dinnertime, and they welcomed me as if I were a member of the family.

After two days of tender, loving care we got back on the road bound for New York City. We made it to the Texas border by nightfall on the second day and decided to stop to refuel and have a bite to eat. Most of the gas stations were located off the highway in small towns thick with locals and their customs. As soon as I stepped out of the car, I could feel a chill wind raising the hair on the back of my neck. The place was packed with motorcyclists, and the few cars parked out front had mammoth steer horns on their hoods. I wanted to fill the tank and scram. As soon as Ron finished pumping the gas, I went to pay the clerk. It was dark and I couldn't see the rattlesnake in my path, which delivered its warning rattle just as I approached. It was within striking distance and I made a mad dash into the station cafe. The lights inside were dim, but through the clouds of cigarette smoke and the smell of booze, I could see it was full of large men wearing large hats and well-worn cowboy boots. Behind the bar stood a tough-looking woman with tattoos on every visible part of her hefty body. Our fuel bill was five dollars and one cent. I handed her five dollars and turned to leave.

She shot me an evil look, spit on the floor and yelled, "Where the hell is my penny, you fuckin' bastard?!"

Everybody stopped talking and turned toward me. With a shaky hand, I dug into my pocket and found a dime, which I slid in her direction across the counter.

"Sorry, thank you, sorry," I said, my voice cracking.

I must have sounded like a frightened teenage boy. With her eyes burning holes into my back, the walk to the door felt like the second longest walk I ever took. We drove away as fast as we could, and for the next half hour I kept turning my head to look out our rear window, afraid someone might be following us.

Three days later, exhausted from the long hours in Ron's cramped little car, we appeared on Mrs. Roehr's doorstep. She wanted to hear all our news, of course, and invited us to have dinner. I knew Ron was too bleary-eyed to drive home and said he could stay with me that night. When we both began to nod off at the table, Mrs. Roehr ordered us straight to bed. Thank god, Ron didn't have the energy to wash himself with Listerine.

22

Pique Dame

September was a beautiful month in New York City, ushering in the delicious combination of crisp air and bright sunshine. The opening performances of the fall season would begin in a couple of weeks, and I thought it was a good time to contact Felix Eyle at the Met, hoping this time he would agree to hear me play since I was now a card-carrying member of Local 802. I reintroduced myself on the phone, informed him about my union membership and engagement with Stokowski's orchestra, and conveniently neglected to mention that I never played an opera in my life. After some subtle arm-twisting, he told me to show up the following week.

On September 21, 1965, I entered the stage door of the old Metropolitan Opera House once again.

Eyle, in his bookish sweater-vest, was slightly more pleasant behind his impenetrable dark-rimmed glasses, but nevertheless, the first words out of his mouth were, "May I see your union card . . . please?"

I guessed he still didn't trust me.

He examined the front and back of my card carefully, and then said, "The orchestra is rehearsing and we have to wait for the concertmaster and the principal cellist. You can warm up outside my office for a while."

Eyle shoved a chair into the hallway in a narrow pocket of space between instrument cases and clutter, and left me alone. I put my bow to the strings very quietly, hoping not to disturb anybody around me.

A few minutes later, a petite, sylph-like figure emerged from the end of the dim hallway. Wearing an elegant silk robe and ballet slippers, she started to dance to my music, her long hair and the shimmering fabric of her dress floating freely, like an exotic butterfly. She was utterly gorgeous, and I stopped playing to look into her dark eyes as she approached.

"Are you here to audition?" she asked, and leaned in close to whisper in my ear, "I have a feeling they are going to hire you!"

Then she kissed me on my forehead. I could no longer remember why I was there; I just wanted to pull her into my arms in a passionate embrace. But she eluded me, fluttering away. She coyly glanced over her shoulder with an irresistible smile, and I stood up, trying to stop her.

"I am Leszek. What your name?" I yelled after her.

"I am Teresa. Teresa Stratas."

Not wanting her to escape, I asked quickly, "You are dancer?"

In the distance, she said with a giggle, "No, no. I am a singer," and scampered toward the stage chirping, "Good luck, good luck."

As soon as the rehearsal ended, Gniewek and Chardon showed up in Eyle's office. Eyle invited me inside, but asked me to practice in the back of the room while they talked business at his desk. Playing off in the corner felt odd, but I practiced my repertoire and pretended no one was there.

Eyle finally stopped me and said, "We heard enough. You are a good cellist and we would like to call you from time to time to play performances as a substitute."

I was confused. That was my audition? They didn't even want to hear any opera excerpts? I had taken some strange auditions over the years, but this was one of the strangest. At least I got a toe in the door of the great Metropolitan Opera. Teresa, whoever she was, must have been my good luck charm.

Eyle explained the terms of my employment. The salaried Met musicians were obligated by contract to play seven performances every week, but sometimes individuals would ask to be released from one or two performances. In these instances the orchestra needed substitutes. I could be called on short notice and would have to be prepared.

With a stiff handshake and a modest attempt to crack a smile, Eyle said, "You will hear from me."

When Gniewek and Chardon invited me for coffee afterward, I couldn't wait to ask, "Who enchanting singer is with name Teresa Stratas?"

Gniewek grinned knowingly and described her as ethereal and quixotic, revered by her adoring fans and considered one of the greatest singing actresses of the twentieth-century. At almost five feet tall and not even one hundred pounds, she was known as "The Baby Callas." He explained that the company was rehearsing Tchaikovsky's *Pique Dame* (*The Queen of Spades*) for opening night, and the soprano star of this new production was none other than Teresa Stratas. The performance was to be conducted by the magnetic, and extremely handsome, Thomas Schippers and feature the world-renowned, incredibly intense, Canadian tenor Jon Vickers. The legendary mezzo-soprano Regina Resnik rounded out the cast. My brief, but magical, encounter with Stratas sent me into a reverie about a future life with the Met, but that would have to be added to my list of dreams. The stark reality was that for now I had to remain at Juilliard, take advantage of my scholarship and the foundation grants, play in the American Symphony, and hope the Met would call often. After all, I had an obligation to continue supporting my family in Poland.

On my first day of the Juilliard fall semester, Gordon Hardy said that as a full scholarship student I qualified for free room and board at International House (known to everyone as "I-House"), across the street from school. I-House accommodates graduate students and visiting scholars from major New York institutions like Columbia University and Juilliard. The residents include more than seven hundred students from over one hundred countries learning about each other's cultures, traditions, ways of intellectual thinking and friendship. I loved the words inscribed above the entrance to the building: "That brotherhood may prevail."

On October 3, I moved from Mrs. Roehr's entirely too fancy apartment to a puny room, number 315, at I-House. Wasting no time, the pianist from my Juilliard trio took me under her wing and introduced me to her bed. I was so out of practice in the game of love, I didn't even realize she had romance on her mind. The relationship was open and welcome. I lived rent-free in a virtual united nations of young people, had a casual girlfriend, a start at the Metropolitan Opera, and a prestigious job with Stokowski. Nineteen sixty-five was looking up.

My first rehearsal with the American Symphony in Carnegie Hall was eleven long months after I last stepped foot on this stage, the night before I defected. Returning to this grand temple of music, all the memories of my defection and the nerves that went with it, came flooding back, including the same uneasiness in my stomach. Was I really good enough to satisfy Stokowski, I wondered? A half hour before the start of the rehearsal, I was already in my seat practicing the music. Within minutes, the great maestro himself showed up.

On his way to the podium, he stopped at my chair with an outstretched hand and said, "Good morning, Mr. Zawistowski. Welcome."

I was surprised by his perfect pronunciation of my name. Before every rehearsal that season he approached me with a personal greeting.

I loved working with Stokie. Never using a baton, his conducting style was dramatic and graceful. He danced with his arms and moved his hands like a sorcerer, drawing glorious colors from the orchestra. Stokie insisted on free bowing, which meant the string players moved their bows in different directions from each other. Visual unanimity in an orchestra, rigorously insisted upon by nearly every other conductor, was of little importance to the maestro. What mattered to him was the luscious, rich sound he was famous for producing.

My first concert with the American Symphony was very emotional. I earned my way back onto the Carnegie Hall stage as an individual, not as a puppet of the Polish government, and I was very proud. Almost all of the important people in my life in America came to hear the performance: Father d'Anjou with Halina Rodzinski, Marek and Julia Mayevski, Lydia Savoyka and her sister Vera, Basia Hammerstein with her son Andy, and some new friends from I-House. Stasio was working at the Plaza and the Mikruts did not dare cross the East River into Manhattan—once had been enough for them.

After the concert we all went to Carnegie Tavern on Fifty-sixth Street, next to the stage door, for a glass of champagne. It was almost midnight when I finally headed home on the subway bound for 125th Street. At that hour the car was practically empty, so I took a seat in the corner, cradling the cello case in between my legs, and began reflecting quietly on everything that happened since I appeared in Carnegie Hall with the Warsaw Philharmonic.

The train stopped at Ninety-sixth Street and three teenage boys made a noisy entrance. They were rowdy and aggressive, testing each other to see who was the alpha male and glancing around to see where they could stage a display of dominance. When they saw me, I was clearly an easy target. The boys moved toward me slowly and bounced jokes off each other in a slang I didn't understand as they approached. All of a sudden, one of them kicked my cello case. I froze, helpless and horrified. I gripped the case firmly, counting every interminable second until my stop. Just before we screeched to a halt, my cello got one more kick and I felt a sharp punch on the back of my head. The doors opened and I shot out of that train like a lightning bolt. They didn't follow me. Once again, I had the all-too-familiar sense of vulnerability that plagued me for the past year. My circumstances changed, but still I didn't feel safe.

Eyle called a few days later and hired me to play a performance of *Pique Dame* the following Tuesday night.

"When is the rehearsal?" I asked, in Polish.

He said in a sarcastic voice, "We already rehearsed. Besides, I thought you knew this music."

I lied to Eyle when we first met, and now I tried to reassure him I really had played that opera in Poland.

"It never hurts to rehearse again," I offered, "because the Metropolitan Opera is the best."

He appreciated the sentiment and, with a satisfied grumble, said in his formal manner, "I expect to see you at the appointed time on Tuesday. And make sure to wear a tuxedo. Goodbye."

Just like that.

I went to Juilliard's music library immediately and checked out the score and a recording of *Pique Dame*, which was based on a story by Pushkin. Intently following the notes on the page, I listened to the three-and-a-half-hour recording as many times as I could, and tried to commit the music to memory. It felt like I was fifteen years old again, hiding under my covers at night with a flashlight, delighting in reading Pushkin in the original Russian. The libretto of *Pique Dame* was dark and intense, about obsession, love and gambling, with Gherman, the main character, ultimately descending into madness. I could hardly wait until Tuesday.

Two days before the performance I made a dry run to see how long it would take to get to the Met from I-House. From there I went to Macy's to buy a new shirt to go with the tuxedo Stasio loaned me. After standing in front of the store directory for some time, I figured out that the men's department was on the sixth floor. When I entered the elevator a young woman, the elevator operator, wearing a pillbox hat and a slimming uniform, greeted me with a plastic smile and held the door open for other passengers.

There was nobody else around, so she stepped inside, closed the door and asked me, "Which floor, sir?"

"Sex please." I replied.

She looked at me in disbelief and, taking a hasty step backward, asked, "Excuse me?"

More slowly this time, trying to clarify my poor English, I said again, "SEX, please."

She yanked open the elevator door quickly and ran out onto the floor screaming, "Security! Security!!" With no security in sight she shrieked even louder, "SECURITY!"

While I stood by myself in the middle of the elevator, she was hollering outside. People started to gather, emerging like curious forest animals from the racks of clothes, and I had no idea what was going on. With meddlesome shoppers pointing at me, seconds later two large men built like rhinos came running. The bigger one was a uniformed security guard and the other, an intense-looking official in civilian clothes. After they listened to the elevator operator's story, which she told in frantic whispers, gesturing wildly in my direction, the men grabbed me under the arms and dragged me to a small office.

The official asked for my name and identification papers. The only documents I had were my Juilliard student ID and my union card.

To my surprise, the official asked in very poor Polish, "What are you doing in Macy's?"

I tried to explain that I was going to play my first performance at the Met Opera and I wanted to buy a new shirt. What is happening?

"What did you say to the girl?" he continued.

"I said, 'sex, please,'" and the security guard looked like he was going to kill me. "She asked me what floor and I told her 'sex, sex.' What is problem?! I just want sex floor!"

Both men exploded in laughter.

The guard said, "Let me give you a free English lesson, Mr. Polack. 'Sex' in English means you stick the thing you have hanging in between your legs into a woman," waving with his billy club at my crotch. "And 'SIX' is the number you were looking for."

He put down his club and held six fingers menacingly in front of my face.

"Now, show me six fingers." He grabbed my hand. "This is SIX. Understand?"

Then he escorted me to the men's department on the sixth floor and helped me purchase a shirt.

On the way out he shook my hand and said with a smile, "My name is John, and I don't want to have any trouble from you again. Don't forget the difference between 'sex' and 'six.'"

I felt like such a fool.

It was pouring rain that Tuesday evening, and when I entered the Met stage door and bounded down the slippery concrete stairs to the locker room, I almost slid the whole way in my wet shoes. Henry Kaston, grinning from one oversized ear to the other, greeted me and introduced some of the orchestra cellists, including Carlo Pitello, who would be my partner on the last stand of the cello section. The pit was so crowded, the string players had to adjust each chair very carefully to have enough room to move freely without poking a neighbor in the eye with the tip of his bow. One of the double bassists actually took out a tape measure to make sure his colleagues didn't have one inch more space than he did. His neighbors rolled their eyes. Apparently, the tape measure made a regular appearance. I wished I had been honest with Eyle about never playing *Pique Dame*. Here I was, playing the performance of a lifetime, and I was sight-reading the music. Carlo sensed my anxiety and tried to be helpful, leading me through the music. In the middle of an aria, a cockroach suddenly crawled across the page. This time it didn't come from my cello; it was a Metropolitan Opera resident roach. Carlo, with his bow, swiftly sent the bug airborne toward the first violin section.

When we finished the first act, Carlo was very complimentary and told me not to worry, that my playing was fine. As soon as we broke for intermission, before I knew it, Ray Gniewek, Carlo and another elderly cellist led me out the stage door, into the rain and across the street to Blecck's Bar—pronounced

"Blake"—which was the hangout for personnel from the Met, *International Herald Tribune* writers, and performers from the big Broadway theaters. The bartender was standing behind the forty-foot long bar and delivered drinks to my colleagues immediately. They didn't even have to order. I could not believe we were performing in the most venerated opera house in the world and these guys were having a drink during the intermission! I stood by and watched them lubricate their spirits while I declined. Ten minutes later, off we went, back to the orchestra pit.

Before the second act began, and after the double bass player again measured the distance between the chairs and the music stands, I had a moment to look out at the massive chandelier that lit the theater's resplendent ceiling. Playing in the orchestra and listening to my enchantress Teresa Stratas singing on the stage, was surreal. By the time we got to the third act, my nerves gave way to a giddy joy. I was able to play the opera without any problem and loved every moment.

Jon Vickers, with his characteristic vigor, sang Gherman's most famous line, "What is our life? A game," and I wanted to cry out, "Life is but a fantastic game!"

The Old Met

I t was already a year and a half since my defection, and I didn't feel like a foreigner any longer. The memories of my past struggles and recent fears were fading. By 1966 I integrated into the student community at Juilliard and felt comfortable with the residents of I-House. The balancing act between my dual student and professional status was precarious, however, and had to be kept quiet. It would not be the first time I danced around the truth as a matter of survival, but I hoped it would be the last.

In the meantime, my social life in New York blossomed. I was invited to parties with Polish expatriates, artists and socialites. One afternoon I received a phone call from a lady who claimed to have met me at some function or another. She sounded intelligent and had a very sexy voice. Following that first enticing conversation, we spoke over the phone frequently and became more and more flirtatious with each passing day. I knew her only by her first name, Zofia. Otherwise, she was a mystery. She offered scant information about herself and answered my questions with vagaries followed by lustful diversions, but somehow she seemed to know a lot about me.

After two weeks of this telephone courtship, the elusive Zofia invited me to her apartment for dinner and I didn't hesitate. She lived on Park Avenue, so I assumed she was rich. I took extra care dressing—splashing cologne on my cheeks and donning my silk ascot—wanting to appear refined and experienced in the ways of love. Carrying a bouquet of red roses, I arrived punctually and eagerly asked the doorman to phone her apartment. He eyed my flowers, and me, suspiciously, and after what seemed an eternity, Zofia answered the house phone and bid me to come upstairs. I was so excited to meet her I practically had an erection in the elevator. Before I even had a chance to knock her knocker, the door eased open and in the very dim light of the entry hall I saw the silhouette of a naked lady a few yards away. Wearing a see-through chiffon robe and nothing else, she spoke to me in her familiar sexy voice and invited me inside. Finally, I was going to get my hands on her. I closed the door and swaggered down the hallway ready for our long-awaited embrace. But, as my eyes adjusted to the light and my gaze lifted from her figure to her face, I saw that the lady before me was at least as old as my mother, if not older. I tried to deflect her outstretched arms with my bouquet of flowers, but she was quick as a fox. She threw her naked body against mine and kissed me passionately on the lips. *Oh shit.* How could I escape, and quickly?

I distracted Zofia with the roses, pushing them between us again, leaving many of the stems as broken as my ego. She cooed at the flowers and blissfully spun around to fetch two glasses of champagne. I did not want to insult the Madame, so I sipped my bubbly and then did a swift job of feigning nausea.

"I feel sick all of a sudden. It must be the champagne," I told her, rushing to the bathroom and kneeling beside the door making loud vomiting noises.

Zofia insisted I lie down on her bed. "I'll make you a cup of tea."

She pranced off to the kitchen in her transparent negligee and I, like a cat, tiptoed to the front door and straight out of the apartment. Instead of waiting for the elevator, I ran down the many flights of stairs to the lobby where the doorman nodded goodbye with a scowl. As the cold night air hit my lungs, I really did feel like throwing up.

In early spring I was invited to play an important concert with two very well-known Polish artists, violinist Roman Totenberg and pianist Arthur Balsam, for the Kosciuszko Foundation's big gala event honoring Arthur Rubinstein. I was relieved that Zofia was nowhere in sight. After the performance Rubinstein made a speech.

He thanked us and said, "Even I could not have produced the same singing tone on the piano as *Pan* Leszek's superb playing did on the cello."

I was happy he didn't remember that in 1958 I was the very same cellist in Warsaw's Hotel Bristol trio that had played a cheap version of his beloved Chopin *Nocturne*, much to his displeasure.

Eyle was also at the Kosciuszko event and listened to my successful performance with obvious satisfaction. He was not a man to take risks, and whatever doubts he harbored about me early on were finally dispelled. Soon afterward he hired me to play Puccini's *Madama Butterfly*, and I was sure I detected a hint of enthusiasm in his voice. I arrived in the pit and sat in my customary last chair, but to my surprise, Chardon, with a sly grin on his face, asked that I sit with him on the first stand. I presumed such an action was against orchestra regulations, and as expected, it was met with harsh glares from some of the regulars who felt slighted. Chardon was an impetuous, eccentric Frenchman and waved them off. Only my friend and fourth stand partner, Carlo Pitello, was visibly pleased, but I paid dearly with continued hostility from a few of the others in the section. In the music world, it is said that the mellow nature of the cello produces warm, friendly cellists. That is not always the case.

A few days later I received a letter from the Kosciuszko Foundation awarding me their annual prize for a Polish musician in New York, and with it, a check for $500. After the humiliating experience in the president's office, I was surprised by their show of generosity and was tempted to tear up the check and send it straight back. But, I did need the money very badly. Anyway, I was sure Halina Rodzinski and Arthur Rubinstein were behind the grant and I didn't want to appear ungrateful, or worse, create a mini-scandal in the Polish-American community.

For the next couple of months, that check helped me to provide a comfortable standard of living for Piotr, and by extension, Regina. I longed for news about my son, but received none. I wrote letters to him and asked his mother to read them aloud. That was wishful thinking. Regina probably never even reminded Piotr that he has a father at all. I also sent money and news to my parents, but not to Zdzisław, who had punished me mercilessly with his lies and abuse for so many years. My brother openly hated me all my life and that wasn't easy to forget. Besides, he had become a skilled electronics technician and I was confident he would find work.

Sure enough, in Mother's next letter she wrote, *Zdzisław got a well-paying job at a television station in Warsaw.* For her sake, I was glad.

❧

Because Dezso Vaghy was a serious, detail-oriented fellow whose sole ambition was the promotion of his quartet, the business dealings for the group fell squarely on his shoulders. In the second week of March we had two important concerts, one at Greeley College in Colorado, and the other in Portland at the University of Maine. Unbeknownst to the rest of us, Greeley and U Maine were recruiting for resident string quartet and music faculty positions. Without consulting the other three members, Dezso decided it was in the best interest of the group to audition for these jobs. I had no idea.

The local reviews were full of praise, and a week after our concerts both schools made offers. There was an excited lilt in Dezso's voice when he shared the news with us, and my colleagues were ecstatic about the prospect of a steady paycheck. After a brief conversation, they chose Portland and gloated about the fabulous opportunity, ready to pack their things. I was speechless. I couldn't imagine living in such a provincial town, even though people familiar with Portland claimed it was a cultural beacon. All I saw was a residential community undergoing an unsightly mix of demolition and construction. Worst of all, at night the streets were empty. No way. I loved New York and didn't want to leave it. Of course, I understood that being on the faculty of a university would be prestigious, and for this reason alone I was momentarily tempted. I tried to be supportive of my colleagues and did not immediately refuse the job, but deep down I knew it would never work.

The decision was made for me at the end of the month. The New York Philharmonic—which I first heard while hiding in the wings of Carnegie Hall watching Leonard Bernstein command the stage—announced an opening in its cello section. My cello professor Maurice Eisenberg, who earned a spot as principal cellist of the New York Symphony as an adolescent in 1918, urged me to seize the moment.

He said, "In this country you need to hustle, take chances. There is no government behind you. You are on your own. Go and play. It will be a good experience."

I contacted the Philharmonic orchestra manager Joseph DeAngelis, and was accepted to audition.

When I arrived, there were several dozen candidates. Each of us played individually in front of the jury of musicians. I was grateful for my orchestral training in Warsaw and my familiarity with symphonic repertoire. The jury advanced me to the semi-finals and then on to the finals. I was so close to securing a spot with the New York Philharmonic, I could taste it.

Mr. DeAngelis summoned me and one other fellow to his office and said, "The final decision is in the hands of the Philharmonic's music director Leonard Bernstein, who is in Europe now. You will have to wait until his return in the fall. Mr. Zawistowski, can you please stay for a moment?"

After the other finalist left, DeAngelis asked, "The Philharmonic needs a cellist for our post-season summer Stravinsky Festival. Are you available?"

"Yes, with pleasure!" I was so excited and told everybody. Well, except for the Vaghys.

By that time I couldn't keep my decision to stay in New York to myself any longer. Naturally, Dezso, Tibor and Ron assumed I would be joining them for the big move. I fortified myself with a couple of glasses of wine and confronted them the next night over dinner.

"I auditioned for the Philharmonic and there is good chance I will get the job," I blurted out uncomfortably. Then I said, nearly choking on the words, "I won't join you in Portland."

As expected, Dezso and Tibor were livid, cursing me in Hungarian. They had no idea I was thinking of jumping ship, and Dezso had already signed a contract with the University of Maine.

"You didn't give us fair warning," they accused me, and I responded with the same argument right back.

"You not tell me concerts were auditions." Still, I felt bad.

My relationship with the Vaghy String Quartet ended on that sour note, but I was extremely relieved to hear that they soon found a replacement cellist and fulfilled their contract without me.

The 1966 Met season ended on April 16, which marked its final performance in the historic, old Metropolitan Opera House. The life of this grand theater came to an end in a blaze of glory with a spectacular gala concert. After the summer the company would be moving to its new home in Lincoln Center. In the meantime, the Met was preparing for its annual spring tour. The American Symphony season was also over and, of course, I had broken ties with the quartet. The only job on my calendar before fall was the short, three-week stint with the New York Philharmonic, but that wouldn't begin until June. I was facing two months of unemployment and had no savings.

Just as suddenly as my financial situation teetered, Eyle called. He needed an additional cellist for the Met's post-season tour and wanted to know if I was free. The timing was perfect. It was a good thing Eyle did not deliver the news in person, or I would have grabbed him by his sweater-vest and kissed him squarely on the cheek. Not only would I be traveling with this great company, I would be saved from financial ruin.

Two days past my twenty-eighth birthday we boarded the company trains bound for Boston. Our home for the next six weeks would be a couple of sturdy iron horses, one for the orchestra and ballet, and the other for the chorus, stagehands and additional Met personnel. After Boston we would ride the rails to Detroit, Cleveland, Atlanta and Minneapolis, spending a week in each, and would split a week between Memphis and Dallas. We played eight performances every Monday through Saturday, each of a different opera—*Il Trovatore*, *Andrea Chénier*, *Il Barbiere di Siviglia*, *Faust*, *Pique Dame*, *Lucia di Lammermoor*, *Don Giovanni* and *La Bohème*. While the workload was challenging, the pay was fantastic. I would be making $190 per week for the privilege of performing with a who's who of world-famous singers: Renata Tebaldi, Gabriella Tucci, Roberta Peters, Anna Moffo, Dorothy Kirsten, Regina Resnik, my muse Teresa Stratas, Franco Corelli, Richard Tucker, Jon Vickers, Sandor Konya, Nicolai Gedda, Robert Merrill and Cesare Siepi. I would have a front row seat at the most spectacular productions performed on the American operatic stage every night.

Our train trips from city to city bordered on the bacchanal, a cross between the lustful spirit of eighteenth-century French opera and a pre-adolescent American Boy Scout camping trip. We were all given sleeper compartments for the journey, and as soon as the train whistle sounded, there began a bout of drinking, gambling and screwing. One car was occupied by poker players who never slept; the dining cars were packed day and night with the intoxicated; and the passageways in between housed our bedrooms, almost all with their privacy curtains drawn. To walk down these corridors was to encounter an inevitable chorus of moaning and screams of delight. Just like my tours with the Warsaw Philharmonic, I was usually found among the drinkers. I never understood the frivolity of gambling away one's hard-earned money and I was too chivalrous to be a playboy.

We typically arrived at a new station early in the morning, with no time to recover from the evening's revelries. Orchestra members and stagehands alike looked like zombies, stumbling out of compartments to collect their belongings, often forgetting where they left their clothes. Dancers in pointe shoes and negligees hobbled past brass players in their underwear, all of them squinting in the early morning light.

In Atlanta, two of the young members of the orchestra, percussionist Herb Baker and bassoonist Lenny Hindell, invited me to join them at an inexpensive, out-of-the-way Southern diner to nurse our hangovers. How peculiar, I thought, the place is packed with men only. There isn't a single woman in sight. Behind the counter stood the restaurant boss, a very heavy-set man with a crimson face from the heat of the griddle and an unusually thick neck that threatened to burst when he barked at the line cooks and waiters. We ordered and my colleagues were served coffee almost immediately. But not I. Their breakfasts arrived a few minutes later, but still nothing for me.

Herb called a waiter over and asked, "Hey, what's going on? Where's his food?"

The owner maneuvered in front of me and with his knuckles on the counter he leaned forward, his arms flanking my empty place setting like a silverback gorilla.

Then he spit out his answer. "I don't serve people from the North!"

My colleagues erupted in laughter, nearly choking on their food.

Lenny decided to taunt the big guy and spoke in a loud voice for a wider audience to hear, "Hey mister, don't worry, he's not a Yankee. He's a foreigner . . . from RUSSIA!"

Forks fell and the whole establishment quieted down. There were one hundred eyes staring at me like I was an alien from outer space. And then they turned to look at the boss, whose blood drained from his face down to his protuberant chin. In the middle of Atlanta, at the height of the Cold War's "Red Scare," a fearsome Russian suddenly dropped from the sky expecting eggs and bacon. The boss elbowed the closest waiter who, with his hands shaking, quickly served me a cup of coffee. And in short order, my hot breakfast arrived.

After the incident in the diner everyone in the orchestra called me the "Polish Yankee."

My friends from the tour had a lot of fun with me, and my European ways. I was a Polack; a living Polish joke. In Minneapolis I brought them to a shoe store to help with a possible purchase. Typical American men's shoes looked very klutzy, with soles so thick they could be used for coal mining, or working a farm. I did find a handsome Italian pair and tried them on, to the dismay of my colleagues.

"Are you crazy?" they balked. "This is embarrassing. Look at those pointy tips. They're only good for killing cockroaches in corners!"

On Tuesday afternoon during our week in Detroit, Lenny and Herb took me to my first baseball game. The Detroit Tigers were hosting the Boston Red Sox at Tiger Stadium, known as "The Corner," where home plate once stood at the intersection of Michigan Avenue and Trumbull Boulevard, in an historic section of town. In Poland I loved the fast-moving games of European soccer and English rugby, whose teams were composed of young and very athletic players. I never saw this American sport and didn't know the first thing about it. When Lenny and Herb told me it is played with a ball and a bat, I thought, *This is going to be interesting*.

The stadium was full of aggressive spectators wearing those ugly American shoes and crushing through the entry gates as if they were rushing to catch a train. I decided to root for the Boston team because one of their players was a Polish-American left fielder, Carl Yastrzemski. Most of the crowd was supporting the Tigers, of course. A local celebrity sang an off-key rendition of the National Anthem, and then a bunch of guys emerged from inside the stadium to thunderous applause. From what I could tell, the players were older than I was and slightly overweight. They sprinted onto the field wearing funny-looking outfits that looked like long johns. I wondered if they were still in their pajamas.

The game began and I tried to figure out the roles of the pitcher and batter. The pitcher throws the ball and the guy with the club is supposed to try to hit it. The pitcher stares down the batter; the batter spits into his palm. The pitcher spits at the dirt; the batter steps up to the plate. The pitcher stands stock-still on a mound of dirt, nods his head 'yea' or 'nay,' and after all these quirky antics, eventually, he throws the ball. One pitch comes after another, with long breaks of spitting and hoofing the dirt in between, and more often than not the batter swings and misses. The fans were going crazy, but I grew less and less interested. Two hours passed and nobody on the Boston team could hit the ball. What kind of ball game is it if men in long johns can't hit the goddamned ball?

The crowd occasionally roared in upswells of emotion, and my friends yelled, "Leszek, wake up! This is an incredible game!"

For me it was like playing a four-hour Baroque opera. Boring, boring, boring. The Tigers won the game 8-0 in a shutout. A shutout was exciting? Only one side scored and the other couldn't even hit the ball?! My colleagues insisted baseball was an athletic, strategic, and marvelous team sport. You couldn't have convinced me of that in 1966.

In every city, patrons of local Metropolitan Opera clubs threw lavish fêtes for the company. After our first performance in Cleveland I was introduced to a few wealthy Poles who attended this particular party, and before I knew it, I found myself being introduced to the Cleveland Zawistowskis. There stood my American cousins, in the flesh.

They announced to everyone within earshot, "We are so proud of Leszek. What a perfect time it is for a family reunion!"

I stared at them in disbelief. These same cousins, who were shaking my hand and grasping my shoulders with foolish grins on their faces, had no time to meet me when I was a desperate Polish cellist with the Warsaw Philharmonic not so long ago. Now that I am traveling in the distinguished company of the famous Metropolitan Opera, they are ready to welcome me into the family bosom. A cold chill ran through my veins.

Stiffening I said, "I am sorry. You must be mistaken. I do not have any family in the U.S."

Their faces fell in confusion and embarrassment.

With a brusque, "Goodnight," I turned around and left.

I was conflicted after this encounter. Perhaps it would have been good to connect with some family. They might not have realized the profound effect of their rebuke. Ultimately, I decided that I am too proud to forget—or forgive— their treatment of me when I had been so vulnerable.

Those six weeks on tour came to an end faster than I would have liked. It was hard work, but I bonded with many of the musicians from the orchestra and felt at home among them. Carlo had become close and was the ideal stand partner. He knew all the ins and outs of orchestra playing and was happy to share his knowledge and experience.

As soon as I got home, with barely any time to catch my breath, I began rehearsing with the New York Philharmonic for the Stravinsky Festival. Lorne

Munroe, the principal cellist, greeted me warmly when I showed up on the first day, but he was really the only congenial member of the orchestra I came across. Unlike the Met, there was a cutthroat competitive edge that dominated this orchestra, and the atmosphere was very tense as a result. The New York Philharmonic was an exceptionally fine ensemble, but as an outsider, I felt uncomfortable and scrutinized.

Shortly after the Stravinsky Festival ended, Carlo invited me for dinner and shared some unexpected news, "There is a contract opening in the cello section of the Met. One of our cellists went to buy new shoes for the opening night performance in Lincoln Center. The poor guy collapsed in the store with a massive heart attack and died. The audition for the position is in two weeks."

Carlo urged me to give it a try and not wait for Bernstein's Philharmonic decision.

"You are young and independent. The Met's performance structure is flexible and allows musicians to accept outside engagements, like playing chamber music concerts. Symphony orchestra contracts are much more restrictive. Besides, the Metropolitan Opera Orchestra is like a family."

I already felt like one of them and took Carlo's advice.

There were roughly twenty players competing for the job in front of a jury of string section principals and a group of conductors. I played the most difficult, flashy pieces from my solo repertoire and sight-read various opera excerpts. After finishing, I paced up and down the corridors for at least an hour, which seemed like an eternity, and was finally asked to return to the audition room.

The jury surrounded me, and Eyle in his typically restrained manner said, "Congratulations Mr. Zawistowski, you got the job."

My heart began to race and I felt light-headed. Less than two years after my defection, I was hired as a full-time member of the Metropolitan Opera Orchestra. I could not believe my ears. There were welcoming smiles and enthusiastic handshakes from everyone.

Carlo was beaming and said, "Come home with me to celebrate!"

We spent the evening exchanging stories and drinking one martini after another until I collapsed on his couch. I woke up the next morning with a fabulous new job and a major hangover. Little firecrackers kept going off in my head making it hard for me to think straight. Piecing together my fuzzy thoughts, I realized that I would now be playing in the grand opening night performance of the new Metropolitan Opera House in Lincoln Center. I couldn't wait.

24

Lincoln Center

It was a spirited summer in New York, with anti-war protests, the Black Power movement and mini-skirts dominating the news, and I was starting to feel nostalgic for my escapades with the Met Orchestra that had ended in June. The gala performance of the Met's inaugural season in Lincoln Center was scheduled for September 16, 1966, with *Antony and Cleopatra*, the world premiere of a commissioned work by American composer Samuel Barber. Designed and directed by the glamorous Italian, Franco Zeffirelli, the production was billed as one of the most extravagant spectacles in operatic history. An all-American roster of over twenty singers, featuring soprano Leontyne Price as Cleopatra and bass Justino Diaz as Antony, was joined on the stage by three hundred thirty additional cast members and a team of horses, camels and goats.

The new Met would become the largest opera theater in the world, with three thousand seven hundred eighty-eight seats and state-of-the-art acoustics uncompromised by the size of the space. Forty-five and a half million dollars endowed a technological marvel of stagecraft, as well as very comfortable working conditions for everybody. No more roaches crawling over the music, or mice underfoot. The first time I entered the theater, I lifted my gaze from the lustrous red and gold interior to the ceiling, and had to catch my breath. Above me twenty-one chandeliers were floating, like celestial fireworks, with one thousand bursting metal rods housing forty-nine thousand individual pieces of crystal. They were a gift from the Austrian government and fabricated by the world's preeminent crystal company, Swarowski. Especially captivating was the main chandelier, the largest starburst of all, hanging one hundred feet off the floor and stretching eighteen feet in diameter across the ceiling. These chandeliers, which came to be known as "sputniks," symbolized our entrance into a new age—a space age—and standing under them I was transported.

I exited the theater with stars in my eyes and turned around. Two massive oil paintings framed either side of the entrance, measuring thirty by thirty-six feet. They were painted by the internationally-renowned Russian artist Marc Chagall, in gratitude for the American hospitality he received after fleeing Nazi-occupied Europe. He named the works *The Sources of Music* and *The Triumph of Music*. I snuck out to the front of the house a few times to watch in awe as Mr. Chagall put the finishing touches on the canvases that conveyed a story of the power of music. With a messy clump of silver hair atop his head, there he stood at the age of seventy-nine, perched on the scaffolding and looking as if he were ascending into the clouds. He reminded me so much of my father, a quiet and mild-mannered gentleman decked out in gray slacks with a shirt and tie under his painter's smock, meticulously attending to his craft. I felt like I was ten years old again, watching my father work, both of us in peace. Chagall noticed that I was peering up at him and asked me something in French. In my poor English I said I only spoke Polish and Russian.

He smiled broadly and asked in perfect Russian, "Are you a singer?" I laughed at the thought.

"No, I am a cellist from Poland," I responded in his native tongue. "I escaped from my country and just got this job."

He replied, "I also left my country, but that was a long time ago. You are a courageous boy. Good luck!"

I didn't try to prolong our chat for fear he might fall off the towering scaffolding. *What a privilege,* I thought after speaking to this great artist, *to be at the right place and time in the history of the Met.*

For weeks the entire company was immersed in a whirlwind of preparations before christening the new hall. The orchestra rehearsed in an oversized, high-ceilinged room, paneled in beautiful blond ash on three of its walls. On the fourth was a Raoul Dufy mural depicting a French sidewalk café scene with the Paris Opera in the background. Our rehearsal schedule began with Richard Strauss's masterpiece, *Die Frau ohne Schatten* (*A Woman Without a Shadow*), conducted by Karl Böhm, an iconic figure in the classical music world. He was a champion and colleague of the elder Strauss and used the composer's original score. A bespectacled, stern-looking German, he sat with his butt on the edge of a tall stool on the podium and occasionally lifted his body off the stool to emphasize a particular phrase.

Die Frau was an incredibly intense work and perfectly suited to the temperamental maestro. In the third act, Strauss wrote a melodic solo line for the two fourth-stand cellists, in this case, Carlo and me. For some reason, when we got to this section in the music, Carlo froze and stopped playing. Having never played the piece, or even heard it, I followed his lead. We sat motionless, looking at the podium. Böhm rose from his chair, his posture as stiff as a commandant, and was seething. The livid maestro slammed down his baton and lashed out at us in his heavy accent, "Vot are you doink? Vot, vot are you doink dehr?!?"

Carlo started to tremble uncontrollably, visibly upset by the tyrannical conductor's ire. Somehow, I was not intimidated and answered back, "Maestro, vot you vant us doink?"

You could hear a pin drop. All eyes were on me, the insane Polish cellist who dared make fun of Böhm's English pronunciation. Böhm seemed to swell on the podium, like Godzilla standing up, the corners of his mouth descending into a menacing scowl.

Gniewek quickly got up from his seat between Böhm and me and said, "Maestro, Mr. Zawistowski is not mocking you. He just came from Poland and this is the way he speaks. Like you. Please understand."

Böhm digested that for a moment and then, as suddenly as he fell into a rage, he burst forth with a hearty laugh and the tension was broken. From that day on, Maestro Böhm kept his eye on me and I was always well-prepared. Off the podium he was friendly and occasionally asked about my English.

I had such high regard for Carlo's absolute professionalism and his ability as a cellist, but I didn't understand why he stopped playing at the beginning of that cello passage. One of my colleagues explained in private.

"Whenever Carlo has a solo, even a few notes, he has an attack of nerves. Carlo was brilliant when he was young, a successful cellist. After the U.S. got into the war, he was drafted and assigned to a commando intelligence unit responsible for risky assault missions. He was sent behind enemy lines. The experience took such a heavy psychological toll on him that even in peacetime he could no longer function as a soloist. Too much pressure. He loved to play, but could only do so with an ensemble."

It was sad for me to think this warm, joyous man was harboring terrible demons. Carlo loved people and he continually delighted me with amusing stories from his past. My favorite was his encounter with Albert Einstein. Professor Einstein was an amateur violinist and relished playing string quartets for pleasure. Princeton University made every effort to please their illustrious scientist and invited top New York City players to join him for informal chamber music sessions. One of these musicians was Carlo. When he returned from his first trip to Princeton, his colleagues were eager to hear all about it.

"Did you really play with that mathematical genius? Tell us everything. What was he like? Was he any good?"

Carlo responded nonchalantly, "As a matter of fact, the afternoon was not fun at all. Einstein kept losing his place in the music. The professor simply cannot count!"

As we approached opening night, during most rehearsal breaks the orchestra held long meetings that made my colleagues unusually tense and agitated. Two brass players were stationed in the doorway of the meeting room and they refused to allow me inside. I wasn't used to such hostility from my colleagues who were normally so friendly.

"The order was issued by the chairman of the orchestra committee. You know, he is a power hungry violist," one of them said under his breath.

It was horrible to be singled out. I felt insignificant and uncomfortable standing in the hallway by myself and asked Carlo what was going on.

"The orchestra has been performing for two and a half years without a contract and is now negotiating a new agreement with the management," Carlo explained.

After the dress rehearsal of *Antony and Cleopatra* on Tuesday, September 13, representatives from the orchestra and the musician's union went public with an announcement: "The Metropolitan Opera Orchestra will go on strike, but not until the day after the opening night gala."

Max Arons, the union president, made a statement to the press. "The first performance of the Metropolitan Opera in its new Lincoln Center home is our gift to the world of music and to the cause of the performing arts in America."

Coming from a Communist country, I was never involved in a labor dispute and for me, the thought of it was horrifying. In Poland a strike meant a one-way ticket to prison, or worse, to a dark grave in Siberia. All of my friends, except Lydia, tried to reassure me that such protests are normal.

"Forget about Poland. This is America," they said.

Lydia, on the other hand, was mindful that I still didn't have residency status and urged me to refrain from making any comments about the dispute.

In the days leading up to opening night, in front of Lincoln Center and by the stage door, orchestra members formed picket lines displaying large posters and held signs screaming of unfair labor practices. New York was abuzz with chatter in restaurants, bars and subway cars. "The musicians are sabotaging the opening season of the new Met," was the refrain heard from one end of the city to the other.

Most of my friends were as uninformed about the issues as I was and unsympathetic to the strike. I was very confused.

Since my Met paychecks had already begun coming in, one day, on a whim, I decided to buy a brand new tuxedo for opening night. Walking down Broadway toward my favorite store—Macy's—I watched my colleagues demonstrating for their rights and got a sick feeling in the pit of my stomach. I didn't want Friday night to be the last time I wore formal attire and played with the Metropolitan Opera.

When I reached Thirty-ninth Street, what I saw left me stunned. Where the old Metropolitan Opera House once stood, the grande dame of American culture, there was nothing but rubble. The front of the building, as well as the auditorium, had been demolished. Only the stage, basking in the noonday sun and surrounded by a few patron's boxes, was left intact. Gaping into this ruined chamber, I imagined the ghosts of Enrico Caruso and Amelita Galli-Curci rising from the smoke and standing triumphantly before adoring crowds.

On the occasion of the Met's final performance in this legendary theater, Leopold Stokowski stood on the podium and pleaded with any who would listen, "I beg you to help save this magnificent house."

His words fell on deaf ears. Now, in one blow a massive wrecking ball was released from its clutch, obliterating a huge portion of the southern wall, which went crashing down onto the stage right before my eyes.

I blinked and was suddenly transported twenty years into the past, returning to the streets of Warsaw as a seven-year-old boy after my wartime exile, only to find the city in a state of total devastation, the air thick with dust and debris. Standing alone on the edge of the sidewalk, with tears streaming down my cheeks, I felt like I was attending the funeral of a friend who had been abandoned by an unfeeling world. The pedestrians around me paid no attention, oblivious to the destruction in progress. They continued to move in deliberate forward motion, each in his, or her, own world. Eventually, I also had to turn away from the scene. I pocketed my sadness and slowly made my way downtown toward Macy's. After passing through its big, revolving doors I headed straight for the elevator.

This time I asked the operator, with extremely careful enunciation, "Sixth floor, please."

On the greatest night in the modern history of the Metropolitan Opera, I arrived at Lincoln Center in my slick tuxedo more than an hour before the performance was to begin. I wanted to savor every exciting minute of the evening. The image of the new house, resplendent at sunset, was magical. With all its lights ablaze, Chagall's brilliant paintings facing the plaza for thousands of people to enjoy, the sumptuous red and gold interiors, and the chandeliers drizzling gilt onto its spectators like champagne bubbles, it was the unfolding of a fairy tale.

Among the attendees were Lady Bird Johnson, the First Lady of the United States, with Imelda Marcos and her husband, the Philippine president Ferdinand Marcos, and an impressive assembly of international and American dignitaries. The diamonds, rubies, emeralds and gold bursting from the audience competed with the brilliant sparkles from the chandeliers. Marylou Whitney alone was said to have two thousand diamonds oozing out of her tiara.

The lights dimmed, Thomas Schippers lifted his baton, and we raised our instruments to play the American national anthem. The audience stood en masse, proud to sing their country's praises. When the final note sounded, one voice held the high B flat longer than anyone in the audience, to the amusement of everyone.

Carlo turned to me and said, "That's the one and only Licia Albanese, Toscanini's favorite soprano. She is never to be outdone."

The powerful conclusions of each act of *Antony and Cleopatra* were, however, less dramatic than the behind-the-scenes tension building offstage. During both intermissions the orchestra convened in the rehearsal room.

"The negotiations are off limits to you," I was told again.

By the end of the second intermission, the musicians emerged with smiles of victory brightening their faces. We all took our seats in the pit, and before the last act curtain went up, Rudolph Bing, General Manager of the Met, strode onto the stage in his dignified, patrician manner.

"It gives me pleasure to announce that a new contract agreement has been reached with the orchestra. There will be no strike!"

The thousands of society aristocrats, bankers, diplomats and glamorous members of the audience exploded in cheers. Throughout the first two acts, the public was decidedly reserved in their applause for Samuel Barber's music, but they gave Mr. Bing a thunderous ovation. I still didn't understand what had happened in that room.

At the end of the performance Carlo said, "Bravo, you are now a member of the highest paid orchestra in the world."

"Excuse me, what you said?" I asked, thinking I must have misunderstood.

Carlo filled me in on the details of the new contract.

"By the final year of our three-year agreement, the minimum weekly pay for a musician will be $355. In addition, the number of performances per week for each of us is reduced from seven to five. There will be four weeks paid vacation and full medical insurance, with fifty-two weeks sick leave after ten years of service."

He went on and on.

In Poland there was no such thing as "negotiation." Under Communism, contracts are drawn up with no input from workers, whether they are musicians or garbage collectors.

This was my first encounter with democracy in the American workplace and I told Carlo, "Is too good to be true."

"Believe it," he said. Then, with a slap on my back, "Welcome to America."

25

Departures

By October of 1967, I was insanely busy with the Metropolitan Opera, the American Symphony and my own solo concerts. I didn't have a moments rest during the day, was performing in the evenings, and had puffy, dark circles under my eyes. There was really no time for Juilliard. Though I never took for granted the important role the school played as my lifeline, my heart wasn't in my studies. With the encouragement of Professor Eisenberg and Lydia—who told me my green card was all but assured—I withdrew. At the age of twenty-eight, my student days were finally over.

As a result, I had to move out of International House. My departure was bittersweet, but I was more than ready to put down roots in my own apartment. With the help of some Met orchestra colleagues, I found a duplex at 211 West Seventieth Street on the third and fourth floors of a brownstone. It was five blocks from the Met, and I fell in love with it at first sight. The narrow foyer led to a large living room with a kitchenette off to one side and a flight of steps to a second-story bedroom and bathroom. There were two tall windows downstairs facing south that filled the place with cheerful sunlight for most of the day. The monthly rent was less than one week of my salary, so I signed the lease without hesitating, thrilled to find my own hideaway in that jungle of a city.

The Met issued a series of commemorative posters by Marc Chagall in honor of its opening season at Lincoln Center. One was a detail taken from "*The Triumph of Music*," ablaze with red in the spirit of *Carmen*, and the other a forest scene from *Die Zauberflöte* (*The Magic Flute*) with a blue angel playing her trumpet to the creatures below. Together they were a perfect combination to enhance the ambience in my living room. I stood a few feet away, admiring my diptych and thinking of Mother. She must have had a similar feeling when she went scavenging for a piece of art in the streets of Warsaw and came back with the kitschy pastoral tapestry that she proudly hung on our wall. I smiled at the thought.

In typical Halina fashion, she set to the task of helping me with furnishings. Knowing that Nela and Arthur Rubinstein were about to move out of their luxurious apartment on Park Avenue, Halina took me there hoping to collect some hand-me-downs. When we arrived, Nela led us straight to her overstocked kitchen.

"Please take anything you'd like," she said, sounding anxious to unload as much as possible. "We've already moved what we are keeping."

The cabinet doors were all open and empty. Piled high on the counters were dishes and glassware galore, small appliances, utensils of all variety, a smorgasbord of cookware. Julia Child would have cooed at the sight. Halina urged me not to hold back, and by the end of our visit I managed to equip my entire kitchen with the Rubinsteins' unwanted inventory. The most precious items I took were a set of crystal wine glasses and a marvelous mint green, hand-cranked stainless steel juicer that weighed as much as a cement block.

I settled into my bachelor pad in no time, living on my own and supporting my family in Poland with ease. I loved establishing a household routine that began with mornings of freshly squeezed oranges from the Rubinsteins' juicer and a copy of *The New York Times*. *The Times* was a constant presence in my home and the best English teacher. I purchased it at the corner deli every day and poured over its pages with a dictionary by my side, trying to absorb as much news as I could about my new country and world events. Most disturbing was the news about the Vietnam War and reports that so many people my age and younger were dying in the fields. I shared American's hatred for Communism, but did not think war was the way to rid the region of that evil. I strongly believed the day would come when the millions of oppressed would rise together against Communism and liberate themselves.

I invited friends to celebrate November 15, the two-year anniversary of my flight to freedom, and my personal Thanksgiving Day. I labored for days, using the Rubinsteins' fancy pots and pans to make traditional *bigos*, simmering the sauerkraut, cabbage, grated sour apples and garlic, pork shoulder, bacon, Black Forest ham, sausage and smoked goose, wild mushrooms, juniper berries, peppercorns and a bottle of Madeira until it exploded with the flavors of Eastern Europe. For the time being my spirits lifted.

As expected, with the approach of the holiday season came a flood of thoughts about Piotr. Other than my mother's letters, the only communication I had from Poland came in the form of official currency receipts from the agency that sent my dollars to Regina. I didn't exist, except to provide money. Mother contacted Regina a couple of times, hoping to visit her grandson, but Regina refused her requests. Instead, my mother went to Piotr's school occasionally to sneak a look at him on the playground through the fence. She wrote to me afterward, *He is so handsome and seems very healthy and happy.* Her words helped, but they weren't enough to fill the void in my heart.

Walking to work at the Met on Christmas and New Years nights, I recognized a familiar nostalgia on the faces of cab drivers, bellhops, deli clerks and delivery boys, street poets and painters I passed along the way. Like me, they probably had roots far from the tiny island that lured us to her shores, and we wandered the city blocks with mixed expressions of burden and bliss remembering the lives we left behind. In my reverie, I thought about the year before when I was cheerfully stringing lights with Steffi and Melanie across every corner of their home. A few days after the New Year, Luther called to tell me Steffi was terribly ill. She kept it a secret from her family for as long as she could, but finally had to unmask the truth. Her body was riddled with cancer. Melanie was only nine years old. I tried to believe in a miracle.

Professionally though, my life was flourishing. Stokowski asked me to play the solo part of the Bacewicz Cello Concerto for him again, which he remembered from my audition. After hearing it for the second time, he decided to program its New York premiere performance with the American Symphony. Since only one set of parts existed, and they were in Warsaw, our orchestra manager David Katz wrote to Poland requesting to borrow the music (standard procedure between orchestras). Katz's letter included the fact that I would be the cello soloist. The answer came three months later: *We will not loan you the parts.* End of story. Of course they wouldn't cooperate. After all, I was a persona non grata, an enemy of the Polish People's Republic. The project didn't happen, and in reality, I had no regrets. My focus had shifted dramatically to my job as a regular member of the Metropolitan Opera Orchestra, and that was more than satisfying.

Late May brought the devastating news that Steffi was dying. The mounting hospital bills forced Luther to hustle for extra work in order to keep up with the payments. Melanie had to grow up overnight. She assumed the responsibilities of the household, taking care of her beloved mother, cleaning, shopping, cooking, and playing host to Steffi's coterie of devoted companions who visited frequently. At two o'clock on the morning of June 3, surrounded by family and friends, Steffi died. This beautiful woman, a great wife and mother, with such an indomitable spirit, was only forty-seven years old. She had been so good to me. It was a tragic loss for Melanie and Luther, and also for me.

Two days later I was confronted by a different kind of bombshell. On page one of *The New York Times* was a headline in bold type announcing the attack on Israel by Arab armies. The horrors of World War II, and my brother's death in Auschwitz those many years ago, came rushing back. What was to become of my Jewish friends and colleagues from Poland who had emigrated to Israel? After suffering untold harm at the hands of the Nazis, again their lives were in mortal danger. The shock was not mine to endure alone. Tension and fear cast a dark cloud over all of New York City. The prevailing question on so many people's minds was, '*Is Israel on the brink of a second Holocaust?*'

Without waiting for the inevitable invasion, Israel destroyed the heart of Egypt's Air Force, dealing the first of many fatal blows to Arab attempts to defeat it. In only six days the Israeli Army prevailed. *The Times* printed emotional scenes of victorious Israelis praying and weeping at the Wailing Wall. They also reported that Poland summarily broke diplomatic relations with the State of Israel. This coincided with a renewed wave of anti-Semitism in Poland that was beyond my comprehension. Father d'Anjou shared my outrage and issued an order to fly the Israeli flag atop the steeple of his Church of the Sacred Heart of Jesus in Port Chester, New York. It was a show of support for the Jewish community with whom he maintained close ties after leaving Poland. As a priest in America, he vigorously preached against intolerance and was proud to wave that flag over his church.

With the approach of summer, I was grateful that Professor Eisenberg had arranged for me to get away for a while to participate in an international music festival in Cascais and Estoril, Portugal, and to play a recital at the

International Cello Center in London. It made me sick to think that being relatively close to Poland, I wouldn't be able to visit Piotr and my parents. As a defector, the Polish government would have gladly taken me back in, locked me up, and thrown away the key. I did relish the idea of going back to Europe, nonetheless.

To get the necessary visas for Portugal and London, I had to have my U.S. residency papers, but they hadn't come through yet. I could not leave the country until they were finalized. Throughout the spring I showed up at the Immigration Office every week, hoping to expedite the process, but when the Met season ended I was still waiting for my damned green card.

An Immigration official advised me to buy my plane ticket for Portugal anyway because, according to him, "Your papers are in order and you will receive them soon."

His "soon" was not soon enough. My departure was less than two weeks away. Starting on the Monday before I was to leave, I went to the Immigration Office every day and waited. Nothing happened.

Finally, it was Friday and I had my ticket to fly to Lisbon on TWA the next day. As soon as their doors opened, I sat in the same uncomfortable wooden chair in the front office of the Director of Immigration with my heart pounding in my chest like a jackhammer. The secondhand on the clock lumbered forward in slow motion; it was hot and my dislike for the bureaucrats in the room began to turn to rage. At three o'clock I noticed a few of them shuffling stacks of papers and getting ready for the weekend. Still, I had no papers. The director's secretary put away her things and started to paint her fingernails, no doubt in preparation for some Friday night partying.

I approached her and asked, with as much restraint as I could manage, "Where my documents are?"

She did not lift her gaze from the stream of red polish bulging over the side of her cuticle and threatening to ruin the whole cosmetic endeavor.

"Listen," she said with obvious annoyance, "you don't have to wait around any longer. Come back Monday."

At this I lost my temper. Out of sheer desperation, I stormed past her desk and straight into the director's inner office. The secretary screamed, and before I knew it I felt the barrel of a gun pressing against my back.

"Raise your hands over your head."

Seated before me was a pleasant-looking young man, unfazed by my intrusion. He gave the security guy an order, "Leave us alone."

In a patient tone of voice he asked, "Now tell me, what is going on? What is the problem?"

Sweating profusely and very upset, I tried to explain, "I am concert cellist, member of Metropolitan Opera. I have invitation to play concerts in Portugal and London. I have plane ticket flying in few hours, expensive ticket. But I cannot leave country; I can do nothing without my papers. I wait for months, and for whole week I sit in office every day. I need U.S. papers!"

In a voice gushing with enthusiasm, the director said, "Please sit down. I am very happy to meet you. My wife and I love the cello and we attend Met performances all the time!"

While he was touting the many splendors of opera, he thumbed through a stack of documents in a box.

"Ahhhh," he said gleefully, "Here are your papers! Wait outside while I take care of the remaining minor details."

For the next few minutes the security guard watched me like a hawk and the secretary glowered. The seconds seemed like hours, and I half expected the director to flee the building down the fire escape from his office to avoid signing and stamping my forms. I had become so paranoid. Finally, the director came out of his office and personally handed me my documents.

"Mr. Zawistowski, congratulations! You are now a legal permanent resident of the United States. Have a nice flight. I wish you great success with your concerts and I hope to hear you play someday."

I stood there like a statue, numb. I meant to thank him, but the words never left my mouth. My two and a half year legal battle was actually over. I was so emotionally drained I couldn't even be joyous. Holding the precious papers close to my chest, in a daze I wandered out into the streets.

For all the years as a Polish student, a soloist and a member of the Warsaw Philharmonic, whenever I played concerts outside my country's borders, the government arranged my plane tickets, booked my hotels, organized my meals and practically scheduled my trips to the bathroom. I had to behave like an obedient child and didn't dare take a step out of line. And now, for the first time in my life, I am boarding a flight that I chose myself and paid for with my own money. *I can fly to the opposite end of the earth if I want to!*

Sitting in my seat as the plane idled on the runway, I began to feel very disoriented, not scared or excited, but unhinged, the same way I felt at the end of the war when I didn't have Rokossovsky to guide me or make decisions for me. I was just suddenly let loose.

A half-hour into our flight over the Atlantic, I started to cry out loud. My body was shaking involuntarily and I had a hard time catching my breath between sobs. The passengers around me called for help, but I was beyond help. Nothing the stewardess said made any sense, in fact, I couldn't even hear her through the pounding in my head.

"Is there anyone on the plane who speaks Polish? We need your assistance," she called on the intercom.

An elderly gentleman from first class appeared and asked in perfect Polish, "Are you sick, sir? What happened? Is something hurting you? I am a doctor. I can help you. Trust me."

He held my hand gently, made me look into his eyes, and in a soothing voice asked me to answer a simple question. "What is the matter?"

I looked up at him and said in Polish, "Doctor, I am free." And louder, "I am free!" And then I stood up on my feet, looked at all the passengers, and yelled, "*JA JESTEM WOLNY!*"

Everybody must have thought I was crazy. The doctor coaxed me back into my seat and ordered vodka for both of us.

Still holding my hand he asked, "What do you mean? We are all free here. Of course you are free."

I replied, "Two and a half years ago I defected from Poland, and now, for the first time ever, I bought my own plane ticket. I am flying across the Atlantic to another country, on my own, without anyone's permission. Do you understand what I'm telling you?"

The doctor gave me a vague nod and a paternal smile. I gulped down the vodka and felt better, but very embarrassed.

"Thank you so much, Doctor. Would you explain to everyone that I could not help myself? Please apologize for my outburst."

When we landed in Portugal I felt lighter than air. Eisenberg had arranged a very easy schedule for me, knowing how overworked and stressed I had been in New York. I stayed in a little villa by the sea, in the fishing town of Cascais, and had time for reflection and rest.

One of my concerts was at the Sintra National Palace, a medieval castle, preserved over the centuries as a national treasure. The entrance to the building and passage to the stage were lined with dozens of uniformed, armed soldiers, and military personnel were stationed throughout the hall. They carried machine guns and seemed on edge. It was a very upsetting scene and reminded me of my days with the Russians during the war. After the concert I was told that Portugal's infamous dictator Salazar was in the audience and demanded military protection at all times.

From Portugal I flew to London to play an all-Chopin program at the International Cello Center. It was my first visit to England since my days with the Warsaw Philharmonic, and it felt strange to be there again. Unpleasant memories came pouring forth and made me nostalgic for my nest in Manhattan. Before I knew it, I was on a plane bound for New York. The weeks abroad were therapeutic, but it felt wonderful to be back in my cozy apartment, looking forward to rehearsals at the Met.

We would open the season with the most fantastical production of Mozart's *Magic Flute*, designed by Marc Chagall. The repertoire also included two Wagner operas, *Die Walküre* and *Die Meistersinger*, and I had never played either. Herbert von Karajan, considered the greatest maestro in the world, was making his Metropolitan Opera debut as conductor, director and designer of the new, extremely dark production of *Walküre*. Maybe he was a fabulous conductor, but it was common knowledge that he had been an early card-carrying member of the Nazi Party. The mere anticipation of his arrival threw the company into a frenzy.

In the middle of the first rehearsal, one of the clarinetists played a note slightly off pitch, but Karajan didn't stop to correct it. Instead, during our break he marched straight into Rudolf Bing's office to register his complaint. Bing then had to call Eyle, as the personnel manager of the orchestra, who in turn, had to call for a special meeting of the orchestra committee, a group that was made up of the clarinetist's own peers. And finally, the poor clarinetist had to face the committee and be told about Karajan's dissatisfaction. In the orchestra world, when there are phrases that don't please the conductor he always confronts the musician directly to make the corrections. Not Karajan. He didn't want to soil his own hands. Such cowardly behavior doesn't exist between conductors and players who are making music together. Even though fear spread throughout the ranks of the orchestra, I wasn't intimidated by an arrogant ex-Nazi. And, as it turned out, neither was the soprano.

Singing the role of Brunnhilde was Birgit Nilsson, one of the opera world's most beloved Wagnerian sopranos, also known for her sharp wit and sense of humor. Karajan positioned her at the farthest depths of the dimly lit stage. As stage designer he insisted there be little light. When she was supposed to sing her first few notes, there was silence. We tried the passage again, and again, not a sound.

Karajan yelled at her impatiently, "Miss Nilsson, I cannot hear you!"

From almost total darkness, she yelled back, "Maestro, I cannot see you!"

The following morning, Nilsson appeared on stage for her entrance wearing a coal miner's helmet with a floodlight beaming directly at Karajan's baton. She had the last laugh. Karajan was not amused.

As the months passed, I immersed myself in learning new operas and grew more and more comfortable in my independence. I spent the evening of December 31, 1967, alone, without revelry or even a television for some boisterous company, but was content listening to the Budapest Quartet play Beethoven on my cheap radio. It didn't occur to me to feel sad. I had no inkling my life was about to change dramatically.

MAREK MAYEVSKI

SU. 7-1363

2 WEST 67TH STREET
NEW YORK 23, N. Y.

Marek Mayevski's calling card
(given to Leshek at Carnegie Hall the day before his defection), 1964

Leshek's first days in America, with Josef and Maria Mikrut, 1964

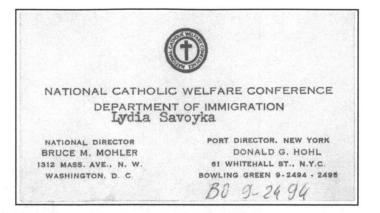

NATIONAL CATHOLIC WELFARE CONFERENCE
DEPARTMENT OF IMMIGRATION
Lydia Savoyka

NATIONAL DIRECTOR
BRUCE M. MOHLER
1312 MASS. AVE., N. W.
WASHINGTON, D. C.

PORT DIRECTOR, NEW YORK
DONALD G. HOHL
61 WHITEHALL ST., N.Y.C.
BOWLING GREEN 9-2494 - 2495

Lydia Savoyka's business card, 1964

Basia Hammerstein

Luther Henderson

Melanie, Steffi and Luther Henderson

Halina Rodzinski

LEOPOLD STOKOWSKI

16 March 65

Mr. Leszek Zawistowski is a well-schooled cellist, and
sensitive artist with a fine instrument. I can recommend
him with confidence for Chamber Music or Symphonic Music.

Maestro Leopold Stokowski's letter of recommendation, 1965

Feliks, Zdzisław and Michalina Zawistowski, c. 1965

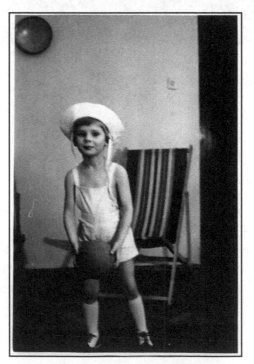

Piotr Zawistowski, c. 1966

Leshek (center) on the beach in Portugal, 1967

MINNEAPOLIS SYMPHONY ORCHESTRA STANISLAW SKROWACZEWSKI, MUSIC DIRECTOR • CABLE MINNORK
NORTHROP AUDITORIUM • MINNEAPOLIS, MINNESOTA 55455 RICHARD M. CISEK, GENERAL MANAGER • PHONE: 612/373-2525

April 22, 1965

To Whom It May Concern:

May I take this opportunity to recommend Mr. Leszek
Zawistowski who was for the last eight years the 'cellist
of the Warsaw Philharmonic. He now lives in the United States
and this year will obtain his Masters Degree from the Juilliard
School of Music.

I have known Mr. Zawistowski for several years as an excellent
instrumentalist. He first came to the Warsaw Philharmonic as
a young and very promising musician when I was conductor of that
orchestra, and very quickly he has developed his abilities to the
point that he became a solo 'cellist, giving many concerts.

He is also a very fine and reliable person.

Sincerely yours,

Music Director

SS:nmo

MAINTAINED BY THE MINNESOTA ORCHESTRAL ASSOCIATION: JUDSON BEMIS, PRESIDENT, CLARENCE R. CHANEY, EXECUTIVE VICE PRESIDENT, CLARKE BASSETT, VICE PRESIDENT, WENDELL T. BURNS, VICE PRESIDENT.

Maestro Stanislaw Skrowaczewski's letter, 1965

Metropolitan Opera SEASON 1965-1966

Tuesday Evening, September 28, 1965, at 8:00

SUBSCRIPTION PERFORMANCE
NEW PRODUCTION
FIRST TIME THIS SEASON

PETER ILICH TCHAIKOVSKY

Queen of Spades

Opera in three acts   Based on Pushkin
Libretto by Modeste Tchaikovsky
English translation by Boris Goldovsky
Conductor: Thomas Schippers
Staged by Henry Butler
Sets and costumes designed by Robert O'Hearn

The Countess	Regina Resnik
Lisa	Teresa Stratas
Pauline (Daphnis)	Rosalind Elias
Gherman	Jon Vickers
Count Tomsky	John Reardon (debut)
Prince Yeletsky	William Walker
Chekalinsky	Paul Franke
Surin	Lorenzo Alvary
Chaplinsky	Gabor Carelli
Narumov	Louis Sgarro
Master of Ceremonies	Gene Boucher (debut)
Chloë	Mary Ellen Pracht
Masha	Carlotta Ordassy

Act II, Scene 1—Ballet "The Faithful Shepherdess"
Choreography by Alicia Markova
Naomi Marritt, Ivan Allen and Corps de Ballet
Chorus Master: Kurt Adler
Musical Preparation: Martin Rich
The new production of QUEEN OF SPADES *was made possible*
by generous and deeply appreciated gifts from Mrs. Albert D. Lasker
and Mr. Francis Goelet

KNABE PIANO USED EXCLUSIVELY

The audience is respectfully, but urgently, requested
not to interrupt the music with applause

Leshek's first performance with the Metropolitan Opera, 1965

26

Daphnis and Chloe

On January 3, 1968, I had an American Symphony rehearsal with the eminent conductor Ernest Ansermet, well-known for establishing the Orchestre de la Suisse Romande. He was academic and boring when I worked with him in Warsaw and Montreux a decade ago, and couldn't possibly have any more pep now at the age of eighty-four. Even though the featured work on the program was the sublime *Daphnis and Chloe* Suite No. 2 by Ravel, I still wasn't expecting an inspired two and a half hours. At least I would be sitting on the first stand of the cello section in Carnegie Hall, a refreshing change from my position in the back at the Met. Taking my seat, I was immediately struck by a stunning new orchestra member in the front of the violin section only a few feet from me. *Who is that beautiful girl with her big, dark, sexy eyes and alluring movie star smile?* She looked vaguely familiar, but I was sure we never met.

I had recorded *Daphnis and Chloe* in Poland and practically knew the cello part by heart, so it was easy for me to disregard the conductor and stare at this compelling creature instead. She, on the other hand, was intently focused on the music. I envied Ansermet as the object of her periodic gaze and wanted to be the notes on the page in front of her that she studied with such devotion. It wasn't long before she noticed me gawking at her like a hungry child. At first she tried to ignore me, but I held my gaze, raised my eyebrows up and down, and clumsily flirted with my face. A couple of times she stared back, her expression pleading with me to stop, as if to say, *'Get lost, I'm trying to concentrate.'*

As the rehearsal progressed she grew increasingly frustrated, narrowed her eyes and worked really hard to get me out of her field of vision. I was annoying her, but I just couldn't help myself.

As soon as the intermission began I was drawn to her side like a magnet. Quickly thumbing through the pages of my mini Polish-English dictionary, I tried to apologize for my behavior.

"I am sorry . . . I feel lou-lousy to disturb you." This made her laugh.

"I thought I was doing something wrong, the way you were watching me," she said. Then, anticipating my question, she continued, "My name is Toni Rapport."

I realized immediately why she looked familiar. At the 1965 Aspen Music Festival, Toni was the violinist in the rival quartet. I tried to explain my recollection to her in English, but it came out as a rambling torrent of gibberish. Toni was smiling as I spoke and seemed charmed by my "lousy" English.

"You must be Polish or Russian," she concluded. "My mother came from Russia and last year I actually visited Warsaw myself. Today is my birthday, so please be nice and don't tease me while I play."

I promised not to, but I lied. I was powerless to look away.

After the rehearsal we went our separate ways, but I couldn't stop thinking about Toni, her voice, her laughter, and that pair of penetrating eyes. I was really infatuated. In Ravel's portrayal of passionate romance he composed a masterpiece, and throughout the rehearsals I played it for Toni with all my heart. When I could not resist looking at her, to my delight she sometimes looked back with a warm smile. What was she thinking? I desperately wanted to know.

On Sunday we played an afternoon concert. I gathered my courage and asked, "Will you go for drink with me at Carnegie Tavern after performance?"

"Okay," she said with a shy gleam in her eye. "But my friend Carol Adler is throwing a belated birthday dinner for me, so I can't stay too long."

Under a dreamy painting of Guilhermina Suggia playing the cello, we sat down, ordered martinis, and fell into a steady flow of enthusiastic conversation. From time to time I resorted to crazy gestures when my language skills betrayed me. We were so immersed in each other's company, we ordered a second round of cocktails without paying attention to the time. I was enchanted by every detail of every story and had no problem understanding her English. I remembered from Aspen that Toni had been in Jascha Heifetz' master class in Los Angeles.

"Tell me about that time," I insisted.

Toni was born in Los Angeles, California, and raised by a quiet father and a domineering mother who was admittedly a talented amateur pianist, but who tried to control her every move. Toni's mother Edith was obsessed with her daughter's studies and forbid her from having a social life. Toni was lonely and miserable and begged her parents for a dog.

"My father finally got me an adorable, caramel-colored cocker spaniel puppy and we named her Cinnamon Candy. Mother and 'Cindy' despised each other from the first day," Toni said, a little sadly. "Cindy hadn't been with us for more than a few months when Mother cooked a beef brisket one night. The minute she put the platter of meat on the table, Cindy jumped onto a chair, grabbed the brisket in her teeth and took off. I watched Mother catch her and give her a stinging slap across the face. In response, Cindy bit my mother on the hand. The following morning my poor dog was sent away forever."

Toni shook off that unhappy memory, but continued the subject of her mother, which was a Pandora's box of stories. In 1951, Edith—a member of Local 47 of the American Federation of Musicians—met the pioneering African-American double bass player and conductor Henry Lewis, also a union member, but of the "Jim Crow" wing, Local 767. Henry and Edith joined the campaign to amalgamate the two locals where they worked side by side and became friendly. One evening after a union protest, Edith invited Henry, nineteen years old, tall, handsome, and the youngest member of the Los Angeles Philharmonic Orchestra, to the house for a musicale. Toni was sick in bed with the flu, and Henry arrived with a long-stemmed red rose, which he presented to then nine-year-old Toni. She was bedazzled.

As Toni became more and more accomplished as a violinist, Henry, who also played the piano and was very astute, came over frequently to play sonatas with her and offer musical insights. Edith was ever-present and highly critical during these sessions and increasingly annoyed Henry, while the attachment between Toni and Henry grew.

Toni's face brightened as she went on with the story, "I was nineteen when Henry introduced me to his fiancée, Marilyn Horne, the world-renowned mezzo-soprano—known as 'Jackie' to her family and friends. Marilyn's brother

Dick, who wanted her to be a boy, insisted on calling her Jackie, and it stuck."

Initially, Henry brought Toni and Jackie together, but the connection between the women sprouted on its own. Toni described Jackie as unspoiled by her fame, gregarious and natural, with an infectious sense of humor and an amazing generosity of spirit. Since Jackie's career took her trotting all over the globe, from Europe to Japan to Australia and back to the States, much of the contact she and Toni had, and the confidences they shared, were over the phone. Jackie had become a deeply loyal, treasured friend.

Toni would often complain, to both Jackie and Henry, about her mother's antics. In time Henry became over-exposed to Edith, and in his infinite wisdom, urged Toni to flee as far as she could from her oppressive home life and pursue a promising career as a soloist elsewhere. After studying with Heifetz for three years, Toni was awarded a Fulbright Grant to London for chamber music coaching with the Amadeus Quartet. Acting on Henry's advice she left home, like me, with nothing more than pocket change.

I loved her hilarious description of her trip to England aboard the SS United States. She was confined to a tiny cabin on the poop deck of the ship with three other girls, squished together like sardines. The four of them hardly had room to stand, body to body, in between the bunks, which made it more than inconvenient for their frequent bouts of seasickness. I told her about my wretched bus trips with the Warsaw Philharmonic, and we laughed and laughed, each of us well into our second martini.

"Please, tell me about time in Warsaw," I asked, not wanting our date to end.

One evening shortly after arriving in London, Toni was invited to an impromptu chamber music session with a group of highly regarded musicians, including the violinist of the Warsaw Quintet, Bronisław Gimpel. At the end of a full night of playing quartets, Bronisław suggested that Toni record the Prokofiev D major Sonata for Violin and Piano in Poland for Warsaw Radio. He told her the pianist would be Władysław Szpilman, a name unfamiliar to her. Toni was thrilled by the unexpected offer and didn't pause to inquire about the pianist's credentials. She presumed if he was good enough to record for Warsaw Radio, he was certainly good enough to play with her.

The recording was scheduled for the first week of January 1967, and the thermometer reading was well below zero when Toni arrived in Warsaw.

To a Southern California girl it felt downright glacial. Szpilman's wife picked Toni up at her hotel an hour before the scheduled six o'clock rehearsal in the Szpilman home, situated on a narrow, unlit country road in the suburbs outside Warsaw. Szpilman, who spoke excellent English, greeted her at the door with a stiff, formal handshake and took his seat at the piano right away. The session went very well—he was a marvelous pianist—but lasted an intense four hours. Szpilman remained remote and businesslike throughout and never suggested taking a break, having a snack or even a glass of water. Promptly at ten o'clock Szpilman nodded, handed Toni her warm coat and gloves, opened the front door and pointed toward the pitch-black road.

"Turn right, walk for a block and a half, cross the street, walk on the left for two blocks and, on the other side, halfway down will be the bus going to Warsaw," he instructed.

It didn't matter that there were no street signs; Toni didn't speak a word of Polish and wouldn't have understood them anyway. She left the house, shivering in the frigid air and terrified she wouldn't find her way. Needless to say, she had a bittersweet feeling about their encounter.

Recounting the story to me as we sat in our warm, cozy booth in Carnegie Tavern, it was clear Toni knew nothing about Szpilman's reputation or his importance on the musical scene. I filled her in.

"Your pianist for recording is one of most famous musicians in Poland. When I study and play in Warsaw, Władysław Szpilman, heroic survivor during war and brilliant performer, is like God!"

Toni's eyes widened and flickered with excitement.

Our date flew by. We flirted, Toni dissolved into giddiness, and I felt like a teenager in love. We were both very tipsy when I reluctantly fetched a cab for her. I held the door open, pulled her gently to me, gave her a soft kiss and then she was gone. Walking up Broadway, I kept hearing the music of *Daphnis and Chloe* in my head. I was *Daphnis* and Toni was my *Chloe*. I didn't care where I was, where I was going, about food or sleep—I just wanted Toni to like me. As soon as I got home I flipped through the pages of the telephone book. Carol Adler's number was easy to find and I couldn't stop myself from trying to call Toni. Carol answered and enthusiastically passed Toni the receiver. She sounded happy to hear my voice and asked where I was.

"I am in apartment studying the English and I learn how to spell '*like*.'"

Toni was obviously amused and replied, "So tell me, how do you spell *'like?'*"

I spelled out my answer, "L – O – V – E!"

Toni couldn't control her laughter on the other end of the line.

"There must be something wrong with your dictionary!" she said, with a coy giggle that was both shy and seductive.

I had never been so captivated by a woman, and music was our aphrodisiac.

The next day Toni told me that no more than five minutes after she hung up from my silly call, the house phone from the lobby of the building rang.

Carol beckoned Toni from the dinner table again and said, "A guy approached the doorman looking for a woman in a long, black gown and carrying a violin case."

Standing in front of the door was Toni's cab driver, holding a ten-dollar bill in his outstretched hand.

"You gave me a ten instead of a one," he said.

It was a goodwill gesture, unheard of in New York, and it convinced me there was magic in the air.

Thanks to Toni my English began to improve rapidly. I suppose the best way to learn a foreign language is in bed. In return I taught her some Polish, which she absorbed surprisingly easily. Since Toni always loathed her given name—she received countless letters addressed to *Mr.* Toni Ann Rapport, including an induction notice from the U.S. Army—I called her *Kotuś*, little kitten, and she called me *Skarbuś*, little treasure. It wasn't long before I introduced Toni to all my friends. Halina treated her like a daughter, and Basia and Toni connected instantly. Mayevski and Eisenberg loved her like two dirty old men, both planting wet kisses smack on her lips, which she despised. The two of us were inseparable, and I knew I wanted to spend the rest of my life with my *Kotuś*.

Of course, I was still married, a predicament which needed to be taken care of as soon as possible. I had already written to Regina asking for a divorce, but she did not respond. I tried a second time, reminding her she had tricked me into marrying her in the first place, and we never loved each other. That may not have been the smartest approach. I imagined her plotting revenge from across the ocean. She was determined to punish me for defecting, and this time answered my request for an end to our marriage with a resounding, *NO!*

Through my Polish contacts I learned that Regina's lover—a Communist Party state prosecutor—moved in with her and Piotr. They were all living in the upscale apartment given to me by the Minister of Culture. Regina had also joined the party and became a ministry official. My American dollars were affording her a lifestyle that was the antithesis of Communist orthodoxy. But even that wasn't enough for her.

A musician friend of mine from the American Symphony referred me to his father, a prominent divorce attorney, who assured me I could divorce Regina without her consent.

"I will arrange a Mexican divorce for you," he said. Then he leaned forward in his chair and offered a word of warning, "It could be very costly."

"Money not problem," I told him, naïvely. "I want out."

Of course, I took my responsibility for Piotr very seriously and would continue supporting the two of them, but I could no longer be bound to Regina.

"No matter price," I assured the lawyer.

All told, the fees amounted to a whopping $2,000, an enormous sum for me. I hustled for extra work and barely managed to cobble together the money in time for my scheduled court date in Mexico.

I flew to El Paso, Texas to meet with a local attorney who would drive me across the border to Juarez. He told me in advance to bring only cash. Even though I packed the fat stack of dollars into a hidden money belt, I walked out of the airport feeling more than a little vulnerable. The attorney was waiting and welcomed me into the back seat of a beat-up old car where I sat between two square-jawed, muscular men who accompanied us, presumably as bodyguards. I asked no questions and tried to remain calm as we maneuvered slowly down a dusty road toward the courthouse. At every corner, locals were leaning against fences and doorways, cigarettes in hand, peering suspiciously from under the rims of their hats. I felt like I was in a John Wayne western. Maybe I should have been wearing a holster instead of an Italian leather belt.

As soon as we parked the car, begging children buzzed around us raising their palms up at me. The two husky guys cleared a path into the building.

"If you want your divorce, keep your mouth shut," the lawyer advised.

He quickly ushered me into a stuffy courtroom where a judge asked only for my name and date of birth, no testimony, no grounds for divorce. In a matter of minutes my marriage was dissolved.

I heaved a happy sigh of relief and could feel the goofy smile stretching across my face as we headed back toward the Texas border. I resolved to invite my new pals out for a drink.

Nearing the checkpoint, the attorney turned around and asked, "May I have your green card and re-entry permit please?"

Oh my god. My smile quickly disappeared. When I left New York I was only focused on the divorce and completely forgot I would need those documents.

"I don't have!" I said, with a shaky voice.

My lawyer responded nonchalantly, "I'm sorry, Señor Leszek. You cannot cross the border without a permit. You will have to stay in Mexico."

He motioned to his driver to slow down.

"How long?" I asked in a panic.

He shrugged his shoulders, "Maybe a few days. Maybe a month. Maybe more . . . I don't know."

All the blood rushed to my head. The driver stopped the car, ready to deposit me on the side of the road. I fumbled in my pocket, grabbed a fifty-dollar bill and handed it to the lawyer.

"Do something!" I pleaded.

He beamed and said, "Señor Leszek, lie on the floor."

Obediently, I lay face down on the floor of the back seat and the two big guys covered me with a scratchy, filthy blanket. They planted their feet on top of my back and I could hardly breathe as we drove on. When we got to border control, I heard my lawyer laughing with the guards; obviously, they were very familiar with each other. The trunk was opened for a brief inspection, the men shared another laugh or two, and we drove safely into U.S. territory.

It was a starry Texas night when I checked into my El Paso hotel. I called Toni immediately.

"*Kotuś*, I am divorced! Will you be my wife?"

"Yes, *Skarbuś!* I will marry you. I love you!"

I could have somersaulted over the moon.

With great excitement, Toni wrote a letter to her parents in Los Angeles announcing our engagement. In the envelope she included a photo of me standing in Central Park looking very debonair, wearing a gray tailored suit with a burgundy silk tie, holding a smoking pipe in the corner of my mouth, and cocking my head as if I were about to ask, *'Have you read any Pushkin?'* or, judging by my pose and the way my left foot presented itself to the camera, *'Do you like my fine Italian shoes?'* The photo was intended to impress my future in-laws, but proved to be a bad choice.

George Rapport replied to Toni by return mail with a stern warning.

> *Dear Daughter,*
> *I urge you to think twice about marrying that fellow. First of all, I can tell he is a womanizer, and second, he looks like he was probably married before. Besides, Mother and I don't trust men from Poland.*
> *Your loving Father*

I dismissed his letter as just a father protecting his daughter, and laughed at his ridiculous pronouncements. But Toni was not amused. She knew these words came from her devious mother, who used George as a messenger. Toni explained that her mother was not likely to accept any man she chose to marry, that she had never allowed her to date, and that she always made Toni feel unworthy of affection. Despite her parents' reaction, we had no intention of calling off our wedding plans. We also decided never to tell them about my previous marriage.

The Met honored my request to be released from the spring tour—under no circumstances would I separate from my *Kotuś*. Toni moved into my apartment and we felt like newlyweds. For the month of June, the Guy Lombardo Orchestra in Jones Beach engaged us to play Rogers' and Hammerstein's *South Pacific*. We rented a car for the drive to Long Island where we boarded a floating barge that served as the orchestra stage. Before every show, a sleek speedboat, boasting an oversized American flag attached to its stern and Guy Lombardo at the wheel flashing a triumphant grin to the crowd, raced toward the stage with great fanfare. It was a corny display of showmanship, but I was always moved when we followed Lombardo's arrival with the national anthem. Neither Toni nor I had ever played an American musical and we loved it.

Eisenberg invited both of us to perform in the Cascais-Estoril festival in August. We planned a late July wedding so our trip abroad could double as a honeymoon. Portugal was an ideal destination and we couldn't afford a separate vacation anyway.

Not only did my future in-laws eventually give up trying to thwart our wedding plans, they insisted the celebration be held in their home. The date was set for July 28, two days before our flight to Lisbon. We arrived in Los Angeles a week before the wedding with the unlikely hope that I might establish a bond with Toni's parents, who met us at the airport. Edith and George Rapport waited at the gate looking like a very odd couple. George was tall and handsome, with wavy blond hair, twinkling blue eyes, a slender mustache and a warm, Cary Grant smile. Edith—not so bad looking herself—was standing beside him in a casually elegant silk blouse, pencil skirt and pumps, and was at least a foot shorter than her husband. As a young adult at full height, she only stood four feet ten inches; but now almost fifty years old, with brittle bones to match her temper, she looked more diminutive than that. George embraced Toni and clasped both my hands in genuine welcome. Edith tried her best to do the same, her pinked lips and rouged cheeks stretched into a stiff smile, but I could tell her forced welcome wouldn't last.

In the following days George came to accept me as Toni's intended. Edith, meanwhile, made no effort to hide her disapproval of everything about me, with the exception of my fluency in Russian, her native tongue. She was a fan of Communism and could not understand why I risked my life to abandon such a "glorious" system of government. For Edith my defection was a bitter reminder of her past. In 1923, during the turbulent post-Bolshevik Revolution era, her brave father, Max Rubin, a *rebbe* (Jewish teacher), managed to escape from the Soviet Union with his entire family, including thirteen-year-old Edith, an extremely clever girl with a very pretty face and a tiny frame. She was perfectly happy as a budding party sympathizer, and when they emigrated to the United States she never forgave her father for wrenching her from an imaginary idyllic existence, even though they were among the lucky few who got out. She despised him, and her resentment only grew deeper in the years after they settled in America.

George's parents, the Rappaports, came from a small town called Borzna in the Ukraine, and his father was a very prestigious *Kohane*, a Jewish priest. When they left Borzna for the U.S. and arrived at Ellis Island—before George was born—the Irish immigration officer shortened Rappaport to Rapport. George's father died at about the same time as Edith's mother, leaving Sarah Rapport and Max Rubin, single. Sarah and Max found each other and married soon after, and George and Edith became stepbrother and sister. This was how they met. Of course, Edith was livid that her father took another wife and, predictably, loathed her new stepmother. In order to get out from under her stepmother's roof, shrewd, petite Edith lured George, who was exceedingly attractive and charming, into marrying her. George was neither prosperous nor formally schooled, but he had a brilliant mind and a remarkable command of history, political science and mathematics. He was also friendly and loving by nature. Whatever strengths of personality he had, however, were overwhelmed by Edith's total domination of him. In 1930, at Edith's insistence, the couple moved across the country to start a new life in Los Angeles.

George and Edith had a son, Jay, in 1931, and then Toni, eleven years later. George ran a struggling small business and Edith dabbled as a concert pianist. They lived as active Socialists, outspoken atheists, and were loyal to Judaism by heritage only. Edith was a feisty rabble-rouser and an outspoken critic of Capitalism. She liked to stand outside butcher shops on Fairfax Avenue waiting for unsuspecting customers to exit. As soon as they did, she would rip the paper packages from their hands, throw the meat onto the pavement and stomp on it, all the while deriding the free market system. Her protests landed her in front of the House Un-American Activities Committee in 1952 as an unfriendly witness, and on Senator Joseph McCarthy's infamous black list. Jay left home as soon as he could to join the Army, leaving Toni, his shy and introverted little sister, alone to grow up under a specter of criticism and blame that shadowed her constantly.

During the week before our wedding, Toni took me to visit her mentors, the legendary virtuosos, Jascha Heifetz and Gregor Piatigorsky. The minute we walked into Heifetz's hilltop Bel Air home, with its stunning views overlooking all of Los Angeles, I sensed a special connection between him and Toni. He was reputed to be a cold man, but I found him anything but. He was extremely smart, had a sharp wit and loved to tell jokes without cracking a smile. We relaxed around his pool for a while and when he asked if I would mind making him a cocktail, I smiled to myself, *He has accepted me!* The drink was probably too heavy on the scotch, but he took it happily.

Piatigorsky was far more outgoing and exuberant. He loved Toni and called her "Taawnee, sveetee!" in his heavy Russian accent. Her favorite

Piatigorsky words of wisdom, uttered in his booming bass voice, were, "To be artist you must be stronk like bool!"

He lived in a lavish mansion—his wife Jacqueline was a Rothschild—that reeked of wealth; the walls were covered in museum-quality master paintings. I will never forget the beautiful Modigliani oil that hung in his living room. But for me, the ultimate treasure in the house was his cello. In the middle of his studio, lying on top of a beautifully carved mahogany table, was one of the most famous Stradivarius cellos ever created. It was called the "Batta" after one of its early owners, Alexander Batta, and was made during Strad's "golden period."

We left Piatigorsky in happy spirits and went on to visit Toni's alma mater, the University of Southern California, and every other Los Angeles attraction she could think of. The more hours spent away from her mother, the better.

Edith managed to make every wedding decision, including who would officiate at the ceremony. She chose a rabbi, despite her vocal atheism. At first we thought it was a joke, but didn't argue. We were satisfied that Wilhelm Sanderson, a Reform rabbi, agreed to perform a non-religious ceremony clad in judge's robes. Aside from the family, the entire guest list consisted of Edith's inner circle of friends; only one of Toni's friends, conductor Lawrence Foster, was invited. I had not been asked if there was anyone I wished to include.

I met the rest of Toni's family when we gathered for a "rehearsal" dinner the night before our wedding. Since the event was to be small and simple and held in a home rather than a public space, there really wasn't much rehearsing to be done. We met at a Hollywood restaurant, and I was introduced to Toni's good-looking, sweet brother Jay, Edith's effusive older sister Florence, and George's sister Rose, who was pure of heart and often the recipient of Edith's (perhaps jealous) wrath. Toni's mother was as tense as one of her piano strings throughout the meal. At the end of dinner, after some encouraging words from Florence and Rose, I kissed Toni affectionately. Edith exploded, unleashing a barrage of insults and accusations.

"Your behavior is unacceptable. I am ashamed to be seen with you!" she shrieked.

This tiny woman, sitting at the head of the table and barely visible above the flower arrangement, staged a tantrum that stunned not only the family, but the surrounding restaurant patrons as well. We paid the bill and made a hasty exit.

Back at the house Edith called Toni and me into the living room and, in a serious tone, launched into a monologue about her parental duty.

"Obviously, I have known Toni all her life. Leszek, you have only known her for seven short months."

At this she turned up her nose disapprovingly.

"I believe it is my responsibility to tell you about the girl you are marrying. Toni is lazy, selfish and inconsiderate, and has no desire to accomplish anything worthwhile in her life. She also lacks discipline, which I am surprised you could not figure out yourself just by looking at her, smeared with lipstick like a whore. Anyway, as her mother, I must do you both a favor before it is too late and speak the truth."

I thought my poor, pale-faced *Kotuś* was going to faint. Her father sat in his chair, motionless, with tears welling up in the corners of his eyes. Edith's tirade, and George's reaction to it, brought me back to the day my mother threw me out because I refused to become a doctor.

I looked unflinchingly at Edith and asked, "*Mother*, you are finished?"

Edith seemed very pleased with herself and nodded her head.

"With permission, I like to say something."

"By all means," Edith replied, like a self-satisfied queen holding court, settling deeply into her chair.

"I love your daughter very, very much. Your words about Toni are not truth. *Mother*, I think what you said was description of yourself."

She sat up straight as if stuck by a pin in her rear end and her eyes narrowed like a cobra's, ready to bite. I was prepared for an eruption, but instead, she got up and stormed out of the room. George's body bent over like a weeping willow, and he was sobbing into his hands.

Toni and I hardly slept that night, lying alone in our separate rooms, anxious to just get through the following day and get out. I couldn't wait to rescue Toni from this poisonous atmosphere.

We were awakened early on the morning of our wedding by a high-pitched yelp coming from Edith's room. Running to her immediately, we found her sitting on the floor clutching one of her feet.

"I broke my toe!" she wailed.

We tried to take her to the emergency room, but she refused, insisting, "Nothing can be done."

For the remainder of the day, Edith had to be carried from room to room in supreme melodramatic fashion, wearing a bedroom slipper on her allegedly injured foot and a high-heeled shoe on the other. With all the attention showered on Edith instead of the bride, her spirits miraculously lifted. We exchanged our vows on the outdoor terrace of the Rapport home, in a small garden enclosed by citrus trees. Toni looked radiant, wearing a floor-length white lace dress and white baby roses in her pixie-like, short-cropped hair. At two o'clock on the afternoon of Sunday, July 28, 1968, or, as the rabbi enlightened us, the fifth day of the Jewish year 5728, we were pronounced husband and wife. After breaking the glass with my foot, everybody shouted "*Mazel tov, mazel tov!*" and we embraced each other in an extended, passionate kiss. We couldn't have cared less what Toni's mother thought.

Throughout the reception Edith greeted her guests as if she were the star of the event. She was seated in a chair twice her size, accepting congratulations on the marriage and condolences for her toe. She smiled from ear to ear and presented me with great enthusiasm to her friends in a performance that would have rivaled Norma Desmond in *Sunset Boulevard.*

She boasted, "He is the most wonderful son-in-law I could have hoped for. Last night he already started to call me '*Mother*'!"

Not knowing any of the guests and feeling like a fish out of water, I waited impatiently until seven o'clock when I finally escorted my *Kotuś* to the Bel Air Hotel for our wedding night. The room was like paradise on earth, and we felt like *Daphnis and Chloe.* A chilled bottle of champagne awaited us along with the biggest California king bed I ever saw. We made love until the first birds of a glorious new day began singing their messages of love and freedom.

27

Newport

We slept through the alarm and dashed out of bed to pack for Portugal before meeting Toni's extended family for a bon voyage brunch. The staff at the Bel Air Hotel restaurant treated us like dignitaries and everybody ate like kings. Mimosas flowed and toasts were made. With every succulent bite of Edith's smoked salmon, a forkful of the tension from the previous week disappeared into her gullet. She behaved like an angel for the duration of the meal, never once mentioning her toe, and on a couple of occasions I even caught her glancing affectionately at her daughter, betraying a glimmer of pride. For the first time, she endeared herself to me; that diminutive woman giggling champagne bubbles from across the table. Then abruptly, she stood to go. As if on cue, the rest of the family got up as well, thanked us for the meal, and with hugs, kisses and wishes for safe travels, they departed, leaving us holding the very expensive bill. And so our marriage began, with a sizeable credit card debt.

Driving Toni to the airport, I felt like a knight whisking his damsel to magical far away shores, and Portugal was to be our sanctuary. At the Lisbon Portela Airport we rented a Fiat with a manual transmission—the only option—that was smaller than our bathtub at the Bel Air. I looked forward to gallantly delivering my bride to the doorstep of our honeymoon suite, but immediately encountered the first problem: how to cram our luggage and my huge cello case into the trunk. That was nothing, however, compared to the difficulty I had maneuvering the stick shift. The little chariot, as I liked to think of it, lunged forward, bucked, and then stalled every time I put it in first gear. A line of cars formed behind us, cursing and bellowing as I struggled with our car. Stuck in the middle of a busy traffic circle, we switched seats and Toni took over. Coming from Los Angeles, she was an exceptionally skilled driver.

"People in L.A. learn to drive before they learn to walk," she said with a laugh. "At the end of my first driving lesson when I was fifteen, Father directed me straight onto a six lane freeway."

I found it incredibly sexy to watch her command that vehicle. It appeared it was I who actually needed to be rescued.

Toni got us safely to our villa, next door to the estate of the exiled King of Italy, Umberto II. From our second story windows we had views of Umberto's beautiful gardens and the sea. In the upcoming weeks, together we performed the Brahms Double Concerto for Violin and Cello and the Kodaly Duo. Toni played Copland and Prokofiev sonatas and Bach's *Chaconne*, and I played a Bach cello suite and the Chopin Sonata. It was a lot of work and we tried to play our best on stage, but love came first. Our colleagues in the festival, all rambunctiously single, often teased us about our public affections.

One evening I took Toni out for a romantic dinner and to see Franco Zeffirelli's *The Taming of the Shrew,* starring Elizabeth Taylor and Richard Burton. When we emerged from the theater, the parking spot where our little Fiat had stood was empty. Our car was gone. Toni and I headed straight to our lodgings to report the theft. Four of our colleagues, all of them cellists, were lounging downstairs when we arrived.

"Is anything wrong?" they asked, desperately trying to suppress their laughter.

"Our car ... it is stolen! Toni and I watching *Timing of Screw* ..." I said, "and when it finished, no car!"

The four of them, with Toni joining in, exploded in laughter. "What is funny?" I asked, very confused.

"Come, we'll bring you to your car," a colleague said, explaining that the four of them had picked up our tiny Fiat and carried it around the corner while we were sitting in the theater. "And in the meantime, you can tell us all about the *timing of your screw!*"

Their stunt was obviously not nearly as funny as my English.

During our three-week stay Toni and I bought a few Portuguese souvenirs, including a three-foot-tall, hand-painted, ceramic rooster that functioned as a floor vase and weighed a ton. It was nearly impossible to fit everything into our mini chariot for the return trip to the airport. Not only that, we had the divine misfortune of being booked on the same flight as a missionary group from Our Lady of Fatima. The Lord's servants took every available seat, leaving none for the rooster. To make matters worse, our two seats were in the very last row, the one that doesn't recline. For eight endless hours across the Atlantic, Toni and I were strapped in, sitting upright, and taking turns holding that monstrous bird on our laps, feeling more and more numb with each passing hour. Crossing our New York City threshold with the rooster still intact was a huge relief.

A beautiful, hand-written letter from Halina was waiting for me:

> *My loving son, synusiu,*
> *With all of my heart I am delighted that you finally found happiness, which you deserve so much. I hope that God will bless both of you and grant you joy for the rest of your lives. Congratulations on your successful concerts in Portugal. I am very curious to learn of your future plans. I wish you all the best in the world.*
> *Your adopted mother,*
> *Halina Rodzinski*

She was right; I did find the happiness that eluded me all my life. I was glad to tell her about our honeymoon and how much I loved my *Kotuś*. Our future plans, however, were a topic I preferred to defer because I knew Toni and I would soon be spending a lot of time apart, with me at the Met and Toni pursuing a solo career that could take her far and wide. We braced ourselves for the impending separation until one hot August afternoon when I was called into Felix Eyle's office.

The orchestra manager said, "*Panie Leszku*, you might want to know that we have an opening position . . ." and his mouth lengthened slightly into a reserved, characteristically Polish, smile, "in the violin section. I've heard your wife is an excellent violinist. Would she be interested in auditioning for the job?"

For as long as Toni could remember, Edith expected her to rise to prominence as a successful soloist, and structured her daughter's life accordingly. As a student living at home, Toni was tethered to her violin and not allowed to indulge in any youthful distractions. Her mother didn't permit socializing with friends, except in the evenings, and only if they gathered for chamber music sessions in the Rapport's living room under Edith's watchful eye. Edith would either sit at the keys of her pride and joy—a seven-foot Steinway grand piano, which she doted on more than her daughter—and accompany the young musicians while they played. Or, she would recline in a corner sipping coffee while surveying Toni and her friends, frequently offering stinging critiques. Toni could never decide which arrangement was more awkward. There was no doubt that Edith considered orchestra playing an unacceptable option for her daughter. For us, however, an orchestra was the greatest "instrument" of all, and being part of a world-class ensemble like the Met Orchestra would be the ultimate reward for our years of unrelenting hard work and sacrifice.

Toni's face brightened and she said with a beguiling smile and no hesitation, "Tell Eyle I'll take the audition."

It was held a week before the 1968-69 season opening night. In those days women were not typically welcome in major orchestras—the New York Philharmonic had yet to accept a woman into its ranks. Toni was competing against dozens of other violinists in front of a jury composed of the orchestra's first chair string players and a venerable selection of conductors, including Fausto Cleva and Zubin Mehta. Toni had performed for Mehta before in Los Angeles and his presence helped to calm her jittery nerves.

After listening to her solo repertoire they put Wagner's Overture to *Die Meistersinger*—which she had never played—on the music stand and asked Toni to sight-read it. I stood just outside the room with my ear plastered up against the small glass panel in the door, and could hear and see everything. I watched Toni gulp, close her eyes, and hold her breath for a few seconds, then launch into the unfamiliar music and sail through it easily.

Later that afternoon Toni was offered the position, which she accepted with great glee, and became only the fourth female member of the Metropolitan Opera Orchestra. Unfortunately, Edith didn't share our joy.

"It's a shame you will spend your professional life in the pit. What a waste," Toni's mother declared over the phone.

Her disappointment didn't dampen our excitement. I took Toni to a fancy French restaurant to celebrate our exceptional status as newlyweds working together in one of the finest musical organizations in the world.

Opera repertoire is very demanding and, as the only married couple, we were under a magnifying glass. Nonetheless, Toni and I were ecstatic to wake up together, have breakfast together, stroll to Lincoln Center, and be by each other's side day and night. I was released from my contract with Stokowski, which gave me even more time with my *Kotuś*.

With two Met salaries and a couple of credit cards, we suddenly felt flush with good fortune and indulged our appetite for a larger apartment. Waiting for us was a one-bedroom on the twenty-second floor of a very new building at 15 West Seventy-second Street, just off of Central Park West and next to the famed Dakota. In high spirits, we signed the lease and immediately embarked on a shopping spree for furnishings. Our first stop was Maurice Villency where we bought an impressive, and much too costly, Danish modern set. The sleek modular couch and two circular swivel club chairs—a combination of royal blue and rose tufted velvet—were a major departure from my old, faded floral cotton, moth-eaten, secondhand furniture. I inherited a love of wood from my father and our new desk, coffee and side tables were made of beautiful teak. I walked into our new living room repeatedly to admire those pieces, never stopping to think about their price. At the legendary art and bookstore Rizzoli, we bought our first artworks—a little print by Chagall and two Karel Appel lithographs. Marek Mayevski dipped into his collection and lent us an etching by Raoul Dufy and an oil by the Polish abstract artist Tadeusz Dominik. Our new home was evidence of the free market system at work; there was no trace of my former life as a struggling student or a Communist citizen.

Before long it was winter in New York, and Toni received a phone call from an old colleague, Adam Han-Gorski, a fellow member of Heifetz's master class. He was in New York for only one day on a mission to sell his splendid Domenico Montagnana violin, circa 1700. Heifetz bought the instrument in 1964 and it was used occasionally in the master class. Eventually, the violin wound up in Adam's hands, but because he had designs on a different one, he hoped the preeminent New York dealer Jacques Français would buy the Montagnana outright. Adam needed the money quickly. Sadly for him, Jacques was out sick, so he called us on the off chance Toni might be interested.

As soon as I laid eyes on that beautiful instrument, there was no question my *Kotuś* had to have it. Considering what we had just spent on accessorizing our apartment, Toni thought I had lost my mind. We were just married, had no savings, and had credit card bills to pay off. We still hadn't settled the charges from our breakfast at the Bel Air. From my perspective, however, it was time to shed the Polish notion that anything I wanted would remain out of reach; the old barriers, limits and frugality were gone, and for me it was *good riddance*. Toni warned me to be practical, but I decided that Montagnana was not leaving our apartment. After some complicated, extended payment arrangements, Adam went home slightly disappointed and Toni became the proud owner of an ex-Heifetz violin.

In February of 1969 New York City experienced one of the biggest snowstorms in its history. No taxis or buses were in operation, trash removal was halted, many people were stranded, and several dozen died as a result. The city was paralyzed and the Met's performances were cancelled for two days. For a Southern California girl like Toni, the blizzard was magical. Unlike most New Yorkers, we went outside to play in the snow. And when night fell, with a bottle of champagne, a small jar of Beluga caviar, and a frosty wonderland outside our window, Toni and I celebrated our one-year anniversary of falling in love.

❧

At the Met we developed a unique friendship with concertmaster Raymond Gniewek, an extraordinary musician and consummate leader. He asked us both to play chamber music in Rhode Island's summer Newport Music Festival, a revival of nineteenth-century Romantic repertoire, and we were honored to accept. Toni was accustomed to performing in a variety of American festivals, like the Carmel Bach Festival and the Marlboro and Aspen Music Festivals. But it would only be my second such experience after Aspen and I couldn't wait.

Newport was an opulent seaport town, its streets lined by magnificent limestone mansions with dramatic views of the Atlantic Ocean. In the summer it was home to a Who's Who of American high society. On its social register were celebrities, magnates, international royals, politicians, famous scholars and artists, names like Doris Duke, John Nicholas Brown, Wiley Buchanan, John

Drexel III, Hugh Auchincloss (whose name was so hard for me to pronounce it was like choking on peppered vodka), Countess Sylvia Szapary, Senator Claiborne Pell and on and on and on. It was a rarified world I never had access to until that summer of 1969.

The festival concerts took place in the spectacular ballrooms of The Elms, Marble House and, grandest of all, The Breakers. These elaborate architectural landmarks overlooking the sea were retreats for the American aristocracy, and became known, smugly, as "summer cottages." In actuality, they were sumptuous estates, brimming with gilt, marble and bronze, surrounded by expansive lawns, ornate gardens, sculpted fountains and showy pavilions that indulged the fancies of their illustrious, warm weather residents.

In the opening week, Toni and I played a concert in the Great Hall of The Breakers that featured Alexander Fesca's *Grand Septuor* and Louis Spohr's *Nonet*. The next day, chief music critic of *The New York Times*, Harold C. Schonberg, a fan of unknown music of the nineteenth-century, wrote a rave review of the piece and its performance that catapulted us into an elevated musical position as festival artists.

Everybody in Newport loved Toni. They, and I, were captivated by her playing and her style. She wore elegant, long gowns and carried herself—despite her modest upbringing—with the grace of an heiress. One of her biggest fans was the extremely classy Mrs. John Barry Ryan. Born Margaret Dorothy Wolff Kahn, but known simply as "Nin" to her friends, she was the daughter of Otto Kahn, the preeminent Jewish philanthropist, financier, patron of the arts and President and Chairman of the Metropolitan Opera Board of Trustees. Nin was tiny, had a miniscule balletic waist, penetrating blue eyes that sparkled like sapphires, and silver, wavy hair, which framed her delicate face. The New York Couture Group named her among the World's Best Dressed Women of 1959, and despite her small stature she couldn't be missed in a crowd. Perhaps because of our Metropolitan Opera connection, Nin invited us to dine with her frequently in her home, "Moorland Farm," or join her for lunch at the private ocean side club for the well-to-do, Bailey's Beach.

Unlike many of the patrician Newport types whose main interest was the source of each other's wealth, Nin was an exceedingly broad-minded, admirable person. She was highly literary, a humanitarian, and grew to be a treasured friend who was always in the audience to hear us play.

Even though our financial status was an ocean away from that of our patrons, we were somehow welcomed into their sphere with open arms. By the end of the summer we felt like the world was our oyster. Unbeknownst to us, however, throughout our stay in Rhode Island, a major labor dispute had been brewing at the Met. The musicians and the Met management were unable to reach an agreement for a new contract.

Rudolph Bing, General Manager of the Met—remembering his bitter, public defeat in the negotiations of 1966—resolved to play hardball with the orchestra and announced, "I am cancelling all performances until a contract is signed!" The orchestra committee had to endure a media blitz that blamed the musicians for shutting down the opera house. Everybody turned against us, including some of our friends. The orchestra remained steadfast.

Working together and collecting paychecks every week was great, but when the Met was on strike, it meant a double loss for Toni and me. After a few weeks we ran out of money, lived off our credit cards, and were bereft for the first time since we met. We cobbled together some freelance work with the American Symphony and the New Jersey Symphony, conducted by Henry Lewis. He and Marilyn Horne had been married for several years by then.

After a rehearsal in New Jersey one afternoon, Henry invited us to their home to listen to a run-through of Marilyn's upcoming Carnegie Hall recital. It was my first introduction to her, and just as Toni told me, she had Elizabeth Taylor eyes and luminous skin.

Radiating warmth, with both hands outstretched to me she said, "So happy to meet you! I'm Jackie."

Toni and I were enchanted by Angela, their beautiful, four-year-old daughter, who sang and danced along with her mommy's music. Being in the midst of this lively, happy child, I couldn't help worrying about Piotr and my future family with Toni, and about how I would be able to support them. Our occasional jobs were nice to have, but didn't do much to help us rectify the financial challenges ahead.

And then, in October we found out that Toni was pregnant. With such joyous news the clouds of gloom began to lift. We enjoyed a temporary state of bliss and hoped an agreement between the orchestra and the management would be reached soon, so we could plan for the arrival of our first child unencumbered. With the country at war and the economy sputtering, it was a terrible time to be burdened with fear and uncertainty.

Ten weeks into the dispute, however, there was still no agreement. All our colleagues were struggling, like we were. After fourteen weeks a meeting was called with the orchestra's attorney, who insisted that we stand our ground.

"You will recoup lost salary for the entire time you were out of work," he boasted.

Toni and I looked at each other. Neither of us thought that sounded realistic. Toward the end of the meeting, Toni, already three months pregnant, grabbed my hand and, shaking like a leaf, stood up to speak.

"With all due respect," she challenged the attorney, "Can you give us a guarantee that we will receive back pay?"

The room fell silent, and after an uncomfortable pause, he answered, "No."

Several of the men in the orchestra were furious at Toni. How dare this new, young woman open her big mouth?! Without actually spitting out the words, the insinuation was that women were a tiny minority of the orchestra and should be grateful to have the job at all. They had no business at the negotiating table. Only a few of the members expressed admiration for Toni's courage. I was extremely proud of my *Kotuś*. My little kitten had turned into a tiger.

A week later, after picketing in the streets for over fifteen weeks and being pushed to the limit, the orchestra voted to accept management's offer— with no retroactive pay, of course—and the strike finally ended. We were flat broke, had accumulated huge bills and could no longer afford to live in our expensive building.

Just before the holidays we stumbled upon an incredible, rent-controlled apartment in the Dorilton, at the corner of Broadway and Seventy-first Street. For one week's Met salary, we were able to rent seven and a half rooms, a much larger space than the high-priced one-bedroom we were leaving behind. But, the apartment was unbelievably filthy because the previous tenants, a mother and daughter, had used it as a sanctuary for city pigeons for over thirty years. Bird droppings covered every inch of the place and the odor was revolting. We began a hideous cleaning process that required nose masks, rubber gloves and scrapers. By the New Year we moved into an Upper West Side palace with high ceilings, three fireplaces, towering windows and shiny parquet floors. It was a fine example of elegant turn of the century architecture, and a very short walk to the Met. We spent the next few months nesting, eagerly anticipating the birth of our baby.

Toni handled her first pregnancy beautifully. She didn't miss a single performance at the Met and cherished every moment as the baby grew and began to kick. She decided to follow the recently-popularized Lamaze Method of natural childbirth and, in order to prepare, we took a series of classes taught by Elizabeth Bing, the method's U.S. pioneer. Halina was so overjoyed by our imminent parenthood that she joined us for Lamaze, practicing breathing exercises together with Toni. It was a very amusing scene—several young women with bulging bellies, and one white-haired, flat-stomached, distinguished lady in her seventies, all lying on the floor inhaling and exhaling in determined spurts, in and out, in and out.

Friends advised us that if Toni went into labor in the middle of the night, we should not try to fetch a taxi ourselves.

"Cabbies don't stop for pregnant ladies," they claimed. "Ask a neighbor to get one for you."

We made arrangements with our dear photographer friend in the building, George Hester, to do just that. On the night of May 16, the contractions began. Our bags were packed and at five o'clock in the morning I called George.

"We're ready, George. It's time!" I yelled, to get him out of bed.

He staggered down to the street, groggy-eyed, and waved down a cab. Toni and I climbed into the back seat and George closed the door, bidding us good luck. I told the driver to take us to New York Hospital, and he seemed unconcerned. As soon as he stepped on the gas, Toni's contractions intensified and she calmly began her breathing exercises. With her first in and out breathing whistles, the driver suddenly realized he had a very pregnant passenger on the verge of delivering in his taxi. The poor man screamed, "Oh shit," and floored the accelerator.

"Lady, don't have that baby in my car. Hold your baby, don't have it in my car!"

He took us on a wild ride across town, speeding through every red light and keeping his eyes on the rear view mirror yelling, "No baby in my car. Lady, hold your legs together!"

For sure, we didn't want our baby to be born in his cab either.

We came to a screeching halt at the curb of the hospital and the driver ran into the building shrieking, "Emergency! Take that woman out of my car! EMERGENCY!"

Toni remained in labor well into the afternoon before they wheeled her into the delivery room. Since it was a natural birth, I accompanied her, and the doctor told us that I was among the first fathers-to-be allowed into a New York City delivery room.

I brought a sturdy camera that would capture the birth in case my consciousness failed me, and I took several shots. Never in my life did I revere anyone as much as my *Kotuś*, who so bravely delivered our little girl. Tanya was born the most perfect, beautiful, healthy baby. When the nurse put our tiny daughter on Toni's chest, we were the two happiest people in the world.

After that crazy, bumpy ride to the hospital, knowing that our jobs with the Met were again secure, I hired a chauffeur-driven limousine to give Toni and Tanya a smooth trip home.

28

The Oath of Renunciation

T oni and I had more than two months to adjust to the sleepless, yet wonderful, state of parenthood before returning to Newport for more concerts.
A festival board member, Bill Crimmins, and his wife Ann, knowing we
had a new baby, invited us to stay in their charming guesthouse overlooking Narragansett Bay. After strapping Toni and Tanya comfortably into our
American rental car, I squeezed in five weeks worth of evening gowns, diapers
and beach towels, along with our instruments and a Polish nanny named
Aldona—who was lovely and very tall; everything about her was long, like an
ostrich—and off we went to the city-by-the-sea.

Newport provided a lavish bubble for us to bounce around in, a therapeutic retreat from the intense day-to-day life in Manhattan. The weeks passed
quickly as we combined doting on our baby, performing in the festival, and socializing at extravagant parties in fabled homes. But, Toni was always mindful
of our eventual return to New York, and increasingly anxious about balancing
motherhood and work. She was nursing and struggled with the idea of being
away from Tanya. At the same time, our financial reality dictated that we didn't
have a choice. Supporting a family in New York City on my Met salary alone
would have been very difficult.

One morning I found my *Kotuś* sitting in a beach chair, the early light
swaddling Tanya as she burrowed into Toni's breast, the cadence of waves roll-
ing to and fro lulling the baby into a peaceful sleep. Yet, the expression on
Toni's face was strained.

"I'm not sure how I'll be able to manage being a good mommy for Tanya and playing at the Met," she confessed.

I stared for a while at the open water and tried to come up with a solution.

"Maybe I invite my mother to stay with us for few months?" I suggested. "Mother will take care of baby while we work, and Aldona will cook and clean. You can be loving mommy and have career!"

We both thought a grandmother's presence would be better than a nanny's. I knew that convincing the Polish government to grant Mother permission to leave would be a trick, but I began the process and tried to be optimistic. Aldona moved into our guest bedroom when we returned to New York, and the fall season at the Met began.

By the end of September 1970, I got word that the Polish authorities approved Mother's visit to America. Toni and I were stunned by the news. I knew Poland's economy was crumbling and they were hungry for Western currency, which I was funneling to my family on a regular basis. It seemed I was being rewarded for sending U.S. dollars. So much for the superiority of the Communist system.

Predictably, Mother insisted on one silly condition prior to the journey: she would only travel by freighter, not by plane.

"I want to see the world," she demanded.

I told her she would not see much from the deck of a boat, but she was unwavering, so I arranged passage on the best Polish freighter and she was satisfied. The floating monster stopped in a handful of European commercial ports before crossing the Atlantic, and arrived at Port Newark a few weeks later.

Mother stepped off the plank with a small tote bag clutched in her right hand. I spotted her instantly; a dignified-looking woman in plain attire, hardly disheveled from the long trip, a familiar rosy shade of lipstick staining her pursed lips, and not a strand of her thinning hair out of place. With Toni and the baby at my side, I embraced her and asked to help with her bags.

"Bags? This is it," she exclaimed, pointing to the tote.

"Mother, no luggage? You are going to stay with us for a long time and winter is coming. What about your clothes?"

She looked at me and laughed like I was a foolish child.

"What did I need to bring from Poland? You and your American wife are successful and can buy me everything, yes?"

Toni was very anxious to make a good impression. She had learned a lot of Polish since we met, but was still nervous about communicating with Mother. Maybe her culinary talents would help break the ice, she thought. My wife was a self-taught gourmet cook and agonized over the menu for that first dinner. The legendary Upper West Side Nevada Meat Market always carried particularly good quality lamb. Since such cuts weren't available in Poland, I encouraged Toni to make her special recipe for marinated butterfly lamb that had seduced me on several occasions. Accompanying the succulent meat would be roasted vegetables and lemon couscous with cured kalamata olives and sun-dried tomatoes. I was sure the scrumptious meal would please my mother.

We sat down and Toni served her beautifully plated creation. Silence. After many minutes passed I asked, "Mother, how do you like Toni's dinner?"

"Eeewww," was her reply, with a turned up nose. No translation was necessary.

For the next few days, poor Toni schlepped all over Manhattan, in and out of department stores, fitting Mother with stockings, underwear, dresses, a warm coat, hats, shoes, scarves, face cream. Her wardrobe cost us hundreds and hundreds of dollars.

As soon as my mother was fully equipped she asked, "When are we leaving for a trip around the country? You must show me your United States of America."

I explained that I could not travel because I had a job in a very prestigious orchestra and couldn't take off on a whim.

"Not only that, I don't want to leave Toni and Tanya. Mother, there is so much to see in New York City. I will be a perfect guide," I promised.

As a start, I offered her a ticket to a performance at the Met. She was furious.

"Why would I go to your opera when we have the best opera house in Warsaw?" she snapped.

Our hopes for a loving grandmother nurturing our baby evaporated as soon as she stepped foot in our previously happy home. She hardly paid any attention to Tanya and spent most of her time crocheting eyelet tablecloths in the living room, staring off into space with her crossed legs bobbing up and down nervously. She treated Aldona like a slave, scowling at her and issuing orders for food and laundry. We had to keep an especially close eye on Mother in the street. She was a confirmed racist and made no effort to hide her obvious disdain for African-Americans, never stepping foot into an elevator if the doors opened to a black person. As a Jewish woman who suffered so much prejudice herself, I couldn't understand her bigotry. But like so many Poles, she completely denied her Jewish roots. That Toni was Jewish had no meaning for my mother. Toni was a convenient tool for her constant triangulation. She created imaginary conflicts between Aldona and me—using Toni as the culprit—and didn't consider that her daughter-in-law was well-schooled in spotting manipulation from her own mother. My poor *Kotuś*. After escaping Edith's tyrannical claws, she was stuck with an unbearable mother-in-law.

One sunny fall afternoon, Mother was in an unusually pleasant mood and decided to take Tanya for a walk in her carriage. I went down to the street level with them to make sure she would not venture beyond our city block.

"You might get lost if you go too far," I warned.

Mother assured me they would stay close. One hour passed, and then another, and they still hadn't returned. Toni and I were panic-stricken. We walked in opposite directions around the block, but could not find them. Terrified, Toni went back upstairs to call 911.

She came down again, her voice shaking with fright. "The police said if Tanya is with her grandmother there is no need for alarm. They refuse to understand. Let's keep looking."

We went dashing through the neighborhood as the sun started its descent behind the skyline. Twilight was upon us when finally, about a mile away, we found my mother resting on a bench, the carriage beside her with Tanya inside, crying. Not only was there no word of apology from Mother, she had a look of rebuke on her face, as if it were our fault that she got lost. Tanya, she said, was fine. We were not. After that horrific experience, we insisted that Aldona not allow Tanya out of her sight when we weren't home.

In the next weeks the situation became increasingly tense as Mother resorted to nastier and nastier behavior. Aldona, who proved to be the most caring, intelligent and responsible caregiver for Tanya, learned never to turn her back on our disagreeable guest. Mother remained with us through Christmas and the New Year, but at the end of January we sent her back to Poland. Four months had been more than enough, and a welcome harmony returned to our household. The following winter and spring passed quickly as we settled into a contented family and work routine.

Our dear friend Nin often attended performances at the Met, seated in the director's box, one level above the parterre. That box was closest to the stage and looked directly into the orchestra pit. It was easy to spot Nin, even though she was barely taller than the wall of the box itself, because she always waved down to us from her perch overhead. Her wave was a special signal that she would come down for a chat during intermission.

Nin occasionally invited us to dine in her sprawling waterfront triplex at the end of East Fifty-second Street, across from Manhattan's exclusive River House. Her apartment spanned the second, third and fourth floors and had an unobstructed view overlooking the East River. Her upstairs neighbor was the mysterious Greta Garbo, who would never ride the elevator with anyone. She appeared in the lobby once wearing all black, her head covered by a broad-rimmed, floppy hat and large, dark sunglasses that hid most of her face. The doorman blocked our path to the elevator and, with his eyes lowered toward the elegantly tiled floor, pressed the number five button on the inside panel. After the doors closed, he apologized sheepishly for the delay. Obviously, the legendary Garbo took great pains to preserve her privacy.

Evenings with Nin were carefully orchestrated. When we rang the bell, the head of Nin's domestic staff, Ann, a plain-looking woman in her sixties with mousey gray hair, opened the door in her starched, black and white uniform, took our coats, and invited us to join our hostess for cocktails in the pecan wood-paneled, double-story library. The interior of Nin's beautifully-appointed, luxurious apartment was like a museum. Staring at us from every wall were paintings by Monet, Manet, Bonnard, Van Gogh and Degas she inherited from her father, Otto Kahn, who had single-handedly saved the old Met when it was on the verge of bankruptcy. On the far wall of the library hung Nin's favorite Monet oil; otherwise, the room, which was furnished in plush floral chintz, housed her prized collection of books that occupied every inch of shelf space, floor to ceiling.

After about a half hour of animated conversation, Ann would beckon us to the graceful staircase that led to Nin's dining room on the next floor. The dinner menu never changed: filet of sole in a light beurre blanc sauce, slightly limp haricots verts, and boiled potatoes sprinkled with minced parsley. The meal invariably ended with a fruit sorbet served in a tiny crystal bowl, accompanied by one shortbread cookie on beautiful Limoges dessert plates. The flower-laden table was covered with a finely embroidered white linen cloth with soft padding underneath, and in the center were dainty porcelain dishes filled with chocolates and nuts. Toni and I were always amused to watch Nin delicately nibbling on the nuts, two at a time, throughout the banter that continued after we finished eating.

At Nin's we spent time with Edward Heath, Prime Minister of Britain until 1974, and David Rothschild, of the English wing of the notoriously wealthy Rothschild family. Free enterprise was still a new concept for me, and David's attitude was especially appealing.

"Capitalism must have a human face," he insisted.

David extolled the virtues of social reform and predicted that without it, free enterprise was sure to fail. I thought about my status as a foreigner in America and was emboldened by David's view. The world I grew up in was so distant, geographically and philosophically. The vision of a progressive society that came into focus in Nin's living room was powerful and profoundly optimistic. It was a vision in which citizens could prosper, not as a socialistic collective, but as humanists sharing social responsibility for the benefit of everyone.

❖

While we were thoroughly enjoying our work at the Met, the previous summer we had joined forces with the spirited Brazilian pianist, Flavio Varani, whose South American flair was irresistible to crowds, and formed the Bergson Trio, named after the composer whose music had brought us together. Our friends from Newport, the Crimminses, offered to sponsor our Bergson Trio debut in Lincoln Center's Alice Tully Hall. How prophetic Carlo Pitello's advice had been many years ago.

"Take the audition for the Met. The schedule is flexible and you will still be able to play chamber music."

For the Tully Hall program we chose three pieces from the neglected nineteenth-century Romantic repertoire, which we loved for its passion and technical challenges: Arthur Foote (American) Trio Opus 5 in C minor,

George Osborne (Irish) Trio Opus 52 in G, and Hans von Bronsart (German) Trio Op. 1 in G minor.

A couple of weeks before the concert, *The New York Times* published an article about our upcoming debut. One of the paper's main critics, Raymond Ericson, wrote, *Anyone interested in romantic music owes it to himself to attend their concert.* We could not have penned better publicity for ourselves on the eve of our appearance. The article created such a buzz that on the night of the concert the auditorium was full. It was a musical and critical success. Harold C. Schonberg wrote in *The New York Times*:

> *In all the music the Bergson Trio responded nobly. Each of these instrumentalists is strong and secure. Mr. Zawistowski has a sweet, pure tone; Miss Rapport has much greater volume. Mr Varani is a very fine pianist. He played all the music with spirit, perfect rhythm and clean-cut technique. These musicians have come a very long way in a few years. May they flourish. They have much wonderful forgotten music to explore; and judging from the applause and cheers that greeted their work and the music, it is a repertory that still has power to enchant a public.*

Nineteen seventy-two began with the thrilling news that Toni was pregnant again. Tanya would be almost two and a half, the perfect age for a baby playmate, and we were nothing short of ecstatic about expanding the family. With Aldona's invaluable help, Toni was comfortable combining motherhood and a career. Our annual summer destination had become Newport. The fresh sea air, romantic music and social scene had restorative powers. The California girl came out in my wife, who tanned easily and looked like a movie star lounging at Bailey's Beach with the most adorable little creature, our Tanya, frolicking in the sand at her feet.

One sunny afternoon in late July, a very pregnant Toni had a solo recital in Newport's spectacular mansion, The Elms, and I decided to bring Tanya with me to hear her mommy play. I was proud to show off our toddler to the society crowd, with her angelic face, the big dark eyes she inherited from Toni, and the most delightful shock of curly, light brown hair bouncing across her shoulders. I took what I thought would be the appropriate precautions by sitting in the back row in case Tanya got restless during the concert. As soon as

Toni stepped onto the stage, Tanya almost flung herself into the aisle, joyfully shrieking "Mommy, mommy, MOMMY." The audience broke into laughter and Toni couldn't help grinning from ear to ear herself.

The last performance of that summer opened with Toni, dressed in a long, satin, ruby red gown, strolling onto the stage. All eyes were on her as she began to play, her protruding belly moving delightfully along with the music. And then, suddenly I heard a pop and saw Toni rush off amidst a collective gasp from the public. I bolted backstage, trailed by two doctors from the audience.

Toni said with a giggle, "I'm not in labor, I just broke a string!"

Changing it quickly, she returned to the stage, provoking yet another round of applause. The morning headlines were all about the scare of a premature birth at the Newport Music Festival.

By the time we got back to New York after the summer, Toni was more than ready for the arrival of our second child. She felt strong and energetic and continued to play. After a particularly out-of-tune performance of *La Traviata* from the soprano, the contractions began. Everyone joked that the sour singing induced labor. Once again I was in the delivery room, and on October 1, witnessed the birth of Monique, a beautiful, delicate, bald baby girl with saucer-shaped blue eyes. Arriving in the world nine days early, determined little Monique must have decided she wasn't going to be stuck in Toni's womb listening to off-key singing for one more night.

In the late fall Mother sent two letters, a joyful one congratulating us on Monique's birth and another describing my father's worsening health. The doctor's diagnosis was cancer. That initial news was followed soon after by a dreadful telegram announcing Father's death. History tricked me into confronting the passing of Feliks Zawistowski before. He was taken from our family twice and returned to us against all odds. Only a couple of months earlier he had written that he wanted very much to visit us in America. For a time I hoped he would appear out of thin air on our doorstep. Father was a survivor, a proud *Szlachcic*, who had faced Nazi bullets, a death camp and a Bolshevik gulag. He managed to revive his spirit over the years, but his body gave out at the age of sixty-three. My terrible sadness was accompanied by a resentment churning in my gut. The Polish government stole my right to grieve at my father's grave because I escaped its iron grip, and I was helpless to change that. From so far away it was difficult to accept that my father was gone. I would never again be able to look into his eyes and draw strength from him.

❊

By the summer of 1973 Toni and I realized that Manhattan was not really a family-friendly place; raising children there, and educating them properly within the limits of our budget, would be daunting, to say the least. Tanya was to start pre-school and Monique wouldn't be far behind, so we decided to look for a house outside the city in Westchester County where the public schools were highly regarded and the environment more suitable for families. Our search ended in the tiny village of Irvington-on-Hudson, a half-hour north of Lincoln Center. In this picturesque hamlet named after American author Washington Irving, we found a charming, converted carriage house that had been part of an estate belonging to the late Cardinal Spellman. Built in 1824, it had old pine walls, exposed beams, and a pretty little pond in the front of the property that was surrounded by the very woods where Irving's Ichabod Crane fled the Headless Horseman in *The Legend of Sleepy Hollow*. We were captivated by it, but had trouble scraping together enough money for the down payment and closing costs. We finally managed and became the proud owners of our first home.

Buying that house was the fulfillment of a dream I never had before coming to America. And to achieve it I didn't have to pull any strings or bribe any officials. Standing with the keys to the front door, I faced a long-standing truth: I no longer had anything in common with the country of my birth or the people who supported its Communist structure. I had an American wife and American children, and I wanted to be an American, too. After living in the U.S. for eight years, it was time to apply for citizenship.

I asked Lydia for help and she gave me an overview of the process.

"It is complicated," she said. "You have to study the names of the best-known presidents and learn about the Constitution and the branches of government. To qualify for citizenship you will need to pass an official test, a symbolic acknowledgment of your allegiance to the United States."

That was fine with me; I already felt like a passionately loyal American.

I hoped my interest in history and knowledge of American civics and government would help me get through the interview. On the other hand, convincing the judge that I had adequate communication skills in English was a different matter—I wasn't even convinced of that myself. I was afraid of slipping up and sounding like a brainless foreigner, not worthy of American citizenship.

At the preliminary examination, an Immigration official began by asking, "Who was the first president?"

"Paderewski . . ." I started to answer, but corrected myself immediately, "George Washington."

The remainder of the test went fairly smoothly. I was asked about the Bill of Rights, to which I had given a great deal of thought, intrigued by the concept of the right to freedom of speech in the First Amendment. Having been so muzzled in Poland, I asked myself how effective the right to speak freely would be without also having the right to be heard. If I were held in isolation, for example, my right to speak would mean nothing. It occurred to me that the official, who administered my exam with such indifference, didn't stop to consider how flimsy his venerable rights are, unless he has leaders who doggedly fight for their protection.

For my final naturalization interview the court required two witnesses. Along with Toni I brought Basia, who introduced herself to the judge as Barbara Hammerstein. The elderly, frail man, reacting to her name, looked down at Basia from the Ben Franklin spectacles perched on the very tip of his nose. She didn't find it necessary to explain that her ex-father-in-law was the famed Broadway librettist Oscar Hammerstein II, and that her son Oscar Hammerstein III was named after his grandfather.

The judge, with curiosity, asked, "Are you by any chance related to Oscar Hammerstein?"

With a straight face Basia answered, "Yes. He is my son."

The poor, bewildered old man abruptly ended the interview. And so, my citizenship proceedings were over. All I could do was wait.

Shortly after Monique's first birthday, our mailman delivered an official-looking envelope from Immigration. Holding it in my hand I remembered November 1964, running out the stage door of Carnegie Hall and into the frigid air with my bare cello under my arm and small change in my pocket. And then I heard myself making a desperate speech in a detention facility before a judge who I never imagined would save me from deportation and a Soviet prison camp. The long journey from Poland to New York had been harrowing, but I never gave up hope. Now my fate came down to the contents of this skinny, white envelope. With my hands quivering I tore it open.

> Dear Mr. Zawistowski,
> The United States Immigration and Naturalization Service is pleased to grant you American citizenship.

I read through the document twice to make sure I wasn't dreaming.

New citizens have the option, free of charge, to change their names before taking the official oath. I took advantage of the chance to turn *Leszek Zawistowski* into *Leshek Zavistovski*, hoping to simplify the tongue twister, at least for some.

On Wednesday morning, October 17, flanked by Toni on one side and Basia on the other, I joined hundreds of people from every corner of the world for the Oath of Renunciation and Allegiance Ceremony in a Manhattan courtroom. The diverse group, dressed in their finest attire, looked like a collection from the International Folk Art Museum. I was clad in my ordinary pressed suit and tie, but surrounding me were immigrants from Africa in their colorful tunics, and others from Asia, the Middle East, and India, all in regional garb. The women carried bouquets of flowers and most of the men held their hats in their hands. Toni's right hand was tightly clasped in my left, and in the other I gripped a miniature copy of the Constitution of the United States and the Bill of Rights.

When we took our seats the room was bursting with emotion. The presiding judge reminded us that it was our duty to, "Support the Constitution of the United States; to renounce and abjure absolutely and entirely all allegiance and fidelity to any foreign prince, potentate, state, or sovereignty of whom or which the applicant was before a subject or citizen; to support and defend the Constitution and the laws of the United States against all enemies, foreign and domestic; to bear true faith and allegiance to the same; and to bear arms on behalf of the United States when required by the law."

If the Polish nation called me to bear arms in its name, I would not sacrifice a drop of blood. For my new country, I would give my life.

The formal pronouncements of the judge were followed by a series of speeches from local politicians about what it means to be an American citizen. Midway through a singularly nationalistic speech, an overzealous stuffed shirt brazenly proclaimed, "From this day forward, as American citizens you will have the right to *think* as you please."

His statement was clearly meant for those of us who had escaped oppressive, totalitarian regimes, and I was stunned by his arrogance. Growing up under the boot of the Nazis and the Stalinists, Poles were oppressed and terrorized day and night. Nevertheless, nobody could stop us from thinking freely—hoping for a better future and wishing for a fate in hell for our tormentors.

Then I heard the words, "All rise and raise your right hands."

I pledge allegiance to the flag of the United States of America . . .

We had all memorized the pledge and recited it in a multitude of accents.

. . . and to the republic for which it stands,

That communal sound was more beautiful than a hundred choruses.

. . . one nation, under God, indivisible, with liberty and justice for all.

With that we were pronounced citizens of the United States of America and the room erupted. In many ways, the war I had been born into only then came to a conclusion. On that day, thirty-five years later, I was finally delivered from its clutches.

Epilogue

Toni and I, with our two gorgeous girls, enjoyed an abundance of happiness in our home on the Hudson. Our passion for chamber music remained alive and we played a second Bergson Trio recital in Alice Tully Hall in 1976. By then, Toni's close college friend and collaborator, the highly regarded, superlative musician Martin Katz had become the Bergson Trio's pianist. The program was all-American in celebration of the nation's bicentennial and included the world premiere of *Yankee Doodleiad*—a National Divertimento by A.P. Heinrich (a hilarious spoof on Yankee Doodle)—and the New York premiere of Leonard Bernstein's Piano Trio Op. 2. *The New York Times* wrote:

> *The quality and diversity of American music were excellently set forward Saturday night at Alice Tully Hall in a concert of unfamiliar pieces played by the Bergson Trio. The trio (Toni Rapport, violinist; Leshek Zavistovski, cellist; Martin Katz, pianist) is a first-rate ensemble . . . plays with individuality and oneness, with an ability to adapt its style to the piece at hand and, most welcome, a flair for deadpan musical humor.*

We worked on the Bernstein premiere with the great maestro himself, which was one of the artistic highlights of our lives.

Many years had passed since Zdzisław and I had any contact. Through Mother, I knew he was working as an engineer at a Warsaw television station, was married with one daughter, and had a steep receding hairline that was the trademark of the men in our family (I had been cultivating mine since high school). The few letters I did receive from Zdzisław always ended with a request for money. His most recent correspondence was a stern warning that congratulated me on my success, emphasized that as my influential older brother he deserved full credit for it, and insisted on $10,000 as compensation. A failure to pay would result in legal action on his part.

This letter gave me deeper insight into my brother's affairs; it seemed he was now in the business of extortion. Our relationship, such as it was, ceased, and we never spoke again.

In 1981 we were thrilled to learn that Toni was pregnant. On September 16, she gave birth to our third child, who we named Katia. She was the sweetest little cupid, with bouncy, yellow curls atop her head and cheeks that looked like they were stuffed with cotton. Tanya and Monique treated her like a living doll and she stole our hearts. The following year Toni was diagnosed with breast cancer. Soon after her final radiation treatment, she got pregnant yet again. Her doctors were divided in their opinions about whether she should be carrying a baby under the circumstances. Some wanted Toni to terminate the pregnancy; others were very supportive. Our desire to have another child, a companion for Katia, was unshakable, and on June 25, 1983, our healthy, adorable son Gregory was born. The obstetrician who delivered him had advised us not to take the risk. As soon as he pulled our baby from the birth canal and held him up proudly, Gregory soaked the doctor with a long, vengeful stream of pee. Gregory had the last word.

Over twenty years had passed since I saw my son in Poland, and I still imagined Piotr as an affectionate three-year-old. Regina never once wrote to me about him or allowed any communication between us.

In 1984 a young Polish lady, who introduced herself as Anita and said she was in America visiting relatives, called me out of the blue.

"Your son Piotr and I are going to be married. He recently graduated from university with a degree in engineering. I can give you his address and phone number if you want to reach him."

Thanks to Anita I was able to contact Piotr without censorship from his mother. We had an awkward, but happy exchange. Regina had kept secret from him all the gifts and letters I sent over the years. We agreed that I would make the necessary arrangements for him to visit us in the United States. A few months later, Piotr arrived at JFK Airport, a tall and handsome young man whom I recognized only because of his resemblance to Regina.

New York City overwhelmed Piotr (much as it had me when I first visited in 1961), and perhaps our domestic tranquility in the American suburbs was, in a more acute way, also too much for him to handle. Our month together passed very quickly and before I knew it he was boarding a plane back to Warsaw. It pained me that so much remained unresolved between us. But I understood that a terrible void must have formed after living without a father for so many years, and for the time being, it was too deep to fill.

The Eastern Bloc was undergoing a groundswell of change throughout the 1980s, and in Poland the popular Solidarity movement was gaining momentum. For her part, my seventy-five-year-old mother, who was much diminished in stature, used her artistic talent to paint clandestine posters for the opposition.

In the middle of the night, she would tuck a stack of the distinctive posters, featuring the Polish flag and a bright red "*Solidarnosc!*," under her coat along with a jar of homemade glue, and meet her brother Stasio on the street. Stasio played the role of a feeble old man and the elderly pair would stroll nonchalantly toward the Communist Party headquarters in Warsaw. Entirely unnoticed, they would plaster Mother's rebellious handiwork on all sides of the shadowy building. When they woke the next morning they would return to the scene of their crime, stand in between cheering early morning commuters, and watch exasperated Communist Party workers trying in vain to scrape Mother's posters off the concrete. Their efforts took long enough for everyone in the area to get the message loud and clear: Soviet authority over Poland was going down. A decade later the first democratically held presidential elections took place in Poland, and the leader of the Solidarity movement won. My brave mother, Michalina Zawistowska, was able to live out her last few years in the free Poland she had fought for. In 1995 she passed away.

Two years later Toni and I, with our two youngest children, Katia and Gregory (Tanya and Monique were married and living out of the house), moved back to New York City. We had grown tired of the provincial life in the suburbs. Irvington had surprisingly little to offer the human spirit (it is no wonder that Rip Van Winkle slept through twenty years in that part of New York), and we moved into an apartment across the street from Lincoln

Center with panoramic views of Central Park, Fifth Avenue and Broadway.

Then, in the summer of 2000, thirty-five years after defecting from my native country, I flew with my family to Warsaw. Piotr greeted us at the airport. He had married Anita and they had two beautiful daughters, Aleksandra and Marysia. He eventually became a successful businessman running his own company, and I was very proud of him.

It felt odd to travel across Poland without constraint. I took Toni, our children, and our son-in-law Adam, to the townhouse of my birth on Ulica Freta, the terrible building in Praga where I lived after the war, my high school, university, the Hotel Bristol, Saski Gardens, Victory Square and, of course, Auschwitz where my brother Henryk was murdered. Our children scanned the Victims Wall for a photo of Henryk, but he was impossible to find among so many.

The next year in Manhattan was marked by the tragic attacks of September 11.

From our windows to the southwest, overlooking Broadway and Sixty-second Street, we could see the smoke from the fallen World Trade Center towers, and for weeks we inhaled toxic air from the wreckage. A little girl from our building, who was no more than eight years old and who used to flit past me in the lobby like a cheerful sprite, stood every day for a week with a pale, twisted look on her tear-stained face, holding her mother's picture and a handwritten sign that read,

Have you seen my mommy? Please help me find my mommy.

Her mother had perished along with the towers. Two wars loomed on the horizon after 9/11, and it seemed that history had taught those in power nothing.

Life in New York would never be the same. Toni and I decided it was time to put our hands to different use and to embark on a new journey. Our last concert with the Met Orchestra was in Baden-Baden, Germany, on August 20, 2002. When we returned home we stored our instruments in their cases, never to touch them again. We had serenaded so many audiences for so long, and now it was our turn to listen, to let go of the pressure of achieving perfection, to allow the water to flow freely through our fingers.

Toni and I purchased a home in Santa Fe, New Mexico, and packed up half a lifetime worth of belongings. Before we left New York, Toni made a quiet farewell dinner. Sitting beneath the window, we gazed out across Central Park in peace with our past and looking forward to our future, and toasted to a century of good health.

Sto lat!

Toni Rapport

Leshek in Central Park
(photo taken by Toni
Rapport), 1968

George and Edith Rapport

Sunday Afternoon, January 7, 1968 at 3:00

and

Monday Evening, January 8, 1968 at 8:30

American Symphony Orchestra

Leopold Stokowski *Music Director*

ERNEST ANSERMET, Guest Conductor

PROGRAM

BRAHMS   Symphony No. 3 in F Major, Op. 90
    Allegro con brio
    Andante
    Poco allegretto
    Allegro

INTERMISSION

DEBUSSY   Six Epigraphes Antiques
    (*Transcribed for orchestra by Ernest Ansermet*)
    Pour invoquer Pan, dieu du vent d'été
    Pour un tombeau sans nom
    Pour que la nuit soit propice
    Pour la danseuse aux crotales
    Pour l'égyptienne
    Pour remercier la pluie au matin

STRAVINSKY   Symphonies of Wind Instruments

RAVEL   "Daphnis et Chloe," Suite No. 2
    Daybreak
    Pantomime
    General Dance

Steinway is the official piano of the American Symphony Orchestra

These concerts are being recorded for future world-wide broadcast
over the facilities of the Voice of America

Leshek and Toni's first performance together, 1968

Leshek with Jascha Heifetz at his poolside, 1968

Toni with Jascha Heifetz at his poolside, 1968

Toni and Leshek's wedding day, 1968

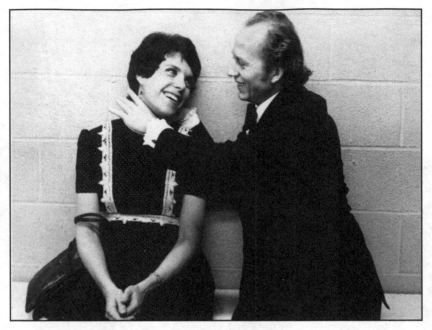

Horsing around backstage at the Met, 1969

Feliks and Michalina, c. 1971

The Bergson Trio, 1971

Feliks, Michalina, Uncle Stasio's wife and Uncle Stasio at the Zawistowski home in Warsaw (with Michalina's beloved tapestry hanging on the wall), c. 1972

Funeral announcement, 1972: "Feliks Zawistowski was a fighter in the Home Army and participant in the Warsaw Uprising. He passed away on 29 October 1972 at the age of 63. The funeral service will be held at the Church of St. Florian in Praga on November 3 at 12 o'clock, followed by burial in the Brodnowski Cemetery in the family plot. With great sadness from his wife, children, grandchildren and entire family."

Michalina (left) with a family friend and Zdzisław at Feliks' funeral, 1972

Letter from Janet Lee Auchincloss (Jacqueline Kennedy's mother), 1972: "Dear Mrs. Zawistowski — Hugh and I were very sad not to have been able to come to your party. We expected to — and at the last minute complications arose. I tried to call you a few days later — and you had vanished. You and your husband gave us so much pleasure at the Music Festival — we look forward very much to seeing you next summer. In the meantime we send you our warm regards and every wish for great happiness with your new baby — and love to your little girl. — Janet Lee Auchincloss"

Toni and Tanya on the grounds of Hammersmith Farm, the Auchincloss estate, 1971

Toni and Leshek backstage at the Met

Leshek performing at Marble House in Newport, Rhode Island, 1973

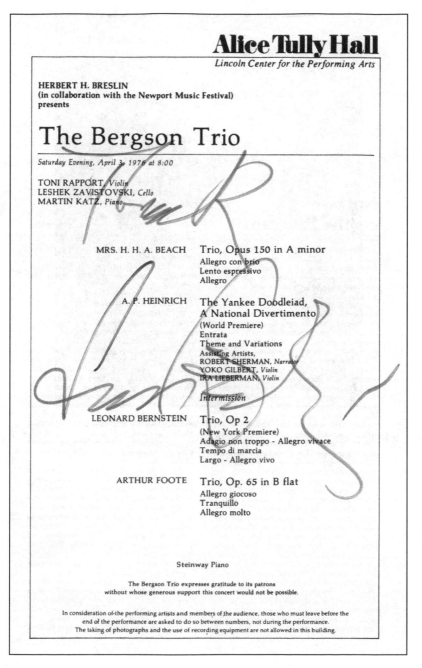

Alice Tully Hall
Lincoln Center for the Performing Arts

HERBERT H. BRESLIN
(in collaboration with the Newport Music Festival)
presents

The Bergson Trio

Saturday Evening, April 3, 1976 at 8:00

TONI RAPPORT, *Violin*
LESHEK ZAVISTOVSKI, *Cello*
MARTIN KATZ, *Piano*

MRS. H. H. A. BEACH	Trio, Opus 150 in A minor
	Allegro con brio
	Lento espressivo
	Allegro
A. P. HEINRICH	The Yankee Doodleiad,
	A National Divertimento
	(World Premiere)
	Entrata
	Theme and Variations
	Assisting Artists,
	ROBERT SHERMAN, *Narrator*
	YOKO GILBERT, *Violin*
	IRA LIEBERMAN, *Violin*

Intermission

LEONARD BERNSTEIN	Trio, Op 2
	(New York Premiere)
	Adagio non troppo - Allegro vivace
	Tempo di marcia
	Largo - Allegro vivo
ARTHUR FOOTE	Trio, Op. 65 in B flat
	Allegro giocoso
	Tranquillo
	Allegro molto

Steinway Piano

The Bergson Trio expresses gratitude to its patrons
without whose generous support this concert would not be possible.

In consideration of the performing artists and members of the audience, those who must leave before the
end of the performance are asked to do so between numbers, not during the performance.
The taking of photographs and the use of recording equipment are not allowed in this building.

Leonard Bernstein's signature on The Bergson Trio's Alice Tully Hall program,
1976

Toni and Leshek's second wedding celebration,
(from left: Leshek, Marion "Oatsie" Charles, Toni, Mrs. John Barry "Nin" Ryan,
Elaine Brownstein, Maestro Kazimierz Kord), 1977

Leshek, Tanya and Toni on the Met picket line, 1980

Anita and Piotr Zawistowski

Leshek with Susan Graham

Toni, Placido Domingo and Leshek

Leshek presents Marilyn Horne with a birthday cake

Marilyn Horne and Toni

Samuel Ramey and Spiro Malas with Leshek at his 60th birthday party,
impersonating Leopold Stokowski

Henry Lewis at the
Zavistovski home

Toni and Leshek in Santa Fe, 1995

The Zavistovski Family in Santa Fe, New Mexico, 2006

Leshek and his sculpture, *Hope,* commissioned by the University of New Mexico
Cancer Center, 2010

Glossary

French

    buerre blanc – butter sauce

    haricots verts – string beans

Italian

    Cosi fan tutte – women are like that

    glissandi – slides over the fingerboard

Latin

    Prima Aprilis – April Fools

Polish

    babushka – grandmother

    bąć spokoiny – be calm

    bigos – hunter's stew

    bimber – precursor of vodka

    chleb – bread

    dzieci i ryby nie mówią – children and fish don't talk

    dziwak – weirdo

    flaki – tripe

    ja jestem wolny – I am free

    kabanosy – finger thin sausage

    karaluch – cockroach

    kotuś – kitten

kurwa – prostitute

Lulai że Jezuniu – *Go to sleep my little Jesus*

odważny – courageous

naleśniki – thin pancake

nie płacz – don't cry

pan, pani, panie – mister, missus, mister

pierogi – dumplings

skarbuś – treasure

sto lat – one hundred years

strona – page

struna – string

suka – bitch

synku – son

szlachta – nobility

szlachcic – nobleman

uważaj – careful

wariaci – crazy ones

woda – water

żądamy chleba – we demand bread

zloty – Polish currency

Russian

balalaika – guitar-like stringed instrument

domra – long-necked stringed instrument

Kazatsky – Russian folk dance

kopek – Russian penny

nyet – no

Yiddish

boychik – young boy

chozzer – pig

gefilte – Jewish fish dish

kishka – stuffed sausage

mazel tov – congratulations

meshuggah – crazy

oy vey – oh pain

shiksa – non-Jewish woman

Acknowledgments

As in all worthy pursuits, our path has been paved with help from many people whose enthusiasm and guidance have been invaluable.

We are grateful for the resources provided us by John Pennino of the Metropolitan Opera Archives, Barbara Haws of the New York Philharmonic Archives, the Kosciuszko Foundation, the Ukrainian Institute of America, the Polish Institute of Arts and Science and the Aspen Music Festival.

Among the characters in *Children and Fish Don't Talk* who enhanced and substantiated stories from decades past are: Cecylia Arzewski, Michael Arzewski, Avron Coleman, Basia Hammerstein, Melanie Henderson, Richard Rodzinski and Vera Savoyka. We thank them all for being a part of the fabric of this book.

The insightful feedback we received from our savvy group of readers, Jerome Adler, Katrine Ames, Adam Parrish King, Beth Lebowitz, Alicia Miller, Lucinda Young and Katia Zavistovski was critical to the development of the book.

Writer Bruce McKenna's brilliant and abundantly professional advice had a profound impact on us. We owe him a debt of gratitude for his confidence in *Children and Fish Don't Talk* and the time he invested in its promotion. We are also grateful to our publisher and editor Jim Smith for believing in our book and taking it under his wing. Very much appreciated was the additional counsel we received from Scott Duncan, Susanna Margolis, Stephanie Ripps,

Debra Rogers, Nick Spark and William Zeckendorf about the intricate world of writing and publishing.

Our family members were the impetus that propelled us forward: Tanya Zavistovski for her encouragement, Katia Zavistovski for her masterful, perceptive edits, Gregory Zavistovski for the title of the book, Adam Parrish King for his astute, provocative suggestions, and Chloe King Zavistovski for reminding us of the purpose of our efforts.

And finally, at the risk of succumbing to hubris, we acknowledge each other. Writing this story together was a cathartic and powerful experience; sometimes heart wrenching, other times uproariously funny, always inspiring and revelatory, it has enriched our lives beyond imagination. We are so fortunate.

—Leshek Zavistovski, Monique Zavistovski, Toni Rapport Zavistovski

Left to right: Toni, Leshek and Monique
photograph by Katia Zavistovski

Bibliography

Allegro, publication of Local 802, American Federation of Musicians, October 1966

Annals of the Metropolitan Opera, the Metropolitan Opera Guild Inc., G.K. Hall & Co., 1989

Haiman, Miecislaus, *Polish Pioneers of Virginia and Kentucky*, Polish R. C. Union of America, Chicago, Ill., 1937

Life Magazine, September 30, 1966

Kolodin, Irving, *The Metropolitan Opera 1883-1935*, Oxford University Press, 1936

Kriwaczek, Paul, *Yiddish Civilization*, Alfred A. Knopf, 2005

Metropolitan Opera opening night program book, September 16, 1966

Ksiegarnia, Nasza, *Wojna i dziecko (War and child)*, 1968

The New York Times, September 11-17, 1966

The New York Times Magazine, September 11, 1966

Poland 1946, Smithsonian Institution Press, 1995

Polish Falcon, *Kosciuszko & Pulaski – Two Geniuses of the American Revolution*, October 15, 1993

Rodzinski, Halina, *Our Two Lives*, Charles Scribner's Sons, 1976

Rokossovsky, Konstantin, *A Soldier's Duty*, Progress Publication, 1985

Rubinstein, Arthur, *My Young Years*, Charles Scribner's Sons, 1973

Stara Warszawa (Old Warsaw), Arkady, 1958

The Department of State Bulletin, Address by President Johnson, *The United States and Poland: Strengthening Traditional Bonds*, November 1966

The Paderewski Memoirs, Charles Scribner's Sons, 1938

The Timetables of Jewish History, Touchstone, 1994

Warszawa – Miasto i Ludzie (Warsaw – City and People), Arkady, 1968

Index

A

B